The Chiron Dictionary of Greek & Roman Mythology

Gods and Goddesses, Heroes, Places, and Events of Antiquity

Translated by
Elizabeth Burr

CHIRON PUBLICATIONS • Wilmette, Illinois

Fourth printing, 2000

Originally published in 1981 as
Herder Lexikon: Griechische und römische Mythologie.
Copyright 1981, 1990, Verlag Herder Freiburg
im Breisgau.

Translation © 1993 by Chiron Publications.

Book design by Elaine M. Hill.
Cover design by Fujii Communications, Inc.
Printed in the United States of America.

Library of Congress Cataloging-in-Publication Data:

Herder Lexikon, griechische und römische Mythologie. English
  The Chiron dictionary of Greek and Roman mythology : gods and
goddesses, heroes, places, and events of antiquity.
    p.   cm.
  ISBN 0–933029–82–9 : $14.95
  1. Mythology, Classical—Dictionaries.
BL715.H4713   1994
292.1'3'03—dc20   93–43989
                                                       CIP

ISBN 0–933029–82–9

English Translator's Note

In general, the German text of the original Herder lexicon has been faithfully adhered to. Occasional minor deviations from the German text have been made where considered necessary for accuracy of content.

Introduction

This little lexicon of Greek and Roman mythology is intended to convey an impression of the multitude of gods and goddesses, heroes and heroines that imprinted themselves on the imagination of men and women in antiquity. For our purposes, they include not only the important figures from famous legendary cycles and the greater gods, along with their spheres of competence and their deeds, but also a selection of the lesser-known figures who were woven into mythical and legendary tales. The wealth of narrative variations resulting from the heterogeneous traditions is often astounding; further, we must be aware of the fact that these accounts are hardly straightforward or consistently reliable. This is evident not only within individual entries, where frequently only a portion of the versions can be presented (or where just the fact that different versions exist is indicated); often this is clear from the preliminary remarks, which may, for example, attribute several parents (singly or in pairs) to the figure in question. Alternatively, despite this multiplicity, certain motifs make repeated appearances, such as the stepmother attempting to seduce her stepson (the Potiphar motif) or the angry father putting his pregnant daughter out to sea.

To ease the reader's task of locating an item, important events have been given their own entries. The separate treatment of the twelve classical labors of Heracles (which are also mentioned collectively in the Heracles entry) exemplifies this practice. Likewise, important places in myths and legends are handled as separate entries.

As a rule, Greek personal names are either directly transliterated (and may not correspond to the most familiar form) or Latinized (sometimes with an alternative spelling added in parentheses to aid recognition). Any attempt to indicate accentuation of Greek names and terms, which would have entailed the introduction of original Greek accentuation ordinarily known only to specialists, has been abandoned.

The mythological material presented here was subject to artistic representation already in antiquity. In the present volume, an effort has been made to supplement the entries by means of illustrations drawn from the most varied periods, with a view to enlivening the textual material. The schematic genealogies dispersed throughout the volume are intended to help the reader begin to unravel the often very complicated kinship relations among a given set of persons, whether mortal or divine. They could also serve as the point of departure for a lengthier look at one or another individual of interest from mythology and legend.

Abdera A Greek port city on the Thracian coast, founded ca. 650 B.C., it was destroyed by the Thracians and then resettled. The home of the philosophers Leucippus, Democritus, and Protagoras, among others, its legendary founder was Heracles.

Abderos The weapons-bearer of Heracles and a son of Hermes, he was the eponym of *Abdera. He was torn to pieces by the horses of Diomedes.

Abydos An ancient Greek city on the Asian side of the Hellespont. It was from here that in 480 B.C. Xerxes I transported the Persian army to Greece on two bridges made of boats. Abydos was reputed to be the home of *Leander. During the Trojan War, its inhabitants allied themselves with Troy.

Acamas One of the numerous sons of *Antenor and Theano, he shared the supreme command of the Dardanian troops in the Trojan War with Aeneas and Archeloos. Acamas was killed by Meriones.

Acastus King of Iolcus and the only son of Pelias and Anaxabia (in another version, Phylomache). He married Hippolyte (probably a granddaughter of Cretheus) or Astydameia, and became the father of several children. Counted among the Argonauts, Acastus also took part in the Calydonian boar hunt. He organized the celebrated funeral games for the murdered *Pelias. His own death was connected with *Peleus and the Potiphar motif: his wife, who had fallen passionately in love with Peleus but been rejected by him, avenged herself by maintaining that Peleus had intended to seduce her. Acastus then attempted to kill Peleus. Peleus escaped, however; later he conquered Iolcus and slew the royal couple.

Acca Larentia A Roman courtesan from the time of *Ancus Martius, she was the lover of Heracles and wife of Faustulus; in addition, she was often considered the foster mother of Romulus and Remus. According to another version, she put herself in Rome's debt by bequeathing to the city the riches she had received from Heracles or from her husband. It is likely that Acca Larentia derives from an Italian goddess, to whom new legends were attached after her original significance had been obscured.

Acestes The son of Crimnisus of Sicily and the Trojan Segesta, for whom the city of Segesta was supposed to have been named. A companion of Priam in the Trojan War, he later offered hospitality to Aeneas when Aeneas visited Acestes on his journey from Troy to Italian Sicily. Acestes assisted in the burial of *Anchises and won the archery contest at the funeral games.

Achaea This coastal region in the northern Peloponnesus of Greece, named after the Achaians, was first a loose alliance of twelve city-states with a common sanctuary of Zeus at Aegium. The point of embarkation for Achaian colonization in southern Italy, Achaea was later used by the Romans to designate the whole of Greece as a Roman province.

Achelous A river in western Greece, personified in myth as the highest of the river gods. The son of Oceanus and Tethys, he was the brother of the other river gods and the father of the Sirens. Of him it is traditionally told that he got into a fight with Heracles over Deianira. Possessing the power to alter his form, Achelous turned himself first into a snake and then into a bull, one of whose horns Heracles broke off. Heracles gave the horn back to his defeated adversary and received in exchange from him the horn of *Amalthea filled with fruit and flowers.

Acheron In Greek mythology, one of the rivers of the underworld.

Aeacus—Endeis
Telamon
Peleus—Thetis
Achilles—Deidameia
Neoptolemus

Achilles A hero of Greek legend and the foremost figure in the *Iliad*, he was the greatest of the Hellenes who fought at Troy. His parents were *Peleus (hence his epithet *Peleides*) and the sea goddess Thetis. In order to endow her son with immortality, his mother sought to destroy his mortal part by anointing him with ambrosia and holding him over the fire at night. According to another version, she immersed the boy in the river Styx to make him invulnerable;

only the heel by which she held him remained vulnerable. When her husband surprised her in this endeavor, he snatched Achilles away from her and brought the child to the renowned centaur *Chiron, who raised him. Knowing to her grief that her son would die at Troy, Thetis tried to remove him from the war. Dressing him as a girl, she took him to the court of *Lycomedes of Scyros, where he won the love of the king's daughter, Deidameia, who bore him a son, *Neoptolemus. Meanwhile, the Greeks searched for Achilles, because an oracle had said that without him Troy could not be conquered. Odysseus and his companions found him out at Scyros and exposed his true identity by showing the disguised girl both jewelry and weapons. Responding with a burning interest only in the weapons, Achilles was revealed. He then accompanied his friend Patroclus, his teacher Phoenix, and the Myrmidones with 50 ships to Troy. On the way, and before the siege of the city began, he had already performed many heroic deeds, including conquering a string of cities.—The *Iliad* (*Homer) portrays the quarrel between Achilles and Agamemnon in the last year of the war. This quarrel was triggered by Agamemnon claiming for himself the concubine of Achilles, *Briseis. The wrath of Achilles was so great that he refused to take any further part in the fighting, even though the position of the Greeks was increasingly threatened. Finally he let himself be persuaded to lend his friend Patroclus his own armor and to send him into battle. But Patroclus fell at the hands of Hector after he had repelled the enemy. Only then was Achilles prepared to intervene again in the war himself. His mother provided him with armor forged by Hephaestus and with weapons. He drove the enemy back into the city except for Hector, whom he killed in a duel and then dragged into the Greek camp, tied to his chariot. When the aging Priam appeared at the camp to ransom his son for burial with the proper rites, Achilles showed his magnanimity.—Achilles himself met death from an arrow shot by Paris, which Apollo directed into his vulnerable heel; according to another ver-

Achilles on a Greek amphora

3

sion, Apollo killed him unaided, and a later tradition tells of his assassination in the temple of Apollo. When the corpse was recovered, Odysseus and Aias the Great achieved prominence contending for the armor of the fallen hero, which was finally awarded to Odysseus. After the events described in the *Iliad*, the shade of Achilles lived on in Hades; in another version, his mother brought him to the island of Leuce or to Elysium, where he enjoyed a happy existence. As a hero, Achilles had a number of cult places in Greece. He became a subject for literary treatment from an early date: Aeschylus portrayed him in his *Psychostasia*, Euripides in his *Scyrians*, and the Roman poet Statius in his epic *Achilleis*. Episodes from his adventurous life were also given expression in art.

Acis The son of a nymph and lover of the beautiful *Galatea. After he had been killed by his rival, *Polyphemus, his blood was transformed into a spring and he himself became a river god.

Acrisius King of Argos, he was the son of Abas and *Okaleia, and the twin brother of *Proetus. He married Eurydice (in another version, Aganippe) and became the father of Danae. He and his brother quarreled from childhood on, and later Acrisius banished Proetus from Argos. Eventually the realm was divided into two kingdoms, with Proetus assuming authority over Tiryns.—An oracle warned Acrisius that he would be killed by a son of Danae. For this reason the king confined his daughter to an ivory tower; but Zeus visited her there in the form of a rain of gold, and she became the mother of *Perseus. When Perseus had grown to manhood he inadvertently killed his grandfather with a discus, so that the oracle was fulfilled.

Acron 1. A king who was killed by Romulus after the rape of the Sabines. 2. A friend of Aeneas who was killed by Mezentius.

Actaeon An outstanding hunter, he was the son of *Aristaeus and Autonoe, a daughter of Cadmus. The centaur Chiron raised him and instructed him in hunting. After Actaeon had seen Artemis naked in her bath, the goddess turned

Apollo ┬ Cyrene
Aristaeus ┬ Autonoe
Actaeon

him into a stag. Not recognizing him, his own hounds tore him to pieces.—In another version, Actaeon boasted arrogantly that he was a better hunter than Artemis; she then punished him on account of his hubris. According to still another tradition, Actaeon met his death when he pursued Semele, with whom Zeus had fallen passionately in love.

Actium A peninsula in the Acarnanian region of Greece, where the decisive naval victory of Octavian over Antony and Cleopatra occurred in 31 B.C. It was the site of the so-called Actian games, which were held every four years in honor of Actian Apollo.

Admetus King of Pherae, the eldest son of Pheres and Periclymene (Clymene), and the husband of *Alcestis, he was the father of *Eumelus and of Perimele. Admetus took part in the Calydonian boar hunt and in the Argonautic expedition. Because Apollo had murdered the Cyclopes, he was punished for his crime by having to serve Admetus for a year as a shepherd. The two became friends, and Apollo helped Admetus when Artemis revenged herself on him (because he had forgotten to make the customary offering to her before his marriage) by sending snakes into the bridal chamber. Apollo exacted a promise from the *Moirai that, when Admetus's hour of death should come, he would be allowed to live if someone else would die in his place. At the decisive moment, only Alcestis was willing; but she was saved by Heracles, who appeared opportunely and rescued her from the underworld.

Adonia The private mourning festivals in honor of *Adonis, which were celebrated at different times in the Near East and Greece. As a rule, they lasted from two to eight days. Important parts of the cult were the mock burial of the god and the little *Gardens of Adonis.

Adonis In Greek mythology, the son of *Cinyras and *Myrrha (or Smyrna). A beautiful youth who lost his life while hunting, he was beloved of Aphrodite. She entreated Persephone to let Adonis live on the earth for six months of the

5

year.—Adonis was probably a vegetation god deriving from the Near East, perhaps Phoenicia (Adon = "Lord" in Phoenician), who represented the cycle of dying and reviving vegetation. His cult was not official, but the *Adonia established in his honor enjoyed great popularity.

Adrasteia (Greek = "the inescapable") Originally a Phrygian mountain goddess, from ca. 400 B.C. she was associated and then identified with the Greek *Nemesis because she too was regarded as a guardian of justice and avenger of all wrongdoing.

Talaus—⌐Lysimache

⌐
Eriphyle
Adrastus ⌐Amphithea
⌐
Argeia—Polynices
Deipyle—Tydeus
Aigialos

Adrastus 1. King of Argos, and the son of *Talaus and *Lysimache (in another version either Eurynome or Lysianassa was his mother). After *Amphiaraus had murdered the father of Adrastus, the latter fled to Polybus, his grandfather or uncle, from whom he inherited dominion over Sicyon. Eventually he was reconciled with Amphiaraus and gave him his sister *Eriphyle in marriage, while he himself resumed the kingship of Argos.—Adrastus led the *Seven against Thebes, emerging as the sole survivor of that expedition because his magic horse Arion saved him. Later he led the *Epigoni. He died of grief upon receiving the news that his son *Aigialos had died. 2. The son of Merops, he was killed in the Trojan War by Diomedes.

Aeacus The son of Zeus and Aegina, a daughter of the river god *Asopos. By his wife Endeis he became the father of Peleus and Telamon, and by *Psamathe the father of Phocus. Because of his piety and sense of justice, he was a friend of the gods, and after his death was made one of the judges in the underworld.

Aedon (Greek for "nightingale") The daughter of Pandareos and wife of Zethus of Thebes (*Amphion and Zethus), she erroneously murdered her son Itylus, mistaking him for a son of *Niobe, whom she envied for her many children. When she attempted to commit suicide, Zeus changed her into a nightingale.—*Procne.

Aeetes King of the legendary land of Aia in Colchis, and the father of *Medea and Apsyrtus. He possessed the *Golden fleece, which he had once received from *Phrixus after the latter's fortunate rescue and friendly reception in Colchis.

Aegeus The father of *Theseus.

Aegialeia The wife of *Diomedes (2), she committed adultery with *Kometes during her husband's absence in the Trojan War.

Aegis The shield of Zeus, made by the renowned smith Hephaestus; the head of the Gorgon (Gorgoneion; *Medusa) was depicted at its center. Etymological misinterpretations led to post-Homeric statements to the effect that the Aegis was covered with the skin of the she-goat Amalthea. The Aegis symbolized the protection of the gods (who also loaned it out); hence the expression, still current today, "to stand under someone's aegis."

Aegisthus King of Mycenae and the son of *Thyestes and Pelopia. Brought up by his uncle *Atreus, he was incited by the latter to kill his father, who however recognized his son. Aegisthus thereupon killed Atreus. During the Trojan War, Aegisthus seduced *Clytemnestra, the wife of *Agamemnon, who was away at Troy. When Agamemnon returned home, Aegisthus and his lover drowned him in his bath; according to another version, Agamemnon was struck down. Aegisthus then ruled at Mycenae until the returning Orestes avenged his father by killing the murderer as well as his own mother.

```
          Pelops ┬ Hippodameia
        ┌─────────┴──────────────┐
   Atreus ┬ Aerope        Thyestes ┬ Pelopia
Agamemnon ┬ Clytemnestra ─ **Aegisthus**
    ┌─────┴─────┐
 Orestes    Electra
```

Aegyptus Son of *Belus, he was the brother of *Danaus, whose fifty daughters, the *Danaids, he forced his own fifty sons to marry. With the advice and help of their father, the Danaids murdered their husbands on their wedding night. Only *Lynceus (1) survived.

Aeneades (Greek, *Ainaiades*) The descendants of Aeneas.

7

Aeneas (Greek, *Aineias*) A Trojan hero, he was the son of *Anchises and the goddess Aphrodite. His fate is fully narrated in the *Aeneid*, though Virgil, the author of this work, may have relied on older authors. It can be assumed that the story of Aeneas mixes historical and legendary features.—Following Virgil's version of the story, Aeneas fled from the flames of Troy with his aging father, *Anchises, on his shoulders; he also managed to save his son, *Ascanius (later called Iulus), and the images of the household gods, but his wife, Creusa, was lost. After adventurous wanderings, which also led him to Sicily and Africa, he succeeded in reaching Italy. There he was informed by the Sybil of Cumae about his future destiny, and he visited the underworld. When he arrived in Latium, King Latinus gave Aeneas his daughter *Lavinia in marriage. After heavy fighting with the Rutulians, Aeneas assumed control (Latinus had since died) and founded the city of Lavinium. His son Ascanius became the founder of *Alba Longa, which was regarded as the mother city of Rome.—Aeneas always played an important role in the history of Rome and the Roman Empire because he represented the bonding of Rome with other Mediterranean communities. As a person, he symbolized less the warrior-hero than the man of piety (the virtue accorded highest value by the Romans) who had saved his father and his household gods.

The Trojan Ancestry of Aeneas

```
                    Tros┬Callirhoe
        ┌──────────────────┴──────────────────────────┐
   Ilos┬Eurydice          Assarakos┬Hieromneme    Ganymedes
 ┌──────┴──┐                   ┌────┴──────┐
Laomedon┬Strymo          Themiste┬Capys
 ┌───────┴────┬──────────────┐      │
Priam┬Hecuba  Telamon┬Hesione   Anchises┬Aphrodite
   │                │                  │
 Paris           Teukros            **Aeneas**
```

Aeneid The twelve-volume epic of Virgil, which tells the story of Aeneas after the fall of Troy: the vicissitudes of his flight to Italy, his battles with the Italic peoples, and the union of Trojans and Latins as the precondition for the rise of the Roman people. At the same time, the work presents a vindication of the Augustan Empire: divine deliberation has called the Romans to world dominion so that they may establish a kingdom of peace on earth.

Aeolus 1. The son of *Hellen and the nymph Orseis, he was the husband of Enarete, who bore him seven sons and seven (in another version, five) daughters. He reigned in Magnesia in Thessaly and was the ancestor of the Aeolians. 2. The son of Poseidon and Melanippe, he was god and highest lord of all the winds. He lived on the island of Aeolus, where *Odysseus landed in the course of his wanderings after the Trojan War, though it was difficult to access. To ease Odysseus's homeward journey, Aeolus (who was disposed to be friendly toward him) gave him a bag of winds as he departed. But Odysseus's companions opened it out of curiosity once they had set sail, causing the winds to escape and the ship to be driven back to the island of Aeolus. Odysseus's request for further help met with refusal from Aeolus.

Aepytus King of Messenia, he was the youngest son of *Cresphontes and *Merope (3). His father and his two older brothers were killed by *Polyphontes (2), who usurped the throne of Messenia for himself. His mother succeeded in conveying Aepytus out of the region and preserving his life. Later when he returned to his homeland, Aepytus killed Polyphontes at a festival of thanksgiving to the gods and entered on his father's inheritance.

Aerope Daughter of the Cretan king *Catreus, she was the wife first of Pleisthenes and then of *Atreus, as well as the mother of Agamemnon and Menelaus. After committing adultery with her brother-in-law Thyestes, she bore him twins. Atreus killed them and served them to Thyestes at a banquet.

Aeschylus Greek poet and playwright who was born in 525 or 524 B.C. at Eleusis, and died in 456 or 455 at Gela on Sicily. The earliest of the three great Attic tragedians, he preceded *Sophocles and *Euripides. The Greek myths supplied him with the subject matter of his

Aeschylus: of the some 90 tragedies that Aeschylus composed, seven have survived:

Persians
Seven Against Thebes
Suppliants
The *Oresteia* trilogy
Prometheus Bound

9

plays. His great themes are the power of the gods, and the hubris of mortals and its punishment. Of the 90 or so plays that Aeschylus wrote, seven have survived.

Aesculapius The Roman name for the Greek god of healing, *Asclepius. Worship of Aesculapius began in Rome in 293 B.C. when a plague broke out there. A Roman legation brought the god to Rome in the form of a holy serpent, and in 291 B.C. a temple was consecrated on Tiber Island to the new divinity. Treatment of the sick in the name of Aesculapius was handled in Italy much the same as in Greece.

Aeson King of Thessaly, he was the oldest son of *Cretheus (1) and Tyro, the husband of Alkimede, and the father of *Jason and Promachos. The tradition relates that he compelled his half-brother *Pelias to relinquish the throne and commit suicide. According to another version, after the return of his son Jason from Colchis, Aeson was boiled in a cauldron at the instigation of his daughter-in-law Medea, ostensibly to bring back his youth; on this occasion, however, Medea did not use the rejuvenation magic that she had at her disposal.

Aether The heavens, arising from the union of *Erebus and *Nyx.

Aetna A volcano on the island of Sicily. In Greek mythology it is one of the locations suggested for the workshop of the smith-god Hephaestus.

Aetolia A region in west-central Greece located north of the Gulf of Patras, which according to legend was named after Aetolus, the son of Endymion. The kings of this land, whose inhabitants were long viewed by the Greeks as semi-barbarians, included Hippodamas and Oineus. Aetolia was the setting for the legend of *Meleager and the *Calydonian boar hunt.

Agamede A daughter of *Augeas, she was among the first to use herbs for the cure of illnesses.

Agamedes A legendary Greek architect from Orchomenus and the son of *Erginos, who was decapitated by *Trophonius.

Agamemnon A legendary king of Mycenae, he was the son of Atreus and Aerope and the brother of *Menelaus, the husband of *Helen. He married *Clytemnestra after eliminating her first husband and a child from that marriage. Clytemnestra bore him *Chrysothemis, *Electra, *Iphigenia, and *Orestes. In the Trojan War Agamemnon, who had a certain preeminence among the Greeks, assumed the supreme command over them. Before the fleet could set sail, however, he was obliged to sacrifice his daughter Iphigenia, in order to appease Artemis, whom he had offended, and to secure a favorable wind from her (or the stilling of a severe storm, according to another version). The *Iliad* (*Homer) narrates the harsh arguments at Troy between Agamemnon and Achilles, whose concubine Briseis Agamemnon claimed for himself. When the war was over, the king returned to his homeland with the prophetic Cassandra among his spoils. Meanwhile Clytemnestra, who never forgave her husband for the sacrifice of Iphigenia, had entered into an adulterous relationship with *Aegisthus. She and her lover murdered Agamemnon treacherously and also killed Cassandra. Aegisthus ascended the throne, but once Electra succeeded in bringing Orestes safely to Phocis, the murderers met a similar fate: Orestes with his friend and kinsman Pylades killed Aegisthus and Clytemnestra.—Agamemnon's homecoming and death received their most meaningful treatment in Aeschylus's *Agamemnon*.

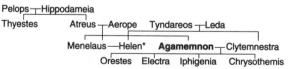

Pelops—Hippodameia

Thyestes   Atreus—Aerope   Tyndareos—Leda

Menelaus—Helen*   **Agamemnon**—Clytemnestra

Orestes   Electra   Iphigenia   Chrysothemis

*Helen is usually regarded as the daughter of Zeus by Leda

Agapenor King of Tegea in Arcadia, he founded the city of Paphos on Cyprus and built a temple to Aphrodite there. As a suitor of Helen, he took part in the Trojan War and commanded Agamemnon's fleet. He purchased Arsinoe, the wife of Alcmaeon, as a slave.

Agasthenes King of Elis and the son (in another version, brother) of *Augeas, whose throne he inherited, he was one of Helen's suitors and so joined in the Trojan War.

Agave 1. The daughter of *Cadmus and *Harmonia, she married *Echion and bore him Pentheus, who later became king of Thebes. Agave, who subscribed to the orgiastic cult of Dionysus, killed her son in an attack of madness by tearing him to pieces. According to another version, the *Maenads dismembered Pentheus, and his mother bore his head home in triumph. Her second husband was *Lykotherses, king of Illyria, whom she later killed so that the throne would pass to Cadmus. 2. One of the Nereids.

Agdistis One of the hybrid creatures descended from Zeus in Phrygian mythology. It was also an epithet of the mother goddess *Cybele.

Agenor In the world of Greek legend, a frequently occurring name that referred most importantly to the son of Poseidon and Libya, regarded as the ancestor of the Phoenicians, who was king of Sidon and Tyre and the father of *Cadmus and *Europa, among others.

Aglaia 1. One of the *Charites. 2. The wife of Abas.—*Okaleia.

Aglaos The poorest man in Arcadian Psophis, who was nevertheless happier than King Gyges of Lydia, according to an oracle.

Aglauros The most beautiful of the three daughters of *Cecrops, she was the sister of Herse and Pandrosos. From Athena the sisters received *Erichthonius in a closed container, which they opened out of curiosity despite the strict prohibition of the goddess. As a result, at least two of them went mad at the sight of the snakelike, or snake-enveloped, child.—Another tradition reports that Aglauros was turned into stone by Hermes when she refused to help the god gain her sister Herse's attention.

Agriope Possibly the wife of King *Agenor.

Aia A legendary land in Colchis under the sovereignty of *Aeetes, where the *Golden fleece was kept.

Aias (Latin, *Ajax*) The name refers to two heroes of Greek legend who played significant roles in the battle for Troy: 1. Aias the Locrian, also called Aias the Lesser. The son of King *Oileus of Locris and Eriopis, he led the forty ships that formed the Locrian contingent against Troy. An outstanding runner and javelin thrower, Aias often fought alongside Aias the Great. Yet though Homer celebrates his talents as a warrior, he is nevertheless portrayed in the epic as boisterous and godless. As legend tells it, when Troy fell he seized *Cassandra, who had sought the protection of Athena by fleeing to a statue of the goddess, and assaulted her. Athena took her revenge by destroying Aias's ship on its homeward journey. He managed to hold on to a rock, but when he slandered the gods from that spot Poseidon split the rock with his trident and Aias perished. 2. Aias Telamonius, also called Aias the Great. The son of King *Telamon of Salamis and Eriboea, he was considered the finest Greek hero of the Trojan War after Achilles. His duel with Hector, the foremost warrior on the Trojan side, remained undecided. His noteworthy exploits included helping to retrieve the corpse of Patroclus from an immensely superior enemy force. The inglorious end of Aias occurred after the Greeks had gathered to decide whether to award Achilles' weapons to Aias or Odysseus, each of whom had claimed them on the grounds that he was the most valiant warrior. First Aias gave a speech full of vanity; then Odysseus spoke, and the arbiters awarded him the weapons. Unable to bear this humiliation, Aias in his raging frenzy wanted to kill all the Greek generals. But he was stricken with madness by Pallas Athena and instead unleashed a terrible massacre against some herds of cattle, believing them to be his Greek adversaries. When he realized his error, he fell on his sword, despite the efforts of his beloved concubine Tecmessa to restrain him. Agamemnon for-

Achilles and Aias
Amphora with the scene of Achilles and Aias playing a board game; work of the Attic potter and vase painter Execias (3rd quarter of the 6th century B.C.), who brought the black-figure style to artistic perfection

bade cremation because Aias had committed suicide. The death of Aias is the theme of Sophocles' tragedy entitled *Ajax*.—The question whether Aias the Locrian and Aias Telamonius were originally one and the same figure has frequently been taken up by scholars, but comparison of the sources has yielded no definitive answer.

Aigialos The eldest son of *Adrastus, he was the only one of the *Epigoni who fell in the battle against Thebes.

Aithon One of the four horses of Ares.

Aius Locutius A Roman deity whose voice is said to have warned Marcus Caedicius on the Via Nova, ca. 390 B.C., of an imminent attack by the Gauls on Rome under Brennus. The warning went unheeded but, after the Gauls had been driven out, the Romans built an altar of propitiation to the deity.

Ajax The Latin form of the Greek *Aias.

Akantha A nymph beloved of Apollo, she was changed by him into an acanthus flower.

Akontios and Kydippe In Greek mythology they were a pair of lovers who became acquainted at the Artemis festival on Delos. Akontios, a poor young man from Ceos, devised a stratagem to win the hand of Kydippe, the daughter of a rich Athenian family. During the festival, he threw her an apple with the following message inscribed on it: "By Artemis, I vow to marry no man other than Akontios." Innocently Kydippe read aloud the message, which had the character of an oath. After this, whenever she was supposed to marry another man from a suitable background, she became sick. Finally her parents consulted the oracle at Delphi, which declared itself in favor of Kydippe's union with Akontios.

Aktis In Greek mythology, one of the *Heliades. Together with his brother, he was the first human being to offer sacrifices to Athena. Following his involvement in the murder of his brother *Tenages, Aktis left Rhodes and went to Egypt, where he founded Heliopolis. The Colossus of Rhodes is supposed to have been erected in his honor.

Alastor 1. The name of the horse belonging to Hades on which he carried Persephone down to the underworld. 2. The arms bearer of *Sarpedon in the Trojan War who was killed by Odysseus.

Alba Longa Former Latin city on the Alban Lake whose legendary founder was *Ascanius. It was regarded as the mother city of Rome.

Albion In Greek mythology the son of Poseidon and Amphitrite, he was reputed to have introduced astrology and the art of shipbuilding into England.—Albion was also a Celtic, and later a poetic, name for England.

Alcestis In Greek mythology the wife of King *Admetus, daughter of Pelias, and mother of Eumelus and Perimele. She volunteered to die in place of her husband, but Heracles came to her rescue and released her from Hades. Ever since Euripides, the story of Alcestis has frequently been treated by writers, among them Rilke and Werfel; in opera Handel and Gluck used it.

Alcinous In Greek mythology, king of the Phaeacians. He married his niece Arete and became the father of Nausicaa in addition to five sons. Recipients of Alcinous's help were the shipwrecked Odysseus on his way home from Troy, as well as Jason and Medea during their pursuit by the Colchian fleet.

Alcmaeon (Attic, *Alkmeon*) Son of the prophet *Amphiaraus and *Eriphyle, he led the *Epigoni, who (in contrast to the *Seven against Thebes) captured the city of Thebes. Like his father, Alcmaeon initially refused to take part in the expedition and tried to hide. However, his mother, who had once betrayed her husband for the sake of the precious necklace of *Harmonia, again let herself be bribed (this time by Thersander with the peplos of Harmonia) to persuade her son and *Amphilochus (1) to join the expedition. After his return (in another version, earlier) Alcmaeon murdered his mother, thus faithfully executing the revenge with which his

Oecles—Hypermestra
Amphiaraus—Eriphyle
Amphilochus
Alcmaeon—Callirhoe
Amphoterus   Acarnan

father had charged him. Because of the matricide, the Erinyes pursued him all over Greece. In his flight Alcmaeon married Arsinoe, a daughter of King *Phegeus, who tried in vain to absolve him. Later he married *Callirhoe (1), daughter of Achelous, who succeeded in absolving him. When Alcmaeon attempted to steal the necklace of Harmonia together with her peplos from his first wife, Arsinoe (the two items had passed to her from his mother), in order to present them to Callirhoe, he was killed by the sons of Phegeus. Once her two sons had reached manhood, Callirhoe commissioned them to avenge the death of their father. After murdering Phegeus and his two sons, they consecrated the baneful necklace and peplos to Apollo at Delphi.—Details of the myth vary in different versions. It received literary treatment, e.g., in tragedies by Sophocles and Euripides, but only fragments of those plays survive.

Alcmene The daughter of *Electryon and Andromeda, she was the wife of *Amphitryon. By Zeus she became the mother of Heracles, and at the same time gave birth to *Iphicles, the son she had conceived by her husband.

Alecto One of the Erinyes, she was the sister of Megaira and Tisiphone.

Alexander Another name for *Paris.

Aloades The designation given to the two enormous brothers *Ephialtes and *Otus, sons of Aloeus or Poseidon, who were often counted among the giants. Battling with the gods, they piled mountains on top of each other in order to storm Mount Olympus. They bound Ares and held him prisoner for a month. According to one strand of the myth, the Aloades were killed by Apollo; in another version, they killed each other while zealously hunting with the aim of slaying a doe that was actually Artemis in disguise.

Alope Daughter of King Kerkyon of Eleusis, she was seduced by Poseidon and bore him *Hippothoon. When her father learned of this, he killed her; she was buried by a road running between Eleusis and Megara. A spring rose up on the site of her burial. Alternatively, it is reported that Poseidon transformed Alope into a spring.

Alphenor One of the children of Amphion and *Niobe.

Alpheus The longest river in the Peloponnesus, it originates in Arcadia and empties into the Ionian Sea. A series of legends involves the Alpheus; Heracles is said to have cleaned out the *Augean stables with the river's help. Of the river god bearing the same name, it is told that he pursued the nymph *Arethusa (in another version Artemis as well) until she was changed into a spring by Artemis. The Artemis tradition relates that the goddess disfigured her face and fled from the lustful river god as far as Sicily.

Amalthea In Greek legend she was a nymph who nursed the infant Zeus with the milk of a she-goat. According to another version, Amalthea herself was a she-goat and nourished Zeus with the aid of one of her broken-off horns. Later Zeus turned this horn of Amalthea into a cornucopia, which passed to Achelous and from him to Heracles. The cornucopia also became an attribute of various gods and goddesses. Zeus thanked Amalthea for her care by placing her as a star (Capella) in the heavens.

Amata In Roman legend the wife of Latinus and mother of *Lavinia, she disapproved of her daughter's marriage to Aeneas.

Amazons In Greek legend a warlike race of women reputedly from northeastern Asia Minor who were led by a queen. Various heroes are said to have fought with them (including Heracles, Theseus, and Achilles). Fundamentally hostile toward men, the Amazons engaged in sexual intercourse with them just once a year and raised only girls. Their right breasts were burned or cut off so that they would be unhindered when drawing their bows. On this basis the Greeks explained the name Amazon as meaning "breastless." How the legend of the Amazons arose cannot be determined with certainty. However, it is safe to assume that the Greeks embellished traditions deriving from a pre-Greek, matriarchal culture.—The Amazons

Amazon

Ambrosia

Amor

were often the subject matter of poetry (e.g., Kleist's "Penthesilea") and the fine arts (Polyclitus, Rubens, Feuerbach).

Ambrosia In Greek mythology, the food of the Olympian gods, which together with *Nectar conferred immortality on them.

Amor The Latin name given by the Romans to the Greek god of love, *Eros, when they took him into their pantheon.

Ampelos The son of a nymph and a Satyr, for whom Dionysus felt great affection. He died when he fell into a drunken state.

Amphiaraus An Argive seer, he was the son of *Oecles and Hypermestra, the husband of *Eriphyle (the sister of *Adrastus), and the father of Alcmaeon and Amphilochus. He received the gift of prophecy either from Zeus or from his grandfather *Melampus. Despite severe misgivings, Amphiaraus finally decided to take part in the expedition of the Seven against Thebes, even though he foresaw that all the participants except Adrastus (1) would meet their doom. His own death came as he was trying to escape from the catastrophe at Thebes; together with his chariot, his horses, and his driver, he was swallowed up by a crevasse in the earth, which Zeus tore open with one of his thunderbolts.

Amphilochus 1. A prophet, he was the younger son of *Amphiaraus and *Eriphyle, and the brother of Alcmaeon. As a suitor of Helen, he engaged in the Trojan War and was among the heroes who hid inside the wooden horse. He is also supposed to have been one of the *Epigoni. Whether Amphilochus assisted in the murder of his mother at the behest of his father is uncertain; possibly his brother Alcmaeon did the deed alone. 2. The son of Alcmaeon and Manto, he was the nephew of Amphilochus (1) and, like the latter, endowed with the gift of prophecy. He was brought up by Creon, king of Corinth, and fought in the Trojan War. Amphilochus is regarded as the founder of the oracle at Mallos. He and his half-brother *Mopsus killed each other during a quarrel.—The tradition of these two mythical figures bearing the same name is not entirely clear; much that is told about the uncle is also reported of the nephew and vice versa.

Amphion and Zethus A pair of twins in Greek mythology, they were the sons of Zeus and *Antiope. As a result of their mother's fate, they were exposed on Mount Cithaeron as soon as they had been born, but shepherds found and raised them. The two brothers were utterly different in character: Amphion devoted himself to the Muses, playing artfully on the lyre, which Hermes had given him (in another version, Amphion invented the lyre himself), whereas Zethus grew up to be an expert hunter and athlete. Having driven Lycus (an uncle of their mother) from the throne and killed him together with his wife, they assumed jointly the rulership of Thebes, which was their due. As they were building a wall to surround the city, the stones joined together of their own accord at the sound of Amphion's lyre, but Zethus had to use his great physical strength in the work of construction. Thus the two came to symbolize the contemplative and the practical life, respectively.— Amphion married *Niobe and was killed by Apollo when he attacked the god's temple to avenge the death of his numerous children. Zethus probably married Aedon (Procne), becoming the father of Itylus, whom Aedon inad-

Amphion and Zethus
Amphion, the husband of Niobe

19

vertently destroyed. Amphion and Zethus were buried in a common grave.

Amphithea The wife of *Adrastus (1), king of Argos, who was the sole survivor from the expedition of the *Seven against Thebes.

Amphitrite A Greek goddess of the sea and the daughter of Nereus and Doris, or Oceanus and Tethys, she was therefore a *Nereid or an *Oceanid. Amphitrite married Poseidon, who had pursued and abducted her, bearing him a succession of children, including *Triton. One strand of the tradition relates that at first Amphitrite attempted to flee from Poseidon but was traced by a dolphin and persuaded to return. As a result, it is said, the dolphin was translated to the stars.

Amphitryon Son of Alcaeus, king of Tiryns, he was the husband of *Alcmene, daughter of *Electryon. After killing his father-in-law by mistake, he fled to Thebes, where he had to undergo many adventures in order to obtain absolution. During his absence Zeus visited Alcmene—who remained faithful to her husband—in the guise of Amphitryon and begot Heracles. Very shortly Amphitryon returned to his wife, who then conceived Iphicles by him.— The Amphitryon–Alcmene story has provided one of the most popular themes in world literature since Plautus (who likely had Greek models at his disposal).

Amulius King of Alba Longa and son of Procas, he dethroned his brother *Numitor and killed Numitor's sons. Later he himself was brought down by Numitor's grandsons Romulus and Remus, who restored their grandfather to power.

Amyclae A place near Sparta. The site of a sanctuary of Apollo from an early date, it was said to have been founded by Amyclas.

Amyclas One of the sons of Amphion and *Niobe. According to one strand of the tradition, together with one of his sisters he eluded death at the hands of Apollo and Artemis, who succeeded in killing all the other children of Niobe.

Amycus King of the Bebryces, he was the son of Poseidon and the ash nymph Melia. A renowned and spirited boxer, he challenged every stranger to mortal combat. Amycus was invariably victorious until Polydeuces (*Dioscuri) defeated and killed him.

Amymone One of the *Danaids, she was the daughter of Danaus and Europa. Sent by her father to search for water (in another version she went hunting), she encountered a satyr, who approached her lustfully. At that moment Poseidon appeared on the scene as her deliverer, and Amymone bestowed her love on him. Their son was *Nauplius (1), the eponym of Nauplia. On the site of their union Poseidon created a spring, named after Amymone.

Amyntor The father of *Phoenix (2).

Anacreon A Greek poet of the 6th century B.C. He composed graceful drinking songs and love songs, which were already being imitated in antiquity ("Anacreonteia").

Anadyomene (Greek for "emerging from the sea") Epithet of Aphrodite.

Anatolia (Greek for "land of the sunrise," "orient") Also Asia Minor, it is a peninsula of western Asia situated between the Black Sea on the north and the Mediterranean Sea on the south and west. Anatolia constitutes the greater part of Turkey.

Anaxarete A Greek princess. Because she did not return the love of *Iphis, he hanged himself in despair. Anaxarete proved so thoroughly unmoved at his burial that Aphrodite turned her into a stone.

Anchises King of Dardanus near Troy, he was the son of Capys and beloved of Aphrodite, who bore him *Aeneas. At first Aphrodite did not reveal her divine identity to her mortal husband. When she finally did tell him her name, she forbade him to utter it. Failing to obey her, Anchises was crippled or blinded by Zeus. His son Aeneas carried him on his shoulders out of burning Troy and brought him along on the voyage to Italy. Anchises died on Sicily, where he was honored with elaborate funeral games.— Anchises' connection with a goddess decidedly elevated the genealogy of Aeneas.

Ancus Martius Traditionally the fourth king of Rome, he was the son of *Tullus Hostilius and the grandson of *Numa Pompilius. Reputedly the subjugator of the Latins and founder of Ostia, he was regarded as the ancestor of the later plebeian line of the Marcians.

Ancyra An ancient city in Asia Minor known today as Ankara. Its legendary founder was Midas.

Androgeus The son of *Minos and Pasiphae. An outstanding athlete who won all the races at the Panathenaic festival, he was killed either by his rivals or by the Marathonian bull. In response, his father Minos undertook a successful campaign of revenge against Athens by demanding a yearly tribute of seven youths and seven maidens of Attic descent, who were sacrificed to the Minotaur.

Andromache In Greek mythology, the daughter of Eetion, king of Thebes in the Troad, she was the wife of *Hector and mother of Astyanax. When Hector fell in the Trojan War, she mourned him deeply. At the end of the war she became the slave of Neoptolemus, and Astyanax was killed in an effort to root out the male offspring of the Trojan ruling house. After the murder of Neoptolemus, whose wife Hermione had constantly tormented Andromache out of enormous envy, she married *Helenus. The fate of Andromache was narrated in a play of the same name by Euripides.

Andromeda In Greek mythology the daughter of Cepheus and Cassiopeia, she was supposed to be sacrificed to a sea monster on the Ethiopian coast, but *Perseus succeeded in rescuing her. After her death Andromeda was translated to the heavens as a star.

Anius King of Delos and son of Apollo and Rhoeo. He was raised by Apollo as a priest of the god after his mother had laid him on Apollo's altar at Delos. Later he fathered a son as well as three daughters. The latter—Elais, Oeno, and Spermo—could produce wine, grain, and oil on request. According to one strand of the tradition, thus endowed they provided for the Greeks on the plain of Troy.

Anna Perenna An old Roman goddess, possibly of Etruscan origin. According to one strand of the tradition, she was a sister of Dido and after Dido's death sought refuge with Aeneas, who was living in Latium. Because Aeneas's jealous wife Lavinia persecuted her, she was forced to flee once again and was finally turned into a nymph.—According to another version, during the class conflict in Rome, she sold pastries to the plebs that she had baked herself in order to preserve them from famine.—Her annual festival was held on March 15 in a sacred Roman grove. It had a joyful folk quality and served to usher in the new year.

Antaeus King of Libya, he was a giant and the son of Poseidon and Gaia. He challenged all comers to a wrestling match and always won the contest because he could instantly gain new strength by touching the earth; he would then kill his defeated opponent. Only Heracles succeeded in overpowering Antaeus, which he did by holding him off the ground and strangling him.

Antaeus Heracles triumphs over Antaeus (by H. Baldung Grien)

Anteia The wife of *Proetus, she fell passionately in love with Bellerophon. In Homer she is called Stheneboea.

Antenor A Trojan of aristocratic lineage, who traditionally had fourteen sons and a daughter. He advocated giving *Helen back to the Greeks without resort to arms and received the Greek emissaries who came to negotiate hospitably in his home, but was unable to prevent the outbreak of war. All of his sons except Glaucus subsequently fell in battle. Because the Greeks spared his house when they plundered Troy, he was branded as a traitor. He left Troy and proceeded to Cyrene; in another version he founded Patavium (today Padua).

Anticlea Daughter of *Autolycus, she was the mother of Odysseus by *Laertes, king of Ithaca. The legendary cause of her death was grief over her son's long and danger-filled absence during and after the Trojan War.

Antigone The daughter of Oedipus and Iocasta (Euryganeia in another version), she was the sister of Eteocles, Polynices, and Ismene. Antigone accompanied her blind father into exile, returning after his death to Thebes, where her uncle *Creon (2) had assumed power. After the attack of the *Seven against Thebes was over, the king issued an edict strictly prohibiting the burial of the fallen enemy combatants, including *Polynices. Antigone, however, adhered to the law of humanity and buried her brother, defying her uncle's order. For this she was shut up alive in a rock tomb and there took her own life. When her fiancé, Creon's son *Haemon, broke into the tomb to rescue the bride he hoped was still alive, he killed himself over her corpse.

Menoikeus
|
Creon
Iocasta⎯Oedipus

Antigone
Ismene
Eteocles
Polynices

Antilochus The oldest son of Nestor, he was abandoned on Mount Ida immediately after his birth. Later as one of Helen's suitors, he took part in the Trojan War and was a close friend of Achilles. Killed while defending his father against Memnon, Antilochus was buried (according to legend) in a single grave together with Achilles and Patroclus.

Antimachus 1. In Greek legend he figures as a Trojan nobleman who was renowned as a great warrior. Opposed to the return of Helen to the Greeks for the sake of peaceful reconciliation, he recommended that the Greek negotiators be killed; his sons were later killed in retaliation. 2. A Heraclid, he was the son of Heracles and a daughter of Thespius, as well as the father of Deiphontes.

Antinous 1. Son of Eupeithes and the most importunate of Penelope's suitors. In the name of all the suitors, he announced to the queen that none of them would return home until she had chosen one of them to be her bridegroom. Antinous was the first suitor whom Odysseus killed after his homecoming to Ithaca. 2. Darling of the Roman emperor Hadrian, he drowned in the Nile in A.D. 130. Hadrian elevated him to divine

Antinous Darling of the Roman emperor Hadrian (ancient bust)

status and founded the city of Antinoopolis in his memory.

Antiope Daughter of the Theban king Nycteus and Polyxo, she was beloved of Zeus and became through him the mother of the twins *Amphion and Zethus. Fearing her father, she fled during her pregnancy to Epopeus of Sicyon, who took her as his wife. On his deathbed Nycteus transferred the royal power to his brother Lycus, commissioning him to make war against Epopeus and to bring Antiope back forcibly. Epopeus was fatally wounded, and en route to Thebes Antiope gave birth on Mount Cithaeron to Amphion and Zethus. Compelled to leave her children behind, she served from that time as a slave in the house of Lycus, whose wife Dirce added to her misery. Later in flight from Thebes, Antiope encountered her two sons on Cithaeron. They avenged their mother by killing Lycus and Dirce and assuming control of Thebes. According to one strand of the tradition, Dirce was dragged to death by a bull and then thrown into a brook near Thebes that was subsequently named after her.

Antiphates King of the Laestrygonians on Sicily, he was a giant and a cannibal. When Odysseus's fleet entered the harbor of Telepylos, Odysseus sent three of his companions as envoys to the king, seeking a friendly reception. Antiphates seized one of them immediately and ordered that he be cooked for dinner, but the other two got away. Then the monarch called his people to arms, and the Laestrygonians hurled huge boulders at the ships of the newcomers. The ships burst asunder and the greater part of the crew was killed. Only Odysseus's own ship, which had been moored behind a rock, escaped destruction. After taking on the survivors from the other ships, it sailed safely out of the harbor.

Anubis Egyptian god of the dead in the form of a dog or a man with the head of a dog or jackal, he was identified as the son of Osiris and played a role in the cultic preparation of the corpse for burial. The guardian of cemeteries, Anubis had a series of cult places at various

Aphrodite The so-called Aphrodite with dove; sheet gold, Mycenae

Aphrodite

Aphrodite of the old type

Aphrodite of the Medicean type

Aphrodite of Cnidos, a work of Praxiteles (marble copy)

sites in Egypt. Later as *Hermanubis* he was equated by the Greeks with Hermes, conductor of the souls of the dead.

Aphrodite Greek goddess of love and beauty, she corresponded to the Roman goddess *Venus. Although her origin poses many questions, she was probably of Asiatic provenance and first identified with Astarte. Often conceived by the Greeks as having emerged from the sea, she was on that account also called *Aphrodite Anadyomene*. Whether her epithet "the Cyprian" indicates that the Greeks made her acquaintance on Cyprus remains uncertain. It is evident, however, that both there and on some other Greek islands she received special veneration from an early date. Her arrival in Greece by way of the sea can be assumed.—According to a version found in Homer, Aphrodite was the daughter of Zeus and Dione, and the wife of *Hephaestus, the lame smith-god. In spite of his own ugliness, Hephaestus excelled in the production of objects whose great beauty rivaled that of Aphrodite. In addition to her husband, the goddess had numerous lovers, among them Ares and Adonis, but also the mortal Anchises. She bore them many children, including Eros, Anteros, Harmonia, Deimos, Phobos, and Aeneas.—Plato as well as other philosophers and writers distinguished between the heavenly Aphrodite (*Urania*) and earthly, venal love (*Aphrodite Pandemus*).—Aphrodite was frequently represented in the fine arts; the Aphrodites of Cnidos, Melos, and Cyrene are famous examples.

Aphrodite: the goddess is lifted out of the sea by Tritons

26

Apollo A god receiving great reverence from even the early Greeks and later from the Romans, he was the son of Zeus and *Leto, and the twin of *Artemis. Although his mythical birthplace was the island of Delos, where his mother had found refuge from Zeus's jealous wife, Hera, in reality neither his name nor his origin can be definitively explained. Nevertheless, it is certain that he was not a Greek god to begin with but derived either from the Hyperboreans in the far north or from Asia Minor (probably Lycia). His numerous and varied characteristics and functions, like his many, not always decoded epithets, indicate that, as with his twin sister Artemis, features of local divinities were gradually transferred to him whether they corresponded to his primordial nature or not. In Greece his cult spread mainly from Delos and Delphi. According to legend, shortly after his birth Apollo killed the dragon Python, guardian of the Delphic oracle, made himself lord of the oracle, and organized the *Pythian games.—Apollo had an intrinsically dual nature; on the one hand he could bring good fortune and avert evil, while on the other hand he could inflict disaster. For exam-

Apollo of Tenea (c.a. 600 B.C.); example of an archaic representation of Apollo

Apollo (famous sculptures of Apollo) **1.** Veii Apollo (clay statue, end of the 6th century B.C.). **2.** Belvedere Apollo (2nd half of the 4th century B.C.). **3.** Apollo from the west pediment of the temple of Zeus at Olympia (1st half of the 5th century B.C.)

ple, he caused the Greek camp on the Trojan plain to be overrun by plague and guided the deadly arrow of Paris to the vulnerable heel of *Achilles, brought down the sons of *Niobe, and after defeating *Marsyas in a musical contest had him hung from a tree and flayed alive. Yet he was also god of agriculture and herds, with whom peasants sought refuge, god of expiation and healing (*Asclepius), gatekeeper, protector of law and order, and increasingly god of the arts—above all music—and the sciences; as *Phoibos he was equated with Helios. But he played his most important role within and beyond Greece as lord of several oracular sites, foremost among them Delphi and Delos, which helped to unify the Greeks politically and otherwise.—Already in the early 5th century B.C., Apollo was adopted by the Romans, who associated him with the Sibyl at Cumae and worshiped him chiefly as god of medicine. A temple was commended to him in 433 B.C. in connection with a plague. Soon after the battle of Actium (31 B.C.), Augustus had a lavish temple built for him on the Palatine. Through the attentions of the imperial family, Apollo became an object of special veneration.—Antiquity saw the creation of many representations of Apollo. In the 6th century B.C. he still appears as a bearded god; later he came to embody ideal masculine beauty in the form of a naked youth and was also depicted as a cithara player.

Apollonia *Delios.

Apollonius Rhodius (*Apollonius of Rhodes*) A Greek scholar and poet of the 3rd century B.C. Born probably in Alexandria, he was active at the famous library there. Around 245 B.C., after the change of government at Alexandria, he moved to Rhodes; hence his epithet Rhodius. His major work, the four-volume epic *Argonautica*, narrates the voyage of the Argonauts to Colchis and their return, homeward journey. It is the first complete presentation of this material in which the formulaic language of Homer is largely absent. Its impact on subsequent literature, e.g., the works of Virgil, was significant.

Appiades In Roman mythology the collective name for the five goddesses Concordia, Minerva, Pax, Venus, and Vesta. A temple was erected to them near the Appian Way.

Apuleius, Lucius A Roman writer from Madaurus in North Africa, he was born ca. A.D. 124 and died ca. 180. Apart from his philosophical works, he wrote (also in Latin) the *Metamorphoses*, a novel in which the protagonist is turned into an ass. Among its other episodes is the tale of Amor and Psyche.

Aquilo The Roman equivalent of the Greek north wind, *Boreas.

Arcadia A mountainous area in the central Peloponnesus, named (according to legend) after King Arcas, a son of Zeus and Callisto. The locale of many old cults, Arcadia witnessed the lives and deeds of important gods and heroes. Some of Heracles' adventures took place there.

Arcas King of the Arcadians and son of Zeus and *Callisto, he was rescued by Zeus from the womb of his dead mother (in another version Callisto was turned into a bear) and raised by *Maia. She brought him to the court of his grandfather Lycaon, who killed him and served him to Zeus for dinner. Zeus, however, restored him to new life. Arcas taught the Arcadians agriculture, weaving, bread-making, and other skills; he contributed greatly to the civilization and refinement of his people. After his death he was set among the stars as Ursa Minor; his mother became Ursa Major.

Archeloos (*Archelochos*) Son of *Antenor and Theano, he shared the leadership of the Dardanian troops in the Trojan War with Aeneas and Acamas.

Areion A magic horse, which was even capable of speech. Offspring of Poseidon and Demeter, it saved the life of *Adrastus (1) on the battlefield before Thebes.

Areopagus ("hill of Ares") A hill at Athens where the council of nobles (which was named after it) met in antiquity. This council was originally the central administrative authority of the state and the state court of justice, but after 462–461 B.C. it had jurisdiction only in criminal cases.—According to legend, *Ares was the first

29

Ares as assailant

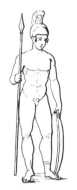

Ares Greek god of war

to stand trial on the Areopagus, in regard to the murder of *Halirrhothius.

Ares Greek war god of Thracian origin; though identified by the Romans with *Mars, he had a much greater significance than the latter. The son of Zeus and Hera, he was regarded as a personification of the wild and unbridled passions of war. Thus in Homer his name could signify simply combat, manslaughter, or war. Despite his inclusion among the twelve great Olympian gods, the cult of Ares was not widespread in Greece; indeed, it was best known on the Athenian Areopagus. The love relationship between Ares and Aphrodite produced, among other progeny, *Harmonia. With other women the god also fathered numerous additional children, who accompanied him into battle often on his swift horses: *Aithon, *Konobos, *Phlogios, and *Phobos. In art Ares was first represented as an old warrior with a beard, whereas later he was shown as a vigorous young man in the manner of the *Ares Ludovisi.*

Arethusa A Greek nymph and companion of Artemis. When she attempted to elude the river god *Alpheus, who was pursuing her, Artemis changed her into a spring on the island of Ortygia near Syracuse.

Arges One of the *Cyclopes, he was the brother of *Brontes and *Steropes.

Argives (Greek, *Argeioi*) The inhabitants of Argos and the Argolid. In Homer the term is used to designate all Greeks.

Argo The ship on which the *Argonauts sailed to Colchis in their search for the Golden fleece. According to Greek legend, it was a longship with fifty oars and built by an Argive, perhaps the son of Phrixus. Athena (in another version, Hera) affixed a piece of wood with the power of speech, from the Dodona oak tree, to its bow. Later the *Argo* was translated to the heavens as a constellation.

Argonauts The name by which those Greeks were called who sailed from Iolcus to Colchis on the ship *Argo* under the leadership of *Jason with the purpose of finding and bringing the

*Golden fleece out of Aia. The foremost participants in this venture were the heroes who had already taken part in the Calydonian boar hunt. They are enumerated in the *Argonautica* of *Apollonius Rhodius, which also portrays the voyage as such in considerable detail. Apart from this list of participants, there are other, divergent lists. After numerous adventures, the Greeks reached their destination. When Jason asked King Aeetes for the Golden fleece, the king attached several arduous conditions to its surrender: Jason had to plough a field by means of fire-spitting bulls, sow the furrows with teeth from Aeetes' dragon, and fight the warriors who sprang into life from the sown furrows. Aided by Aeetes' daughter Medea, a renowned sorceress who had fallen in love with him, Jason succeeded in performing the tasks set for him. Medea gave him an ointment which protected him against the fiery breath of the bulls; and he threw a stone into the midst of the warriors who sprang up from the dragon's teeth, so that they turned on each other and he could kill them one by one. Then when Aeetes still refused to hand over the fleece, Medea drugged the guardian dragon, enabling Jason to steal it. As soon as this was accomplished, the Argonauts fled with Medea and her brother Apsyrtus. On their way Medea killed and dismembered her brother, tossing the pieces of his corpse into the sea in order to delay Aeetes as he pursued them. After many detours and further adventures, the heroes at long last reached Iolcus.—The story of the Argonauts may have grown out of the jour-

Argonauts

1. Cretheus ⊤ Tyro

  Aeson ⊤ Alkimede
           (Polymede)

  Jason — Medea

2. Poseidon ⊤ Tyro

  Pelias   Neleus

  Acastus

Argonauts Depiction on the so-called Argonaut krater (ca. 460 B.C.)

neys made by the Milesians in the Pontus region. It could also be connected with 7th-century colonization. It was enriched with all sorts of mythical and folktale elements, which gradually coalesced around the historical core to form a unity. The Argonautic expedition became a popular theme in world literature.

Argos 1. Legendary Greek king of the domain of Argos, which was named after him. The son of Zeus and Niobe, he was the first son of Zeus by a mortal woman. During his long reign, Argos's kingdom enjoyed an economic and cultural renaissance. 2. The oldest son of Phrixus and Chalciope. After leaving the court of his grandfather Aeetes, he was shipwrecked on a voyage but saved by the Argonauts. He tried to persuade Aeetes to surrender the Golden fleece to Jason.

Argos Panoptes A many-eyed giant with very keen vision (hence the name "Argos eye"). He killed *Echidna and a bull who had laid Arcadia to waste. Finally Hera commissioned him to watch over *Io, who had been turned into a beautiful heifer. But Hermes lulled Argos Panoptes to sleep and killed him.

Ariadne (*Ariane, Aridela*) Originally a Minoan goddess and probably a vegetation goddess, who was worshiped in the Aegean islands. In Greek mythology she was the daughter of *Minos of Crete and his wife Pasiphae. By lending him a skein of wool, Ariadne helped Theseus, with whom she had fallen in love, to find his way

Minos⌐Pasiphae

Phaedra—Theseus
Ariadne⌐Dionysus*

Thoas
Staphylus
Oenopion
Peparethos

*The tradition occasionally names Theseus instead of Dionysus as the father of Ariadne's children.

Ariadne

Ariadne Abduction of Ariadne

out of the labyrinth in which he had slain the Minotaur. They escaped together, but Theseus then abandoned Ariadne on the island of Naxos. There she married Dionysus, to whom she bore several children. After her death Dionysus conducted her to Mount Olympus and set the garland that Hephaestus had given her for her wedding in the heavens as a star (the Northern Crown).—The Ariadne theme has been treated frequently in art (A. Feuerbach), poetry, and music (the opera by R. Strauss). At first the Minotaur part of the story was emphasized, and later the motif of Ariadne abandoned by Theseus.

Arion A Greek lyric poet and musician from Methymna on Lesbos, who lived in the 7th or 6th century B.C. He was the first composer of dithyrambs, which represented a preliminary stage of tragedy, and is also supposed to have been a fine cithara player. None of his works have survived. Herodotus tells the story of how he was thrown overboard by sailors on a voyage back to Greece from Sicily, but then was saved by a dolphin.

Aristaeus Son of Apollo and the nymph *Cyrene, and guardian of beekeepers. He was brought up on nectar and ambrosia by the Horae and so rendered immortal. In another version Chiron was his foster father. When he pursued *Eurydice (1) and she was fatally bitten as she fled, all his bees died. Proteus then advised him to breed new swarms in the carcass of a dead ox, on the basis of the notion that insects of all kinds could be spontaneously generated in carcasses.

Aristophanes A Greek poet and playwright who lived from ca. 445 to ca. 384 B.C. The most important exponent of Old Attic comedy, he expressed sharp criticism of his time in his comedies, using elevated language and drawing on aristocratic, traditionalist sentiments. Of the 44 plays extant in the library at Alexandria that were attributed to him (the authenticity of some is contested), 11 have survived.

Armilustrium A Roman festival dedicated to Mars. Celebrated on October 19 and directed by the *Salii, its main content was the ritual pu-

Artemis The mistress of animals with two does

Artemis So-called Diana of Ephesus (marble with bronze face, hands, and feet); here Artemis is represented as a vegetation goddess rather than goddess of the hunt

rification of weapons at the end of the campaigning season.

Artemis The most popular of all the goddesses in Greek mythology, she was the daughter of Zeus and Leto and the sister of Apollo. The etymology of her name is still not known. As a virgin goddess of the hunt, she gradually assimilated various features that were transferred to her from other, local goddesses. Accompanied by nymphs, she wandered through woods and meadows with her bow and arrow in her capacity as patroness of hunters and mistress of animals. Whoever offended her she severely punished. Thus she killed the daughters of *Niobe, the *Aloades (who intended to storm Mount Olympus), Actaeon because he had seen her naked in her bath, and Orion because he challenged her to a discus-throwing contest or pursued one of her huntresses—perhaps herself as well. Among many other examples, that of Agamemnon is especially noteworthy: because he had offended her, she demanded the sacrifice of his daughter Iphigenia. On the one hand she brought ruin, while on the other she protected life. In her role as Eileithyia, she helped women in labor to have a painless delivery. If a woman died in childbirth, it was believed that she had been struck by an arrow of Artemis; nevertheless, the dead woman's clothes would be sacrificed to the goddess. Brides and bridegrooms, particularly young maidens, entreated her protection by making sacrifices to her before their weddings.—Artemis also appears in mythology as a vegetation and fertility goddess. In connection with the tree cult, her image was hung up in trees and bushes. The masked dances performed in her honor by youths and maidens (often with bear masks), which had a somewhat phallic character, point to Artemis in her capacity as a vegetation goddess, as does the cult image of her adorned with many breast-like formations. In Asia Minor cultic veneration of Artemis was essentially the same as that of the Great Mother. At a relatively late stage, Artemis was identified with the moon goddess *Selene, in whose person she visited the beloved Endymion night after night.—Her role in the Trojan War, following the *Iliad*, was not very glorious, and she finally took refuge with her father, Zeus.—Artemis was frequently represented in art in various guises but especially with her quiver of arrows.

Arval brothers The *Fratres Arvales.

Ascanius The legendary son of Aeneas and Creusa, who followed his father to Italy after the fall of Troy. There he assumed the name Iulus, conquered the Etruscans, and founded *Alba Longa. His descendants reigned for over 400 years, down to *Numitor.—According to another tradition, Ascanius returned to Troy and refounded it.

Artemis as moon goddess

Asclepiadae The practitioners of the healing art of Asclepius.—*Asclepieia.

Asclepieia The sanctuaries of *Asclepius, they were Greco-Roman places of pilgrimage associated with medical schools and sanatoria directed by priest–doctors. Apart from Epidaurus, the focal point of the cult, the most famous Asclepieia were located at Athens, Rome, Pergamum, and Cos.—In their methods of treatment, Asclepian physicians took psychological insights fully into account. Patients first underwent a long, healing sleep (incubation) in the temple of the god; as they slept, Asclepius was supposed to make known to them the correct treatment. In this process autosuggestion played a considerable role, though other therapeutic methods such as exercise, bathing, fasting, and observing special diets were gradually developed and applied too. Thus with time it came about that even scientifically trained doctors (e.g., students of Hippocrates from Cos) often called themselves *Asclepiadae.

Asclepius Asclepian staff, with sacred serpent as emblem of Asclepius

Asclepius Greek god of healing, he was taken over by the Romans under the name *Aesculapius.—At first Asclepius was probably not a god, but rather a hero of Thessalian origin who had been educated by the centaur Chiron, reputed to be an outstanding physician. Asclepius is described in this and other ways by Homer; the poet also refers to his sons, Machaon and Podalirius, as important doctors and fighters in the Trojan War. In other sources it is even said

Asclepius with staff and serpent

that Asclepius was killed by Zeus with a thunderbolt because he had restored the dead to life.—From the 5th century B.C., worship of Asclepius spread throughout the Greek world, with Epidaurus as the chief sanctuary. Meanwhile Asclepius was regarded as the son of Apollo and *Coronis (1) and thereby as the god who was increasingly displacing the old god of healing (Apollo). So-called *Asclepieia sprang up here and there, and at every founding ceremony a serpent symbolizing the god was carried in solemn procession to the new place of worship.—In artistic representations Asclepius is usually shown with serpent and staff (caduceus), surrounded by medically gifted family members, including his daughter Hygieia, who as the personification of health played a special role.

Asclepius enthroned

Asopos In Greek mythology, a river god who was venerated in a region with several rivers of the same name; he was particularly significant as a Boeotian river god. His numerous daughters were the ancestral mothers of the most important Greek heroes, e.g., Ismene, the grandmother of Io. When Zeus abducted his daughter Aegina, Asopos pursued them both; but Zeus prevented him from regaining his daughter by means of a lightning flash.

Asphodel A lilylike plant native to the Mediterranean region, having white, yellow, or pale violet blossoms and bulbous, sugary roots. Among the Greeks and Romans it was associated with the dead and for that reason sacred to Hades and Persephone. The roots were considered food for the dead, who might even be imagined as occasionally wandering through fields of asphodel (Homer). Asphodel was also regarded as a defense against evil spirits. The Greeks often planted it at the graves of the dead to signify their mourning.

Astarte Babylonian Ishtar. A goddess of the sky and fertility, she was also worshiped in Canaan, Moab, Egypt, the Phoenician colonies, and at one time in Israel as well. The Greek goddess Aphrodite may have derived from her.

Asteria One of the fifty daughters of *Danaus.

Astraea Goddess of justice, daughter of Zeus and Themis, and as one of the *Horae usually identified with *Dike.—Astraea left the earth at the end of the Golden Age in order to avoid the human affliction and misery of the Bronze and Iron ages. (In another version she left the earth at the beginning of the Iron Age.) She was translated to heaven as the constellation Virgo.

Astraea Goddess of justice

Astraeus In the Greek imagination, father of the *Winds.

Astydameia Possibly the wife of *Acastus, she fell in love with *Peleus.

Atalanta In Greek legend a female figure about whom the tradition makes rather contradictory statements. She was a famous huntress from Arcadia or Boeotia, either the daughter of *Iasus (2) and Clymene or the daughter of Schoeneus. A participant in the *Calydonian boar hunt, she was the first to encounter the boar, which *Meleager finally killed. Atalanta is also supposed to have accompanied the Argonautic expedition.—One strand of the tradition reports that Atalanta was abandoned as an infant, because her father wanted a son instead, but was nursed by a she-bear and then raised by hunters. A proverbial hater of men, she defended her virginity vehemently. She challenged each of her suitors to a race, killing him once he was defeated. At last she was defeated by Melanion (in another version, by *Hippomenes), who on the advice of the goddess Aphrodite let three golden apples fall onto the race course. Atalanta lost critical time by stooping over to pick them up. Her marriage to Melanion produced a son, *Parthenopaeus. He later set off as one of the *Seven against Thebes against the wishes of his mother, who foresaw his death.— Atalanta and her husband were eventually turned into lions because they had made love in a place sacred to Zeus (according to another version, the place was sacred to Cybele).

Ate In Greek mythology a term for delusion, guilt, and ruin, usually personified as a daughter of Zeus. He angrily banished her from Olympus and dispatched her to earth, where she caused trouble from that time on.

Athamas King of Orchomenus (1), he was the son of *Aeolus (1) and Enarete, by *Nephele the father of *Phrixus and *Helle, and by his second wife (*Ino, daughter of Cadmus) the father of *Melicertes and *Learchus. With the golden ram Nephele saved Phrixus and Helle from the machinations of their stepmother, Ino, who sought to eliminate them. However, only Phrixus reached the court of Aeetes at Colchis, for Helle fell into the strait en route. At his palace Athamas raised the god Dionysus, who had been committed to Ino's care. Furious with him on this account, Hera struck the king with an attack of insanity during which he killed his son Learchus. Together with Melicertes, Ino plunged into the sea, where she was elevated to the status of a goddess, becoming *Leucothea, while her son became the sea god *Palaemon.—*Golden fleece, *Themisto.

Athena Athena in full panoply, just as she was when she sprang from the head of her father (according to one strand of the tradition); from the west pediment of the temple of Aphaea on Aegina

Athena (*Athene*) Virginal Greek goddess of combat and victory, but of wisdom, too, protector of political life, and patron of the arts and sciences as well as handicrafts, she was a daughter of Zeus, according to myth. Fearing that a future grandson might prove dangerous to him, Zeus swallowed his pregnant consort *Metis. In Hesiod's account Athena sprang from her father's head, and in the post-Hesiodic tradition she appeared fully armed. Her name cannot be derived from a Greek source. Probably originating as a peaceful goddess of house and palace in the Minoan period, she acquired new features in the warlike Mycenaean period, remaking her as an armed tutelary goddess of rulers with their citadels and domains. In the *Iliad* she figures as the tutelary goddess of the Greeks and often bears the epithet Pallas ("maiden"). Her

Athena Owl, the animal sacred to Athena, on an ancient Athenian coin image, the *Palladium, was regarded as guaranteeing the preservation of citadels and cities, including Troy. Only if it were stolen could a city be captured by the enemy. At a later stage, when kingship had died out in Greece, Athena became the protectress of free cities, especially Athens, from which she probably also received her name, though the Athenians generally designated her only as "the goddess." The animal sacred to her was the owl, and her sacred tree was the olive. Though usually pictured as a virgin armed with the *Aegis of her father, she was not imagined as animated with the wild, unbridled passion of the war god *Ares. Rather, she interceded on behalf of orderly combat in defense of one's homeland. In such contexts she gave particular support to individual heroes such as Odysseus, Achilles, and Heracles from time to time. She took part in the *Gigantomachy. In her contest with Poseidon, she won dominion over Attica because the Olympian gods preferred her gift to Athens—the olive tree—over the spring that Poseidon caused to gush forth on the Acropolis.—As goddess of peace, and no doubt in continuity with her former identity as goddess of house and palace, *Athena *Ergane* instructed humans in many handicrafts, for example, weaving and pottery making. Occasionally she was also connected with agriculture, and legend reports that she brought not only the distaff and loom but also the plough and rake to mankind. As goddess of domestic peace, she established courts of law in the cities; as goddess of wisdom, she was venerated especially by philosophers and poets.—The Parthenon, one of the most splendid temples in all of Greece, was erected to the virgin Athena on the Acropolis of Athens. The gold and ivory statue of Athena, sculpted by *Pheidias, resided inside the Parthenon. In front of it stood *Athena Promachos*, accentuating her role as a warrior. The *Panathenaia was celebrated annually in honor of the goddess, and the Great Panathenaia (whose main ritual is represented on the Parthenon frieze) every four years.—The Roman goddess *Minerva corresponds to the Greek Athena.

Athena Attic relief (ca. 470 B.C.)

Athena Athena of Myron from the Athena-Marsyas group (ca. 440 B.C.; marble copy of the lost bronze original)

Athena Nike A small temple on the Athenian Acropolis that was dedicated to Athena as goddess of victory.

Athena Parthenos The name given to the gold and ivory statue of Athena Parthenos created by *Pheidias, which stood in the Parthenon. On the basis of descriptions and copies, it can be approximately reconstructed.

Athens (*Athenae*) The modern capital of Greece, situated on the coastal plain of Attica. In antiquity it was the most important Greek city-state after Sparta and the most important center of Greek culture. The zenith of its power and cultural achievement occurred under Pericles (from ca. 460 B.C.). Defeat in the Peloponnesian War (431–404 B.C.) brought with it political decline. During the Hellenistic and Roman periods, its philosophical schools (the Lyceum of Aristotle and the Academy of Plato) made it a center of Greco-Roman education. Thereafter it devolved into a provincial city.—The focal point of ancient Athens was the Acropolis with its many temples.—Athens and Attica together are the locale for a significant body of folklore and mythology.

Athens The Propylaea on the Acropolis at Athens (east facade)

Atlantis A legendary island realm supposed, according to Plato, to have sunk into the Atlantic Ocean after it had ruled Egypt for a long time. Conjectures about its location situate Atlantis in the Aegean, in the lesser Syrtis, or near the Canary Islands. The ancient commercial city of Tartessos in southern Spain was also said to be associated with it. Both the existence and the location of the island, about which no consensus could be reached even in antiquity, remain the subject of scholarly discussion to this day.

Atlas Son of the Titan Iapetus and the Oceanid *Clymene (1), brother of Epimetheus and Prometheus, husband of *Pleione, father of the Pleiades and possibly of the Hesperides. In Greek legend he upheld the firmament on his shoulders. Part of the tradition explained this as a punishment for his having rebelled against Zeus, as one of the Titans. When *Heracles approached the garden of the Hesperides, who guarded the golden apples of the gods, Atlas (being stationed nearby) foresaw his moment of liberation. But though Heracles did indeed assume Atlas's burden while the latter went to fetch the golden apples, he then tricked the Titan into taking back the firmament.

Atlas Hercules and Atlas; depiction on a mirror

Atlas So-called Farnese Atlas (ancient sculpture, now in Naples)

Atreids In Greek mythology, the collective name for the sons of Atreus: Agamemnon and Menelaus.

Atreus Member of the accursed line of the Tantalids (*Tantalus); son of *Pelops (1) and of *Hippodameia; and brother of *Thyestes, with whom he murdered their stepbrother *Chrysippus. Cursed by their father, the two murderers were forced to go into exile. After the death of Pelops, Atreus became king of Mycenae. Thyestes tried to usurp the throne by seducing *Aerope, his brother's wife, in order to acquire through her the golden lamb (a golden ram is also mentioned) that was in her possession and was regarded as the symbol of dominion over Mycenae. Atreus thereupon banished his brother and drowned his wife in the sea. Thyestes succeeded in taking *Pleisthenes, Atreus's small son, with him and raised him as if he were his own child. When Pleisthenes had grown up, his foster father sent him out to kill Atreus. But Atreus anticipated his destroyer and had him killed, without realizing that this was his own child. When Atreus grasped what he had done, he plotted a terrible revenge. Ostensibly intending a reconciliation, he invited his brother to his palace, where he served him Thyestes' own children (whom he had killed) at a banquet. The legend reports that on this day Helios reversed

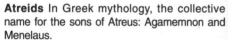

Pelops—Hippodameia
|
Thyestes
Atreus—Aerope
|
Pleisthenes
Agamemnon
Menelaus

his course in horror, following a path from west to east. Thyestes cursed the entire line of Tantalids and obeyed an oracle which said that the son he would engender with his daughter Pelopia would exact revenge for the outrage he had suffered. Atreus married Pelopia and assumed that *Aegisthus, the son his wife bore, was his own. When Aegisthus reached manhood, Atreus sent him out to murder Thyestes. At the last moment, however, father and son identified each other; Aegisthus then slew Atreus. The enmity between the fathers continued into the next generation.—The legendary material with its themes of murder and revenge found a place in literature: Sophocles wrote plays entitled *Thyestes* and *Atreus*, and Euripides wrote a tragedy called *Thyestes*; but these works have not survived except in fragmentary form. Only the *Thyestes* of Seneca is fully extant.—The "Treasury of Atreus," a beehive tomb found at Mycenae, was named arbitrarily after the legendary figure of Atreus.

Atropos One of the *Moirai, she cut the thread of life spun by Clotho.

Attica A region in east central Greece, it was politically united under Athens in antiquity.

Auge 1. An Arcadian princess, daughter of Aleos of Tegea, who consecrated her as a priestess of Athena. She bore a son, *Telephus, to Heracles. When her father, the king, heard this news, he had his daughter and grandson put out to sea in a chest. The chest drifted ashore in Mysia, where King *Teuthras (2) received Auge with her child and married her.— According to another tradition, Auge was sold as a slave by Nauplius to Teuthras, who then married her. After being abandoned by his grandfather, Telephus was raised by shepherds. Later after many wanderings he found his mother again. 2. Goddess of birth; also an Arcadian epithet of Artemis.

Augean stables The stables of *Augeas. In a figurative sense the term is used proverbially to describe extreme disorder and filth.

Augeas In Greek mythology, king of Elis. He may have been the son of Helios, although the tradition names a number of other possible fathers. Augeas possessed vast herds of cattle, whose stables had not been cleared of manure for many long years. *Heracles finally cleaned them by channeling a stream of water through them.

Aulis Boeotian harbor where the Greek fleet assembled before sailing against Troy, and where Iphigenia was supposed to have been sacrificed. At Aulis there was an important sanctuary to Artemis.

Aurora The Roman goddess of dawn, corresponding to the Greek *Eos.

Auster Latin name for the south or southwest wind, *Notos.

Autolycus Son of Hermes, father of *Anticlea, and maternal grandfather of *Odysseus. Instructed from childhood by Hermes, he developed into an expert thief who always knew how to cover his tracks. Sisyphus first gave Autolycus pause by branding the heels of his cattle, which Autolycus was stealing, so that they could be identified.

Autophonos The father of Polyphontes.

Aventine (Latin, *mons Aventinus*) One of the seven hills of ancient Rome, it faces the Palatine and slopes down steeply to the Tiber. The Aventine developed into a plebeian quarter as a result of the influx of plebeians from the municipal zone in 455 B.C. Several temples stood on it; among them, a sanctuary dedicated to Diana is supposed to have been constructed there under Servius Tullius.

Babylon Legendary son of Belus, he was regarded by the Greeks as the founder of the city of Babylon.

Bacchanalia The secret Roman cult of *Bacchus, which was celebrated with sexual excesses. In 186 B.C., the Roman senate prohibited it because of the wave of crime it had

introduced. In spite of stringent regulation, however, the cult did not die out at that time.

Bacchantes The female followers of Bacchus or Dionysus, they were also called *Maenads or Bacchae.

Bacchants Participants in the *Bacchanalia.

Bacchus (Greek, *Bakchos*) Also Liber, the Roman god of wine, he was identified from an early date with the Greek god *Dionysus.

Balios One of the two immortal horses of Achilles; the other one was Xanthus. Issuing from the union of *Zephyrus and the Harpy Podarge, they could run as fast as the wind.

Bassarides Probably female worshipers of Dionysus disguised with fox skins, who belonged to his entourage.

Batieia 1. A *Naiad. Gorgophone in another version, she was the mother of Hippocoon, Icarius, and Tyndareos by Oebalus. 2. Mother of the Trojan race, she was the daughter of *Teucer (1) and the wife of Dardanus, progenitor of the Trojan kings.

Baton (also called *Elato*) The charioteer for Amphiaraus, who accompanied the latter in the war of the *Seven against Thebes. Together with their chariot, the two were swallowed up by a crevasse in the earth that Zeus had created by means of a lightning flash.

Battus 1. The cowherd of *Neleus of Pylos, he was turned into a stone by the enraged Hermes after he broke his promise not to tell Apollo that Hermes had stolen the god's horned cattle. 2. The first king of Cyrene, he reigned for many years and was followed on the throne by a line of hereditary successors. The tradition reports that the Delphic oracle induced him to found the city of Cyrene in Libya. According to legend, he was a stammerer whose fright at the sight of a lion cured him.

Baucis *Philemon and Baucis.

Bear *Arcas.—*Callisto.

Bellerophon (in Homer, *Bellerophontes*) A Greek hero, he was the son of Glaucus, king of Corinth, and *Eurymede. Forced to leave the court of his parents, he went to the court of King Proetus of Tiryns, where the king's wife, *Stheneboea, fell passionately in love with him. When Bellerophon refused her advances, she avenged herself by declaring to her husband that Bellerophon had tried to seduce her. On hearing this the king, who did not doubt his wife, dispatched Bellerophon to his father-in-law *Iobates, king of Lycia, bearing a letter in which Iobates was requested to kill the new arrival. Iobates set Bellerophon various tasks in the hope that he would thus meet his death. However, Bellerophon came through all these trials successfully; he even destroyed the *Chimaera. Finally Iobates gave his guest one of his daughters in marriage and appointed his new son-in-law to succeed him on the throne when he died. Returning at this point to Tiryns, Bellerophon took his revenge on Stheneboea by persuading her to go for a ride on *Pegasus, during which she was plunged into the sea. Later Bellerophon attempted to ascend Mount Olympus on Pegasus, but fell to his death when Zeus repulsed him. In another version, he survived this fall but sank into melancholy.— Bellerophon was venerated in Corinth and Lycia.

Bellerophon persuades Stheneboea to go for a ride on Pegasus

Bellerophon on Pegasus

Bellona Roman goddess of war frequently identified with the Greek *Enyo, and later also with

Bellona Roman
goddess of war

Bellona Roman
goddess of war

the Cappadocian goddess Ma. Regarded as the sister or wife of Mars or Quirinus, she had a Roman temple on the Campus Martius near the altar of Mars. In front of it stood the so-called *columna bellica*, from which the *Fetiales declared war by means of a symbolic spear thrust. This temple was often used as a welcoming site for foreign envoys.

Belus A Greek hero, son of Poseidon and Libya, and brother of *Agenor, he was the father of *Aegyptus and Danaus. Belus may originally have been a Semitic god, who was later taken over by the Greeks.

Benthesicyme Daughter of Poseidon and *Amphitrite, she counted Triton among her several siblings. Benthesicyme married an Ethiopian king and bore him two daughters. She also brought up *Eumolpus, the son of Chione.

Berenice Daughter of King Magas of Cyrene, she lived from ca. 273 to 221 B.C., when she was murdered. In 247 she married Ptolemy III; and for the sake of her husband's safe return from the Syrian campaign, she made an offering of her hair. Berenice appears in the poetry of Callimachus.

Bia Daughter of Pallas and the Styx, she was the sister of Kratos, Nike, and Zelos. Always on the side of Zeus, she helped Hephaestus and Kratos to chain the Titan *Prometheus to a rock as punishment for his theft of fire from the gods.

Biadike Either she or *Demodike was the wife of Cretheus, king of Iolcus.

Bias 1. King of Argos and brother of *Melampus. His first wife, with whom he had several children, was Pero, daughter of Neleus. His second wife, Iphianassa (2), daughter of *Proetus, bore him Anaxabia. 2. One of the *Seven Wise Men.

Bistonians A Thracian people who inhabited the southern coast of Thrace, with their capital city at Abdera.

Bithynia An ancient province of northwest Asia Minor inhabited by Thracians. From 297 B.C. it was an independent kingdom, and in 74 B.C. Nicomedes IV bequeathed it to Rome. Bithynia was the legendary homeland of *Philemon and Baucis.

Biton Son of a priestess of Hera in Argos, and brother of Cleobis. When their mother had no oxen at hand, the two sons drew her wagon to the sanctuary of Hera. They were rewarded for this act with the greatest gift that could fall to the lot of mortals: to sink into eternal sleep. According to another version, when after the sacrifice to Hera they died in their sleep, their mother's prayers were answered.

Boeotia A province of central Greece into which the Boeotians migrated around 1000 B.C. In the 5th century B.C., the Theban League was formed, with Thebes as its capital. Hesiod, Pindar, and Plutarch, among others, came from Boeotia. Within the world of Greek legend, Thebes played an important role.

Boiotos Son of Poseidon and *Melanippe, he was the brother of Aeolus and the father of Itonos.

Bona Dea (Latin for "good goddess") A Roman goddess of female fertility whose annual festival was celebrated at the beginning of December as a mystery cult for women only. The women gathered at night in the house of a high official, who was not himself permitted to participate. Nor was the Pontifex Maximus present, but the Vestal Virgins attended the ceremony. Wine and myrtle were excluded from the cult on the following grounds, as explained by the tradition: Bona Dea, whose real name was Fauna, was the daughter of Faunus and famed for her chastity. Her father conceived a passion for her and sought to win her over by giving her wine to drink. When she still did not succumb, he struck her with myrtle branches. Only after turning himself into a serpent did he attain his objective.— In another version Bona Dea was the wife of Faunus. She voluntarily drank too much wine, and for that reason was beaten to death by her husband with myrtle rods.—The goddess had a temple on the Aventine in Rome, where serpents were kept and healing remedies were prepared. Her cult was still widespread in the imperial period. Greek influences are difficult to determine. It can be assumed, though, that connections existed between Bona Dea and the Greek fertility goddess Damia.

Bonus Eventus A Roman deity who personified success in the sense of a happy outcome. He seems to have been worshiped especially by peasants, but also had a temple in Rome.

Boreades *Calais and *Zetes, the sons of the wind god *Boreas.

Boreas Among the Greeks, a harsh north wind and the son of Astraeus (*Winds) and Eos. He abducted the Athenian daughter of Erechtheus, *Oreithyia (2); carried her off to his homeland, Thrace; and with her engendered the Boreades, Zetes and Calais. The Greeks worshiped him particularly because he had come to their aid against the enemy in the Persian Wars, especially during the sea battle at Salamis (480 B.C.).

Boreas

Bosporus The strait between the Balkan peninsula and Asia Minor, which connects the Black Sea with the Sea of Marmora and divides Europe from Asia. According to Greek legend, the Argonauts passed through the Bosporus

Boukephalos (Greek for "bull's head") The name of Alexander the Great's charger and favorite horse. According to legend, it was supposed to have attained the age of 30.

Briareos One of the *Hecatoncheires, he was the son of Gaia and the brother of Cottus and Gyes. Thrown into Tartarus by Uranus, he was rescued by Zeus, whom he then hastened to help in the struggle against the Titans.

Briseis (actually *Hippodameia*) The daughter of *Briseus of Lyrnessus, she was taken prisoner at Troy, where she served Achilles as his slave and concubine. When Agamemnon was forced to renounce his own concubine because the gods had unleashed a plague in the Greek camp, he claimed Briseis for himself. This led to a fierce quarrel between Agamemnon and Achilles, as a result of which Achilles refused to take any further part in the war, causing the Greeks much distress.

Briseus of Lyrnessus A ruler in the vicinity of Troy. He and his entire family, with the exception of his daughter *Briseis, were killed by Achilles.

Britomartis A Cretan goddess often associated with the goddesses Dictynna and Aphaea. Identified by the Greeks as the daughter of Zeus and Karme, who served Artemis as a nymph, she was also frequently equated with Artemis. When Minos tried to seduce her (in another version, he had seduced her but she sought to elude him), she leapt into the sea and was caught in a net by fishermen (hence Dictynna). As a goddess, Britomartis was worshiped by hunters, fishermen, and sailors.

Brontes One of the Cyclopes, he was the son of Uranus and Gaia, and the brother of Arges and Steropes. Like his brothers, he had only one eye, set in the middle of his forehead.

Broteas 1. Son of Tantalus and Dione, and brother of Niobe and Pelops, he carved the oldest image of the mother of the gods on a rock but refused to do the same for Artemis. In his ensuing madness, sent by the goddess, he scorched himself, which made him think he was immortal. 2. One of the children of Amphion and *Niobe. 3. Brother of Amnon, and an invincible boxer.

Bubona A Roman goddess distinguished for her exceptional beauty and identified with *Epona.

Busiris A king of Egypt who, on the advice of two seers, had all foreigners killed and sacrificed to Zeus in order to avert a drought from his country. He was the son of Poseidon and *Lysianassa, and the brother of Memphis. When this despotic monarch tried to sacrifice Heracles, too, the latter killed both him and his attendants.

Butes 1. An Argonaut, he was the son of Poseidon (in another version, of Teleon) and Zeuxippe. On their way back home from Colchis as the Argonauts were sailing past the *Sirens (with Orpheus attempting to protect the heroes from the sound of their infatuating song by drowning it out with his lyre), Butes jumped overboard, intending to swim to the Sirens. Aphrodite saved him, however. 2. The son of Boreas and half-brother of Lycurgus, king of Thrace, against whom he conspired; thenceforth he lived in exile as a pirate. After he had abducted a princess named Coronis, Dionysus drove Butes mad, with the result that he jumped into the sea and drowned. 3. Son of *Pandion and Zeuxippe, twin of Erechtheus, and brother of Philomela and Procne, he married Chthonia, a daughter of Erechtheus.

Buthrotum The legendary harbor of Epirus, founded by Helenus after the fall of Troy.

Bybassos A goatherd and the father of Syrna, wife of Podalirius.

Cabiri In Greek mythology, the name given to divine beings of unknown, but possibly Phrygian, provenance; some were male and some female. It is not clear how many there were, and they had many obscure features which the Greeks themselves could not explain. Their cult flourished especially in Samothrace, Lemnos, and Thebes. Probably they originated as earth divinities, and the Greeks then associated them with Hephaestus. They were often invoked by persons in distress at sea and by persons working the land. The oldest known testimony about them is contained in *Cabiri*, a lost tragedy by Aeschylus.

Caca Ancient Roman goddess of the hearth, daughter of Vulcan, and sister of *Cacus; at a very early stage, she and Cacus were associated as a divine couple. Caca was replaced by Vesta.

Cacus An old Roman god and son of Vulcan who was first worshiped on the Palatine and later on the Aventine. In legend, he was a fire-spewing giant dwelling in a cave on the Aventine and killing passersby. When *Heracles came along with the oxen of Geryon, Cacus pulled some of them by the tail into his cave. Drawn to the cave by the roaring of the oxen, Heracles entered it by force and killed Cacus.

Cadmea A city founded by *Cadmus. In the historical period, it was the citadel of Thebes.

Cadmus Son of the Phoenician king Agenor (or Phoenix) and Telephassa (or Ariope), he had several siblings, including *Europa. When Zeus abducted Europa, Cadmus was commissioned by his father to go in search of his sister. He undertook a long and fruitless journey, which culminated in his consulting the Delphic oracle. The oracle advised him to follow a cow and, wherever it lay down, to found a city on that spot (*Cadmea). Cadmus stoned to death a dragon that had killed his companions, extracted its teeth, and (on the advice of Pallas Athena) sowed them in the earth. The armed warriors who sprang fully grown from the soil killed each other off until they were reduced in number to five—the so-called Spartoi, who became the ancestral heroes of the Thebans. Because the slain dragon was descended from Ares, Cadmus had to perform some years of slave labor to expiate his deed. Afterward he married *Harmonia. On the occasion of their splendid wedding, she received from Hephaestus a costly necklace, the so-called necklace of Harmonia, which brought disaster to all of its owners.— Cadmus was said to have brought the Phoenician alphabet to Greece, and his Theban reign was reputedly marked by peace and prosperity. Later he moved with his wife to Illyria and became king there. The couple were finally turned into beautiful snakes and removed to Ely-

Agenor—Telephassa

Cilix
Phoenix
Europa
Cadmus—Harmonia

Polydorus
Autonoe
Ino
Semele
Agave

sium.—For the Greeks, the story of Cadmus constituted the founding legend of Thebes, the Theban royal house being traced back to a Phoenician origin.

Caduceus (Greek, *kerykeion*) The herald's staff of *Hermes.

Caeculus An ally of Turnus against Aeneas. According to local tradition, he founded Praeneste.

Caelius (*Caelius mons*) Of the seven hills of ancient Rome, the one that lay farthest to the southeast.

Caeneus One of the *Lapiths, Caeneus was originally a young girl named *Caenis whom Poseidon abducted and then rewarded by granting her a wish. She asked to be transformed into an invulnerable man. This "second" Caeneus was considered impious, and it was asserted of him that he revered nothing except his own spear. Part of the legend tells of how he met his death in the struggle between the Lapiths and the *Centaurs in spite of his invulnerability: his opponents drove him into the ground with rocks and branches.

Caenis The name of the young girl who later became *Caeneus.

Caesar Originally a cognomen of the old Roman Julian gens. It was borne by Augustus as the adoptive son of Gaius Julius Caesar and afterward became part of the title of the Roman emperor. From the reign of Hadrian, it was also applied to the emperor's successor. During the tetrarchy of Diocletian (A.D. 285–306), Caesar was used for the rank below the Augusti.

Caesar Gaius Julius Caesar

Caieta The legendary wet nurse of Aeneas and the eponym of the city of Caieta, where she was traditionally supposed to have been buried.

Calais One of the *Boreades, he was the son of *Boreas and Oreithyia.

Calchas Son of Thestor, he was a famous Greek seer who knew how to divine the will of the gods especially from the observation of birds. In the Trojan War, the duration of which he prophesied, Calchas played an important role for the Greeks. Thus he explained the basis on which Achilles would have to take part in the conflict and why Iphigenia would be sacrificed at Aulis. According to a later version, the stratagem of the wooden horse was his inspiration.— When Calchas lost a contest with the seer *Mopsus (2), he died of chagrin, as had been prophesied.

Callinira One of the *Nereids.

Calliope The *Muse of epic poetry and learning, she was frequently represented with a tablet or scroll and a stylus (writing implement).

Calliope One of the Muses

Callirhoe The name of several legendary Greek figures: 1. Daughter of the river god Achelous and wife of Alcmaeon. 2. Daughter of the river god Scamander, wife of Tros, and mother of various children including *Ganymedes and *Ilus. 3. Daughter of Amphion and *Niobe, who was killed together with her sisters by Artemis. 4. One of the Oceanids, who married *Chrysaor, to whom she bore Geryon and perhaps also Echidna.

Callisto (Greek for "the most beautiful") Daughter of Lycaon, she was a hunting companion of Artemis. In the company of Zeus she broke her vow of chastity and then gave birth to Arcas. To save her from Hera's jealousy, Zeus turned Callisto into a bear. According to another version, Artemis struck her with an arrow or transformed her into a bear. A further tradition reports that Zeus turned Callisto into the constellation of the Great Bear.

Calpe Ancient name for Gibraltar, known in antiquity as one of the "pillars of Heracles."

Calyce Daughter of Aeolus and Enarete, wife of Aethlios, and mother of Endymion. Distinguished for his exceptional beauty, her son may have been fathered by Zeus.

Calydon 1. An ancient Greek city in Aetolia containing a sanctuary of Artemis and Apollo, it was probably the locale of the *Calydonian boar hunt. 2. Son of the Aetolian king Thestius, he was inadvertently killed by his father. 3. Son of

Ares, he was turned into a stone (according to legend) because he had observed Artemis in her bath.

Calydonian boar hunt The most important Greek heroes, led by *Meleager, participated in this hunt for a wild boar that had been devastating the land of Calydon. The hunt was the subject of one of the celebrated stories comprising the Greek (specifically Aetolian) cycle of legends.

Calypso Daughter of Atlas in Greek mythology, she was a nymph who lived on the island of Ogygie (possibly located near Crete or Italy). Calypso offered shelter to the shipwrecked Odysseus, fell in love with him, and kept him with her for seven years (according to another version, even longer). Then at his request and that of the gods, she let him go.—The name Calypso, meaning "to cover" or "to veil," suggests that the nymph may have been a goddess of death. If so, the fact that Odysseus eventually proceeded on his way could be interpreted as a victory over death.

Camasena Possibly the mother of *Tiberinus by Janus.

Camenae Ancient Roman prophetic water nymphs, worshiped in Rome near the Porta Capena, where the vestal virgins drew their daily water. Later they were identified with the Greek Muses.

Camilla Daughter of Metabus, king of the Volsci, and of *Casmilla. A virgin, she was brought up in the sacred woods of Diana to be a huntress and warrior. Camilla fought on the side of Turnus against Aeneas until she was killed by an arrow.

Camillus Son of Hephaestus, he was occasionally identified as the father of the *Cabiri.

Camirus Son of Kerkaphos and grandson of Helios and Rhodos, he was the eponym of the ancient city of Camirus on the island of Rhodes.

Campus Martius The "plain of Mars"; in ancient Rome it was an exercise field and place of assembly dedicated to Mars and located at the bend in the Tiber. Until the reign of Aurelian, it lay outside the city walls. From the last century of the Republic, it was filled with temples, baths, and other public buildings.

Canace Daughter of Aeolus and Enarete, she had many brothers and sisters and was the grandmother of Iphimedeia. One legend reports that she killed herself when commanded to by her father after she had engaged in incestuous relations with one of her brothers.

Candaules King of Lydia who lost his beautiful wife and his kingdom to *Gyes (2).

Canens A nymph and daughter of Janus and the goddess Venilia, she was happily married to Picus. When *Circe pursued Picus and was rejected by him, she avenged herself by turning him into a woodpecker. Canens long searched in vain for her husband and finally, like Echo, was reduced to a bodiless voice. In another version, the nymph dissolved in her own tears out of grief over the loss of her husband.—Picus became a holy bird of Mars; although certainly not regarded as a god, he was accorded a certain reverence.

Capaneus Son of Hipponous, he was the husband of *Evadne (2), the father of Sthenelus, and one of the *Seven against Thebes. During a storm in the city, he insulted the gods by asserting in an act of hubris that not even Zeus could quell the storm. In return, Zeus killed him with a stroke of lightning. Capaneus was not buried together with his warrior comrades but instead (as was customary for one struck by lightning) cremated on a separate funeral pyre. One strand of the tradition reports that Evadne leapt onto the burning funeral pyre of her husband.

Caphareus A cape, or headland, protruding from the island of Euboea. There *Nauplius (2) allowed the ships returning from Troy to crash onto the rocks by sending them misleading fire signals, his aim being to avenge the death of his son *Palamedes.

Capitol (Latin, *Capitolinus mons*) One of the seven hills of ancient Rome; located at the northwest end of the Roman Forum, it was apparently already fortified in the pre-Roman period. It functioned as the religious center of the ancient city. The cult of the divine triad comprising Jupiter, Juno, and Minerva is supposed to have been transferred by the kings from the Quirinal to the Capitol. The temple of Jupiter Capitolinus was erected on the Capitol by Tarquin Superbus and dedicated in 509 B.C. Although this temple burned down repeatedly, it was always rebuilt according to the original dimensions. The triumphal way terminated on the Capitol, which also served as the point of departure for the Ludi Romani (festive games). Caligula linked the Capitol and the Palatine by means of a bridge.

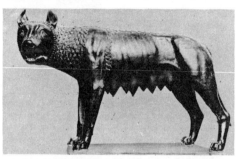

Capitol The Capitoline she-wolf, an Etruscan-Roman bronze sculpture, was set up on the Roman Capitol in 439 B.C. and complemented, in the 15th century, with figures of Romulus and Remus

Capricornus The Latin designation for the constellation Capricorn. Named after his father Aegipan, the half-goatlike Pan, Capricornus was placed among the stars on Mount Ida as the foster brother of the infant Zeus.

Capys A Trojan and companion of Aeneas, who warned the other Trojans about the hazards of the wooden horse. He came with Aeneas to Italy and is sometimes regarded as the legendary founder of Capua.

Car Son of Phoroneus and eponym of the Carians.

Carcinus This large crab was trampled on by Heracles when it rushed to the aid of the many-headed Hydra, which the hero destroyed in the course of his second labor.

Cardea Roman goddess of the door hinge (*cardo*), she was a maiden huntress beloved of Janus.

Caria (*Karia*) A plateau in southwestern Anatolia between the Meander River (today the Menderes) and the coast, it was originally inhabited by pre–Indo-European Carians. The Dorian migration brought Greek settlement to the area. From 546 B.C., it was under Persian domination, and from 133 B.C. it was ruled by Rome. Caria is mentioned by Homer.

Carmenta A legendary prophetess who came to Rome with her son *Evander from Arcadia, where her name was Nikostrate or Themis; she is supposed to have prophesied in verse.—In reality Carmenta was probably an old Roman goddess of birth with a sanctuary on the Capitol near the Porta Carmentalis (named after her). Her festival, the Carmentalia, was celebrated in January by women.

Carmentalia The festival of *Carmenta.

Carna An old Roman goddess whose functions cannot be determined with certainty. Her name likely derives from *caro*, meaning "meat," but it could also have an Etruscan origin. On her feast day (June 1), beans and bacon were offered to her at her sanctuary on the Caelian Hill. Often associated with the cult of the dead and the underworld, she was actually goddess of the bodily organs (heart, lungs, etc.).—Ovid tells a completely different story about Carna. According to his story, she was a nymph who knew how to fend off her many admirers: she would command them to go ahead of her into a cave, and as soon as their backs were turned she would run away from them. This stratagem failed, however, with the two-faced Janus, who was able to win Carna for himself. Out of gratitude for the favor she had bestowed on him, Janus granted her the power to drive away nocturnal, vampirelike creatures.—Carna and the goddess Cardea may originally have been identical.

Carthage (Greek, *Karchedon*; Latin, *Carthago*) Formerly a Phoenician commercial center situated north of Tunis, it was traditionally founded in 814 B.C. from Tyre but in actuality probably somewhat later. Carthage became the capital of the Carthaginian kingdom. As such, it achieved hegemony over all the other Phoenician colonies in the western Mediterranean.—Legend traced the founding of Carthage back to *Dido, who obtained the land for the city from King *Iarbas.

Caryae 1. An ancient city in Laconia. 2. A young girl beloved of Dionysus. After she died she was turned into a walnut tree. Because Artemis made known the death of Caryae, legend records that the goddess received the epithet Caryatis.

Casmilla The wife of Metabus, king of the Volsci, and the mother of *Camilla.

Cassandra In Hellenistic poetry also called *Alexandra*. The legendary daughter of Priam and Hecuba, she was endowed with prophetic powers. Apollo fell in love with her, but because she did not return his affection the god brought it about that her prophecies were never believed. Thus in vain she foretold the fall of Troy and warned her compatriots against the wooden horse. When Troy was captured by the Greeks, she sought refuge with the image of Athena but was taken prisoner by Aias the Locrian and, according to part of the tradition, raped. In the distribution of booty among the Greeks, she fell to Agamemnon, who took her home with him as his concubine. There she was murdered together with her master by *Clytemnestra.—The expression "cry of Cassandra" derives from the thoroughly dark and foreboding nature of Cassandra's prophecies.

Cassiopeia The wife of Cepheus of Ethiopia and the mother of *Andromeda. When Cassiopeia boasted that her beauty surpassed that of the Nereids, at the behest of the latter, Poseidon sent a monster onto the land by means of a tidal wave; the monster proceeded to devour man and beast. An oracle promised deliverance in exchange for the sacrifice of Andromeda to the monster. The princess was chained to a rock for this purpose, but *Perseus succeeded in freeing her. After Cassiopeia died, she became a constellation.

Castalia The name given to both the nymph of the sacred spring on Mount Parnassus at Delphi and the spring itself. The water from this spring was used primarily to purify the temple. In the Hellenistic period, Castalia served as a symbol of poetry.

Castalides This epithet was applied to those Muses connected with the Castalian spring at Delphi.

Castor One of the *Dioscuri.

Catamitus The Roman equivalent of Ganymedes, the son of *Tros (1).

Catreus King of Crete and son of *Minos and Pasiphae, he was inadvertently killed by his son Althaemenes.

Catullus (*Gaius Valerius Catullus*) A Roman poet of the first century B.C., whose very personal, affecting, passion-filled poems treat experiences of nature, friendship, and above all love. In his later poems, Catullus ventured into political themes, with satirical verses directed against Julius Caesar. Even the longer poems and mini-epics showing Greek influence, among them the poem on the marriage of Peleus and Thetis which focuses on the lament of Ariadne, are marked by his own stamp.

Cebren A Trojan river god, and possibly the son of Oceanus and Tethys, he was the father of Asterope and Oenone.

Cecrops The name of several Greek legendary figures, including the following: 1. An earthborn hero, imagined as a serpent with a human body, who was widely considered to have been the first king of Attica. He reportedly built the Athenian acropolis (Cecropia) and issued the earliest laws, contributing greatly to the civilizing of the state. His daughters Herse, Aglauros, and Pandrosos were divine beings like the nymphs, who filled fields and meadows with dew. They were called Agraulides. 2. Son of the Attic king Pandion and grandson of Cecrops (1), whose heroic activity was set in Haliartos.

Celaeno 1. One of the *Harpies and designated as their leader by one strand of the tradition. 2. One of the *Pleiades.

Celeus King of Eleusis, he was the husband of Metanira and the father of *Demophon (2). When Demophon's nurse *Doso (Demeter) in her wish to make her charge immortal held him over the fire, his frightened mother, Metanira, intervened. Demeter revealed herself, ordered Celeus to build a temple for her, and initiated him along with other Eleusinian princes into the "mysteries."

Celmis One of the three oldest *Dactyls.

Centauromachy The battle between the Thessalian Lapiths and the *Centaurs.

Centaurs One of the Centaurs

Centaurs These fabulous creatures, half-man, half-horse, whose name remains obscure, were native primarily to Thessaly. Already in antiquity their origin was often traced back to Centaurus, a son of *Ixion. Some of them, like *Chiron, were friendly and cultured; others, like *Eurytion, who started the battle between the Thessalian Lapiths and the Centaurs (Centauromachy), were wild and uncontrolled.

Centaur and warrior: metope from the Parthenon on the Acropolis of Athens

Centimani The Latin name for the Greek giants with one hundred arms called the *Hecatoncheires.

Cephalus In Greek mythology, the son of Hermes and Herse, he was a famous hunter. *Eos carried him off to Mount Olympus and bore him Phaethon. He married Procris, daughter of

Erechtheus, who likewise distinguished herself as a hunter. Advised by Eos, Cephalus decided to test the fidelity of his wife. This he did by leaving their home for several years and then returning in disguise and attempting to win her over with gifts and protestations of love. Procris finally yielded, but when she recognized her husband she fled, overcome with shame, to King Minos of Crete. He presented her with a spear that never missed its mark (in another version, she received the spear from Artemis). Later the partners were reconciled, and Procris returned to Athens. Despite their reconciliation, Procris remained jealous, and when Cephalus went on one of his frequent hunting expeditions she suspected him of having a mistress. On one such occasion, she hid herself in a bush; believing that the rustling that he heard in the thicket was caused by a deer, Cephalus killed his wife with his spear.—The Cephalus legend has many variants, which touch on the characters and their conduct as well as the spear.

Cepheus 1. King of Ethiopia, he was the husband of *Cassiopeia and the father of *Andromeda. 2. King of Tegea, he was one of the Argonauts and the father of numerous sons. One legend reports that Cepheus had in his possession a lock of Medusa's hair, given to him by Athena, which made his kingdom invincible. During the Argonautic expedition, he gave this lock to his daughter Sterope. He and all his sons perished in a war between Heracles and the Hippocoontides in which they fought on the side of Heracles.

Cephissus (also *Cephisus*) A Boeotian river god, he was the son of Oceanus and Tethys, brother of the other river gods, and father of Narcissus by the nymph Liriope. Other children are ascribed to him, but in those cases his paternity is disputed.

Cerberus Guardian of the underworld, he was the son of Typhon and Echidna. This three-headed dog-monster (according to another version he had up to fifty heads), with serpents on his heads, neck, and back, stood at the entrance to Hades. He granted admission to

Cerberus Heracles overcomes the hound of hell (Cerberus) and takes him out of the underworld; depiction on an Attic amphora

Ceres

Ceres

everyone but permitted no one to go back out again. Only twice was he persuaded otherwise: once by the song of Orpheus, and once by *Heracles, who overcame this hound of hell with his bare hands, showed him to Eurystheus, and then brought him back to Hades.

Ceres Roman goddess of agriculture and all nourishing plants, she was also a goddess of marriage and death. From at least the 6th century B.C., she was identified with the Greek goddess *Demeter. In 496 B.C. construction commenced on a temple dedicated a few years later to the divine triad Ceres, Liber, and Libera. To a large extent Ceres was the goddess of the plebeian class. She saw to it that the tribunes of the people upheld the laws, and her temple served as the religious focus of the plebeian community. Around 250 B.C. a substantial shift occurred in the cult when Greek priestesses reoriented its performance to Demeter, whose search for her lost daughter Proserpina (Persephone) now played a central role in the ritual.

Cerialia The Roman festival of *Ceres, celebrated on April 19; later it was held in honor of the divine triad Ceres, Liber, and Libera.

Ceryneia With its golden horns, the "hind on Mount Ceryneia" was sacred to Artemis, who prohibited anyone from killing it. Heracles pursued it for one year and captured it alive. He then carried it to Argos, where he set it free.— By contrast, Euripides represents the hind as a dangerous monster that was killed by Heracles.

Ceryx 1. Son of Hermes and Herse. 2. One of the Heraclids and son of Eumolpus or Hermes, he was the founding father of the *Kerykes*, a family of priests who served the Eleusinian deities.

Ceto A daughter of *Gaia, she was the sister and wife of *Phorcys.

Ceyx King of Trachis, son of Hesperus, and husband of Alcyone (daughter of Aeolus), he was said to have sheltered the fugitive Heracles and later the Heraclids.—Regarding the king and his wife, a legend involving animal metamorphosis such as frequently occurs in Greek mythology is told: when Ceyx and Alcyone in their hubris called themselves Zeus and Hera, Zeus became angry and turned them into birds.—According to another tradition, Ceyx failed to return from a sea voyage, whereupon the despairing Alcyone threw herself into the sea. Overcome with compassion, Zeus turned her into a kingfisher (in Greek, *alkyon*). The expression "halcyon days" was proverbial in antiquity for beautiful weather because, during the kingfishers' brooding period, the sea tended to be especially calm.

Chalciope The daughter of Aeetes, king of Colchis, and wife of *Phrixus, to whom she bore four sons: Argos, Melas, Phrontis, and Kytissoros. After the Argonauts had saved her shipwrecked sons, Chalciope persuaded her sister Medea to help Jason obtain the Golden fleece.—The legend of Phrixus has a whole series of variants.

Chalcis The chief city on the Greek island of Euboea. In the 8th and 7th centuries B.C., it was an important commercial center with many colonies, especially on the peninsula of Chalcidice. In 506 B.C., it was subjugated by Athens. According to legend, Chalcis took its name from a daughter of Asopos.

Chalcodon King of the Abantes on the island of Euboea, and the father of *Elephenor. He was killed at Thebes by Amphitryon.

Chaos In Greek mythology, the yawning void symbolizing the state of the world before the genesis of living beings, Chaos was also understood as the unordered primary substance preceding all substantiality and its laws. Out of Chaos issued Erebus and Nyx or, according to other scenarios, Gaia (earth), Tartarus (the underworld), and Eros (love). Orphic cosmogony had time (Chronos) generate Aether and Chaos out of himself. The speculations about Chaos were numerous and sometimes quite diverse.

Chariklo A nymph who was the wife of Eneres, the mother of *Tiresias, and a favorite of Athena.

Charis A Greek goddess and possibly the wife of *Hephaestus, maker of exquisite art objects, with whom she was associated as the personification of charm. She received veneration in Sparta, Attica, and other parts of Greece. Since the plural of Charis is *Charites, she may originally have belonged to that group of goddesses.

Charites (Greek for "the Graces") Greek goddesses of grace, they were the daughters of Zeus and Eurynome. They often appear in the entourages of Hermes, Aphrodite, and Apollo. After Hesiod there were usually three of them: Aglaia ("radiance"), Euphrosyne ("joy"), and Thaleia ("the flowering"). Their Roman analogs were the *Graces.—*Charis.

Charon In Greek mythology, the aged ferryman who transported the dead across the rivers of the underworld, including Acheron and Styx, and brought them to the gates of Hades. The prerequisites for his service were the prior burial of the dead person and the payment of an obolus, placed in the mouth of the deceased. Charon likely originated as a god of the dead. In Greek popular tradition, the figure of Charon survived as *Charos*.

Charon The hoary ferryman of the underworld

Charybdis A legendary monster of whom Homer tells in the *Odyssey*. Three times a day it sucked in water and then with a loud roar spewed it out again. Facing Charybdis was the equally menacing *Scylla; together they posed an almost insuperable threat to seafarers. Odysseus himself escaped them only with great effort. Already in antiquity, the monsters were assumed to be located at the straits of Messina.

Chelone A nymph who, according to legend, ridiculed the marriage of Zeus and Hera. Her punishment was to be turned into a tortoise and forever deprived of speech.—Chelone was also the popular designation for a coin from the island of Aegina on which a tortoise was represented.

Chilon An important Spartan statesman and philosopher of the 6th century B.C. He played a decisive role in the internal and external politics of Sparta and is supposed to have strengthened the position of the ephors. A number of sayings like "Know thyself" (*gnothi seauton*) and "Nothing in excess" (*meden agan*) are attributed to him. Later he was worshiped as a hero and counted among the *Seven Wise Men.

Chimaera (Greek for "goat") A fire-spewing monster in Greek mythology, often depicted with the head of a lion, body of a goat, and tail of a dragon or snake; each of these three parts could also have its own head. This composite creature, an expression of the dark and sinister, devastated his surroundings until he was killed by *Bellerophon. Today the term "chimaera" often signifies a vague and foolish fancy.

Chimaera Etruscan bronze, 5th century B.C.

Chione 1. A daughter of *Daidalion, who had many suitors. Particularly loved by Hermes and Apollo, she bore them a pair of twins: *Autolycus to Hermes, and *Philammon to Apollo. One strand of the tradition reports that Artemis shot Chione with an arrow out of envy when she boasted that she was more beautiful than the goddess. 2. Daughter of *Boreas and *Oreithyia (2). She gave birth to *Eumolpus, whom she threw into the sea, traditionally in order to hide her shame. Eumolpus was saved by Poseidon, however.

Chiron The only immortal *Centaur in Greek mythology, he was the son of Kronos and *Philyra. Dwelling in a cave on Mount Pelion, Chiron was distinguished for his wisdom, justice, and goodness. Probably originating as a Thessalian god of healing, he developed into a teacher and counselor of many eminent Greek heroes, among them Asclepius and Achilles. Incurably wounded by Heracles during the latter's pursuit of the Centaurs, Chiron yielded his immortality to Prometheus and was set in the heavens as a star by Zeus.

Chloris 1. Daughter of Amphion and *Niobe, she may have been the only one of their daughters to escape death at the hands of Apollo and Artemis. Chloris married Neleus, with whom she had one daughter and twelve sons. All of her sons except *Nestor died in combat with Heracles. 2. The mother of *Mopsus (1) by Ampycus.

Chromios Son of *Neleus. He and Alkenor were the only survivors, on the Argive side, of a battle between 300 Argives and 300 Spartans. The sole Spartan survivor was *Othryades.

Chrysaor The son of Poseidon and Medusa, he issued from the womb of Medusa together with the winged Pegasus when Perseus killed Medusa. Chrysaor married the Oceanid *Callirhoe (4); she bore him Geryon, a three-headed monster (in another version, three-bodied) who played a role in the adventures of *Heracles. *Echidna may also have been a daughter of Chrysaor.

Chryse The daughter of Halmos and Orchomenus, sister of *Chrysogeneia, and mother of Phlegyas, son of Ares.

Chryseis In the *Iliad*, the daughter of *Chryses, priest of Apollo. She was captured by the Greeks at Troy and made the concubine of Agamemnon, to whom she bore a son, also named Chryses. Because Agamemnon refused to give Chryseis back at the request of her father, Apollo sent the plague into the Greek camp and so compelled Agamemnon to release his slave after a long delay. When Agamemnon then turned his attention to *Briseis, the concubine of Achilles, an explosive conflict arose between the two heroes.

Chryses 1. Son of Agamemnon and *Chryseis. 2. Son of Hermes and co-regent on the island of Paros. 3. The father of Chryseis, a priest of Apollo. During the Trojan War, when the Greeks refused to surrender his daughter (who had fallen into their hands) to Chryses, he prayed for revenge and Apollo struck the Greeks with the plague.

Chrysippus Bastard son of Pelops, whom Laius carried off to Thebes. Hera then sent the sphinx to punish the Thebans. Distinguished for his exceptional beauty, Chrysippus was murdered either by his two half-brothers, Atreus and Thyestes, or by Hippodameia.

Chrysogeneia The daughter of Halmos, sister of *Chryse, and mother of Minyas.

Chrysothemis A daughter of *Agamemnon and *Clytemnestra.

Chthon (Greek for "earth") The meaning of the name *Gaia.

Chthonia 1. Daughter of Kolontas; she established a sanctuary for Demeter after her father was annihilated because he had disregarded the goddess. 2. Daughter of Erechtheus; she married Butes (3), the twin brother of Erechtheus.

Chthonios One of the *Spartoi, he was the brother of Echion, Hyperenor, Peloros, and Udaios.—*Cadmus.

Cicones A Thracian people who were allied with Troy in the Trojan War. On his way home from Troy, Odysseus plundered the chief city of the Cicones. In revenge they killed some of his ships' crews.

Cilix Son of *Agenor (or Phoenix) and Telephassa (or Ariope) in Greek legend, he was the brother of Cadmus and *Europa. After the abduction of Europa by Zeus, Cilix accompanied Cadmus on the search for their sister.

Cimmerians In Greek legend, they were a people living on the far side of Oceanus, whose land contained an entrance to Hades. As the inhabitants of this land, the Cimmerians never saw the light of day. Odysseus visited them on his homeward journey from Troy.

Cimon 1. Athenian general and politician who lived from ca. 507 to 449 B.C., he was the son of Miltiades. From ca. 476 B.C., as one of the annually reelected *strategos*, he exercised political leadership in Athens.—Legend portrays him as the king of Athens who brought the bones of Theseus back from Scyros to Athens. 2. The father of Miltiades, hero of Marathon.

Cinyras Legendary king of Paphos on Cyprus, he was the father of *Myrrha and perhaps also of Adonis. A seer and singer, he is supposed to have founded the famous sanctuary of Aphrodite at Paphos.

Circe One of the famous enchantresses of Greek mythology

Circe A famous sorceress who lived on the island of Aeaea, she was the daughter of *Helios and Perse and the sister of Aeetes and Pasiphae. Circe turned all of her guests into animals, including the companions of Odysseus. To Odysseus, who stayed with her for some time, she bore the son Telegonus (Latinus, according to another version). She figured as an enchantress second only to Medea in ancient mythology.

Cithaeron The name of both a mythological king of Plataea, traditionally depicted as cruel, and a mountain range running between Attica and Boeotia. The mountain range was the locale for a series of legends as well as a focal point for the cult of Dionysus.

Claros A site in Asia Minor near Colophon, Claros was the seat of an ancient oracle sacred to Apollo which underwent a notable revival during the imperial period. At Claros the prophets and priests descended into a kind of sacred grotto, took a drink, and then prophesied in verse, or else they had the results of their consultation rendered in verse.

Cleitus Member of the prophetic line of the Melampodidae and uncle of Amphiaraus, he was abducted by Eos because of his beauty.

Cleobis Brother of *Biton, he was one of the sons of an Argive priestess of Hera.

Cleobulus 1. One of the *Seven Wise Men. 2. A Trojan leader who was killed in the Trojan War by Aias the Great.

Cleopatra In antiquity this frequently used name also played a role in mythology. It was shared by: 1. The daughter of *Boreas and Oreithyia who became the wife of *Phineus (1). 2. The daughter of Idas and Marpessa who married *Meleager and upon his death either hanged herself or died of grief. 3. One of the *Danaids.

Clio The Muse of history.

Clotho One of the *Moirai, she spun the thread of life.

Cloud *Nephele.

Clio One of the Muses

Clymene The bearers of this frequently occurring name in Greek mythology include: 1. A daughter of Oceanus and Tethys who was probably the wife of *Iapetus and had several sons, among them Epimetheus and Prometheus. 2. A daughter of Minyas of Orchomenus who may have been the second wife of Cephalus and gave birth to several children by various men. 3. The daughter of *Catreus and wife of Nauplius (2). 4. One of the *Nereids.

Clymenus 1. Son of Schoeneus of Arcadia and Epicaste, he was the father of Harpalyce, whom he married to Alastor. However, he continued to maintain an incestuous relationship with his daughter even after the marriage ceremony had taken place. Out of hatred for her father, Harpalyce served him a meal consisting of a son or brother. When Clymenus realized what she had done, he killed his daughter and then took his own life. In another version, Harpalyce hanged herself. 2. King of Boeotian Orchomenus, he fell in battle against the Thebans and was avenged by his son *Erginos. 3. King of Olympia and a descendant of Heracles, he revived the Olympian Games or (according to another tradition) inaugurated them.

Clytemnestra Daughter of *Tyndareos and Leda, she was the wife of *Agamemnon, whom she killed in collusion with *Aegisthus. Her children were Electra, Iphigenia, Chrysothemis, and *Orestes, who avenged the death of his father. The role of Clytemnestra in the murder of her husband is variously evaluated in the tradition. Sometimes her involvement is viewed as slight, and sometimes the bloody deed is portrayed as her own act.

Cnidos An ancient city on the west coast of Asia Minor, Cnidos was colonized by Dorians. In its sanctuary of Aphrodite stood the famous statue of the goddess by Praxiteles, which has been handed down through Roman copies.

Cnossos This ancient Cretan city was located south of Herakleion. Above the Neolithic strata at the site, the remains of a palace were excavated dating from the 16th or 15th century B.C. and preserved up to the fourth story. Its foundations can be traced back to a building originating around 2000 B.C. This structure has been wrongly identified with the labyrinth of Greek legend. The different parts of the palace, divided by corridors, are arranged in a confusing manner around a rectangular central courtyard.—In legend Cnossos is connected with Minos and Pasiphae, the Minotaur, and the labyrinth.

Cnossos Faience statuette of a so-called snake goddess

Cocalus The king of Sicily, to whom *Daedalus, constructor of the labyrinth, fled. In one version the legend reports that Cocalus received Minos hospitably at first when the latter appeared and demanded that Daedalus be turned over to him, but Minos was then thrown into hot water by Cocalus's daughters and killed.

Cocytus The name of: 1. A river god and son of Oceanus and Tethys. 2. The underworld river across which Charon, ferryman of the dead, carried the souls of the deceased to Hades.

Codrus The sons of this king of Athens and son of Melanthos were the legendary founders of most of the Ionian cities. According to one strand of tradition, an oracle pronounced that a victory by Peloponnesians who had attacked Athens could be averted through the sacrificial death of the king. After Codrus sacrificed himself, their piety prevented the Athenians from electing another king.

Coeus Son of Uranus and Gaia, he was the brother of the other Titans. He married *Phoebe (2) and became the father of Leto and Asteria.

Colchis The ancient designation for an area situated along the southeast coast of the Black Sea. Colchis was the legendary homeland of *Medea and the destination of the *Argonauts.

Colossus of Rhodes This huge bronze statue of Helios, the god most revered on the island of Rhodes, was erected between 304 and 292 B.C. at the entrance to both main harbors of the city of Rhodes. Toppled by an earthquake in the third decade of the third century B.C., it was considered one of the *Seven Wonders of the World.

Comaetho 1. A priestess of Artemis Triclara at Patrae who had sexual relations with her lover, *Melanippus (3), in the sanctuary of the goddess. As a result of this outrage, both mortals were sacrificed. 2. Daughter of *Pterelaus, king of Taphos, she fell in love with Amphitryon, who did not return her passion. In fact, he killed her because she had pulled out the golden hair of her father on which the latter's immortality depended.

Comatas A goatherd and servant of the Muses on Mount Helicon, he was shut up in a chest after sacrificing a goat but then freed by the Muses.

Compitalia The Roman festival of the *Lares, celebrated at the *compita*, or crossroads, usually at the end of December or the beginning of January.

Concordia An old Roman goddess who personified harmony. After civil war between the patricians and plebeians had ended in 367 B.C., the Roman general and politician Camillus con-

Concordia The goddess of concord; reverse of a Roman coin

71

structed a temple for her at the west end of the Forum, which remained her most important cult place, although another temple to her was erected on the Capitol in 216 B.C.—Concordia also supplied a popular motif on Romans coins, where she was frequently shown with sacrificial bowl and cornucopia.

Consentes (*Consentes Di*) Originally the designation for the twelve Etruscan gods who constituted the council of the gods, it later came to refer to the twelve great Olympian gods, whose statues adorned the Roman Forum.

Consivius ("the sower") Epithet of Janus, who figured in Roman legend as the god of civilization.

Consus Roman agrarian god whose name derives from *condere*, meaning "to save" (conceal) or "to bury." Consus was the guardian of the grain stored in pits, following the ancient Italian custom, and for this reason had an underground altar near the Circus Maximus; from the 3rd century B.C., he also had a temple on the Aventine. The underground altar was uncovered on his feast days (the *Consualia*), August 21 and December 15. Because horse racing (among other activities) took place at his festal celebrations, Consus was erroneously identified as Poseidon or Neptune. Equally false was the derivation of his name from *consilium* and his consequent identification as the god of good counsel.

Copia Roman goddess of wealth and abundance. As the servant of Fortuna, she carried the cornucopia, which was always filled with food and drink.

Corcyra Daughter of *Asopos, she was carried off by Poseidon to the island of Corcyra, where she bore the god a son. Alcinous may have been a descendant of Poseidon and Corcyra.

Coresus A priest of Dionysus at Calydon, he preferred to commit suicide rather than sacrifice Callirhoe, whom he loved.

Corinth This important Greek city of antiquity was situated on the Gulf of Corinth. Its legendary founder was *Corinthus (2), and it was the site of the *Isthmian Games. In 146 B.C. the Romans destroyed the city, but it was later re-founded.

Corinthus 1. Legendary king of *Corinth. 2. A son of Zeus.

Cornucopia In ancient mythology this horn filled with flowers and fruit was an emblem of overflowing prosperity and abundance, as well as a symbol of various gods and goddesses, in-cluding *Fortuna. It was thought to have origi-nated either as the horn of *Amalthea, by which the infant Zeus was partly nourished, or as the horn of the river god *Achelous, which Heracles broke off during combat.

Corona Borealis (*Northern Crown*) In Greek mythology the garland of *Ariadne, transposed by Dionysus to the heavens.

Coronis 1. Daughter of the Lapith Phlegyas and sister of *Ixion, she was loved by Apollo and bore him *Asclepius. Because she deceived Apollo, even while pregnant, by having an affair with the Arcadian Ischys, the god (who was in-formed by a raven) punished her by shooting her dead with an arrow. Apollo rescued the in-fant Asclepius from his mother's body and en-trusted the Centaur *Chiron with his upbringing and education. 2. Daughter of King Koroneus of Phocis, with whom Poseidon fell passionately in love, she was changed by Athena into a white crow. After she brought bad news to Athena, the goddess turned her feathers permanently black. 3. Daughter of Ares. 4. Daughter of Atlas and Pleione, she was one of the *Hyades.

Coronus 1. King of Sicyon, he was a son of Apollo. 2. An Argonaut and leader of the *Lap-iths, he was killed by Heracles.

Corybantes These daimonic beings attended the Phrygian goddess *Cybele. Their orgiastic cult, sometimes extending to states of posses-sion, originated in Asia Minor but had already reached Athens in the 7th century B.C. They were often regarded as children of Zeus who had emerged from the rainwater that he sent down to earth. Whether the Corybantes were identical with the *Curetes, worshiped especially on Crete, or only equated with them at some later time, has not been determined by scholars.

Corybas This legendary Greek figure is occasionally mentioned as the father or ancestor of the *Corybantes.

Corynetes Epithet of *Periphetes meaning "man with a club."

Corythus 1. Son of Paris and Oenone, he led the Greeks to Troy and was killed by his father when he presumed to fall in love with Helen. 2. The husband of *Electra, he founded Corythus in Etruria.

Cos One of the islands of the Dodecanese in the Aegean Sea, it was famed in antiquity for its sanctuary, one of the *Asclepieia. Renowned persons such as Hippocrates and Theocritus were born on Cos or resided there.

Cottus One of the *Hecatoncheires.

Cotys (also *Cotyto* or *Cotytto*) The orgiastic worship of this Thracian goddess spread to Greece and then Italy. Her cult shared features with that of Dionysus, but otherwise she was often identified with Artemis.

Crab (*Cancer*) An animal which already in antiquity appeared under many forms throughout the Mediterranean world, it also played a role in myth and legend. Thus the crab Carcinus came to the aid of the Hydra in its struggle with Heracles and his companion Iolaus. However, the hero succeeded in overcoming the Hydra (his second labor) and in the process crushed Carcinus, who was set among the stars by Hera.

Creon 1. King of Corinth and father of Glauke. Jason and Medea lived at his court for a long time until Jason fell in love with Glauke and decided to marry her. Together with his daughter, Creon fell victim to the revenge of Medea. 2. King of Thebes and son of Menoikeus, he unleashed the drama involving his niece *Antigone when, after the battle of the *Seven against Thebes, he prohibited the burial of his traitorous nephew, one of Antigone's brothers. On humanitarian grounds Antigone disregarded Creon's decree.

Creontiades Son of Heracles and Megara, he was killed together with his brothers by Heracles in a fit of madness.

Cres Son of Zeus and a nymph from Mount Ida, he was the eponym and patron of Crete.

Cresphontes King of Messenia, son of Aristomachus, and husband of *Merope (3), he was one of the Heraclids. Along with two of his sons, he was said to have lost his life in a rebellion led by Polyphontes. The third son, Aepytus, was taken secretly to the court of his grandfather, king of Arcadia, where he grew up. Later he returned to his homeland, killed Polyphontes, and entered into his father's inheritance.

Cressida Not an ancient mythological figure in the proper sense, she is first attested in the medieval legend of *Troilus and Cressida.

Cretan bull A handsome bull sacred to Poseidon, which was sent by the god to *Minos. Minos did not sacrifice it as he had promised but instead incorporated it into his herd. Consequently, the god made the bull turn wild so that it caused great damage. Heracles captured it alive (his seventh labor) and brought it to Eurystheus at Mycenae, but then released it. The panic spread by this monster did not abate until *Theseus killed it.

Crete The largest Greek island, Crete is situated on the southern edge of the Aegean Sea. From early times an important artistic center, it was also the scene of well-known legends.

Crete (Cretan art) Above the so-called priest-king from the palace of Cnossos (16th/15th century B.C.), below a vase with sea-creature motifs (16th century B.C.)

Cretheus 1. Founder and first king of Iolcus, he was a son of Aeolus. Cretheus first married Sidero, then Tyro, and finally Demodike (or Biadike). 2. A companion of Aeneas who was killed by Turnus.

Creusa A name borne by numerous figures of Greek legend, among them the following: 1. Daughter of Priam and Hecuba, wife of *Aeneas, and mother of *Ascanius, who was taken prisoner by the Greeks during the Trojan War but freed by Aphrodite and Cybele; as Aeneas fled from the burning city of Troy, he lost sight of his wife forever. 2. The mother of *Ion. 3. The daughter of King Creon of Corinth, otherwise known as *Glauke, on whom *Medea wreaked her revenge.

Crimnisus A river god and son of Oceanus and Tethys, he married Aigeste, who bore him *Acestes.

Crius One of the *Titans and the husband of *Eurybia. The couple produced three children: Astraeus, Pallas, and Perses.

Croesus As the last of the Lydian kings (6th century B.C.) he subjugated northwest Asia Minor as far as the Halys River. Croesus introduced the coining of gold and his wealth was proverbial; he was reputed to be the richest man in the entire world. It was also said that he sent expensive votive offerings to the Greek sanctuaries, especially to the oracle at Delphi. In 547-546 B.C., he lost his kingdom to the Persians.

Croesus Amphora with painting of Croesus on the pyre from which, accord-ing to legend, he was miraculously saved; by Myson, a Greek potter and red-figure vase painter in Athens (ca. 500 B.C.)

Crommyonian sow This animal, which had been a source of great calamities, was killed by *Theseus near a place called Crommyon.

Crow The bird sacred to Apollo. Originally white, it acquired black feathers because it reported the news of Coronis's infidelity.

Cteatus One of the twin *Moliones, he fought with his brother Eurytus on the side of Augeas in the latter's war with *Heracles. At first the brothers prevailed, but then they were killed.

Cumae (Greek, *Kyme*) The oldest Greek colony in Italy, situated near Naples and founded in the middle of the 8th century B.C. It functioned as the jumping-off point for the dissemination of Greek culture to the Etruscan and Italic peoples. From 334 B.C. it was ruled by Rome.—Cumae was the seat of the Cumaean *Sibyls.

Cupid Roman god of love, analogous to the Greek *Eros.—*Amor.

Curetes Originally the Curetes were probably Cretan vegetation spirits. The legend about them relates that they performed a noisy war dance around the tiny, crying Zeus, Rhea's youngest child, with the intent of fooling Kronos, who threatened to devour his son. Because the

Curetes were servants of Rhea, they were frequently identified with the *Corybantes.

Cybele (also *Magna Mater*) A Phrygian mother and fertility goddess, she was worshiped as the mistress of earth who reawakened nature to new life every spring. An orgiastic vegetation cult celebrated Cybele and Attis, her erstwhile lover, who had killed himself in the mountains after being unfaithful to her. The *Curetes and *Corybantes accompanied her festival with thunderous music, and wild animals drew her carriage. The cult of Cybele arrived in Greece around the 6th century B.C.; there her native land was usually assumed to be Crete, and she was identified with Rhea. Later her cult reached Rome, and from 204 B.C. it was officially recognized with a temple on the Palatine. From the time of Claudius, a great spring festival (March 15–27) was celebrated in her honor, with the orgiastic features much reduced. From the 2nd century A.D. onward, her cult spread through most of the provinces of the Roman empire.— Cybele was also revered as a guardian of citadels and cities, hence the artistic representations of her wearing a mural crown on her head.

Cybele flanked by Hermes (with magic wand) and Attis

Cyclopes These sons of Uranus and Gaia had a single, round eye in the middle of their foreheads. Although their number fluctuates, the tradition most often mentions three giants: Brontes, Steropes, and Arges. They supported Zeus in his struggle against Kronos, forging thunderbolts and lightning flashes for him. Because of their enormous dimensions, the Cyclopean walls of Mycenae and Tiryns were also attributed to the Cyclopes. In addition, legend makes them strong and skillful helpers of *Hephaestus. They were brothers of the *Titans and the *Hecatoncheires.

Cycnus ("swan") The name of several legendary figures: 1. King of Coloni in the vicinity of Troy, of whom one version relates that he was abandoned by his parents, Poseidon and Calyce, and raised by a swan. He married Procleia, who bore him Hemithea and *Tenes. His second wife, Philonome, tried to seduce her stepson but was rebuffed by him. When she then accused Tenes to her husband of having expressed his desire for her, Cycnus in his anger had his son and daughter thrown into the sea in a chest. The two landed on an island whose inhabitants pronounced Tenes their king and named their island after him. When Cycnus discovered that he had been deceived, he punished his wife and went to find his children, hoping in vain to be reconciled with them.—During the Trojan War, the invulnerable Cycnus was stunned by a stone and would have been strangled to death by Achilles if his father, Poseidon, had not turned him into a swan. 2. Son of Ares, he was a highwayman whom Heracles killed in Trachis. 3. King of the Ligurians and friend of Phaethon, he was so grief-stricken when Phaethon plunged to his death in the chariot of the sun that Apollo changed him into a swan. 4. A handsome youth and son of Apollo who loved a man named Phylios. When Phylios left him, he committed suicide and was turned into a swan.

Cyllene 1. A mountain range in Arcadia regarded as the birthplace of Hermes, Cyllene was also the name of the nymph who nursed the infant Hermes. 2. The wife of Pelasgus, king of Arcadia, she may have been the mother of Lycaon.

Cynthia Goddess of the moon. Among the Romans, Cynthia was an epithet of *Diana, and among the Greeks, as Kynthia, of *Artemis. The name Cynthia means "she who comes from Mount Cynthus" (on Delos).

Cynthus A low mountain on the island of Delos, it was often designated as the birthplace of Apollo and Artemis (Diana).

Cyparissus A boy whom Apollo loved. When he inadvertently killed one of Apollo's most beautiful stags, he was transformed into a cypress tree, which took its name from him.

Cypris Epithet of *Aphrodite.

Cypselus 1. An Arcadian king, he was the father of Merope, whom he married to *Cresphontes. After Cresphontes had been killed by Polyphontes, Merope's and Cresphontes' son Aepytus was raised by his grandfather. 2. Son of Aepytus and grandson of Merope, he succeeded his stepfather as king of Arcadia.

Cyrene A nymph and queen of Libya, she was a daughter of the Lapith king Hypseus and a great huntress. When Apollo fell in love with her, she bore him a son, *Aristaeus. The city of Cyrene was named after her.

Cytheria This frequently used epithet of Aphrodite derived from her cult on the island of Cythera (south of the Peloponnesus), which was ancient and widespread.

Cyzicus As king of the Doliones, a Mysian people, he extended hospitality to the Argonauts at his court. They in turn fought with him against his enemies. The Argonauts continued on their way, but the influence of an unlucky constellation as well as a severe storm drove them back to the Doliones, who did not recognize them. In the ensuing scuffle, the king met his death.

Dactyls (Greek for "fingers") The Dactyls were usually thought to be smiths who were associated with Rhea (identified with Cybele) and resided on Crete or in Phrygia. Their number fluctuated: sometimes six giant smiths assisted by five sisters are mentioned or, alternatively, thirty-two magicians and a number of counter-magicians. Another tradition reports that the Dactyls were generated from dust sprinkled by a nymph near the cave where Zeus was born. The remaining fragments of tradition offer further comments but produce no unified, total picture. Thus the legend of the Dactyls is difficult to piece together.

Daedalus (Greek for "skillful") A legendary Athenian and the oldest artist-craftsman among the Hellenes, he was credited with many inventions. After envy drove him to murder his nephew and student *Talos (2) (in another version, Perdix), inventor of the saw, Daedalus fled from Athens to the court of King *Minos on Crete. There he built, among other things, a labyrinth for the king. When Minos tried to detain him in order to secure the talents of this eminent inventor and artisan, Daedalus constructed wings for himself and his son Icarus out of feathers and wax. With these he escaped to the court of King Cocalus on Sicily, but Icarus fell into the sea because he approached too near to the sun, despite his father's urgent warning.

Daidalion The brother of Ceyx and father of *Chione (1). When Chione died (one strand of the tradition reports that Artemis shot her with an arrow because she had boasted that she was more beautiful than the goddess), her father committed suicide out of grief. However, he was saved by Apollo, who turned him into a falcon or some other type of bird.

Daimons Originally a designation for gods, but later used for beings intermediate between gods and humans who could influence human destinies and cosmic processes for good and evil. They had no cult. The Greek philosophers regarded them as the divine component, or divine voice, in human beings. The Daimons were often held responsible for everything fateful, and in this sense they came close to approximating the concept of destiny.

Damastes The real name of *Procrustes, who was killed by Theseus.

Danae In Greek mythology, the daughter of King *Acrisius of Argos and Eurydice. Danae was confined by her father in an ivory tower or an underground dungeon because an oracle had warned the king that a son born to her would kill him. But Danae's encounter with Zeus, who came to her in a shower of gold, made her the mother of *Perseus; later he killed his grandfather by mistake with a discus.— Treated by Aeschylus, Sophocles, and Euripides, the story of Danae was also frequently represented in art.

Danaids The fifty daughters of *Danaus, who were compelled by their uncle *Aegyptus to marry his fifty sons. Because they had married against their will, the Danaids stabbed their husbands on the wedding night with the daggers that their father had secretly given them. Only Hypermestra spared her husband, *Lynceus (1). As punishment for their crime, the Greeks imagined the Danaids in the underworld ladling water into a vessel full of holes.—According to another version, Danaus later gave his daughters in marriage to the winners of a race at an athletic contest.

Danaus The father of the *Danaids, he was also the son of Belus and brother of Aegyptus. Danaus fled with his daughters to Argos, where he supplanted the king. The Greeks considered him to be the progenitor of the Danae.

Daphne (Greek for "laurel") The daughter of the river god Ladon or of Peneus, she was pursued by Apollo, who had fallen violently in love with her. When in her distress Daphne appealed to Zeus to save her, he turned her into a laurel tree. Laurel thus plays a central role in the many artistic representations of Daphne. Also connected with Apollo, the laurel tree was sacred to him and served various functions in his cult.

Daphne Apollo and Daphne; sculpture by Giovanni Lorenzo Bernini (1598-1680)

Daphnis 1. The son of Hermes and a Sicilian nymph, he was exposed immediately after his birth and brought up by shepherds. Daphnis also became a shepherd but distinguished himself rather through his artful singing and flute playing, which he learned from Pan. Having fallen in love with a nymph, he swore eternal fidelity to her, but then broke his vow and was blinded by the victim of his deceit. In another version, he died of unquenchable love pangs inflicted on him by Aphrodite; all of nature mourned him and, according to Virgil, he was eventually divinized.— Daphnis was the legendary creator of bucolic song. Already in antiquity his name had become popular among shepherds, for example, in the pastoral romance "Daphnis and Chloe" of Longus, a poet of the 2nd or early 3rd century A.D., who exercised considerable influence on later pastoral poetry. 2. A shepherd on Mount Ida who was turned to stone by a jealous nymph.

Dardanus In Greek legend, a son of Zeus and Electra. He built the city of Dardania—later called Troy—at the foot of Mount Ida and founded the Trojan royal line.

Dardanus, Mares of Twelve mares who were so fast that no one could catch them. Their father, Boreas, had assumed the form of a horse. Their descendants included *Xanthus (1) and Balios.

Dares A companion of Aeneas on his voyage to Italy. He was killed by Turnus.

Daulis A city in Phocis, located east of Delphi, with nymphs of the same name.

Daunus King of the Rutulians, he was the son of Pilumnus and husband of Venilia, with whom he had two children: Juturna and Turnus. His sword was presented to him by *Vulcan.

Dea Dia A Roman agrarian goddess who was worshiped by the *Fratres Arvales with fertility rites in a sacred grove on the Via Campana during three days in May. Dea Dia, which simply means "goddess," is not a real name.

Decuma One of the three *Fates; the other two were Nona and Parca.

Deianira In Greek legend, the daughter of Oeneus of Calydon and the second wife of *Heracles, to whom she bore several children. After she had sent her husband the shirt of *Nessus and thereby unwittingly killed him, she committed suicide but was changed by Artemis into a guinea hen.—*Achelous.

Deidameia A daughter of King Lycomedes of Scyros. Beloved of Achilles, she bore him *Neoptolemus.

Deikoon Son of Heracles and his wife Megara. When Heracles was suffering from an attack of madness sent by Hera, he killed Deikoon together with the other children from his marriage with Megara, as well as two children of his brother Iphicles.

Deimos and Phobos Two sons of Ares who, according to Homer, rushed into the din of battle with their father and—as their names testify—spread terror and horror all around.

Deiochos A Greek commander-in-chief who was killed by Paris in the Trojan War.

Deion King of Phocis and son of Aeolus and Enarete, he was the husband of *Diomede (1), with whom he had several children.

Deiphobos 1. In Greek mythology, a son of Priam and Hecuba and one of the most valiant Trojans. After the death of Paris, he became the husband of Helen. But when Troy had fallen, *Menelaus, Helen's first husband, reclaimed her as his wife. He mutilated Deiphobos horribly and then killed him. 2. Son of Hippocoon who seized the rulership of Sparta. He had eleven brothers, all of whom (together with their father) were killed by Heracles.

Deiphontes A Heraclid and son of *Antimachus (2). He married Hyrnetho, a daughter of *Temenus (1), with whom he had three sons and a daughter. Because Deiphontes was the chief adviser to his father-in-law, the latter fell victim to his jealous sons. Nevertheless, on account of his wife Hyrnetho's claims, the succession passed to Deiphontes anyway.

Deipyle Daughter of Adrastus and Amphithea, she married *Tydeus and became the mother of *Diomedes (2).

Deipylos Son of *Polymestor and *Iliona, one of Priam's daughters.

Delia Epithet of Artemis (Diana) derived from Delos as her alleged birthplace.

Delios Epithet of Apollo derived from Delos as his alleged place of origin. The annual festival on Delos held in honor of the god was called the *Delia* or *Apollonia*. It was celebrated with speeches in praise of Apollo, with singing, and with games.

Delos Two treeless Greek islands among the Cyclades in the Aegean Sea. As the mythological birthplace of Apollo and Artemis, Delos was one of the main centers of their cult. Since the end of the 19th century, French excavators have uncovered structures there dating from the 7th to the 1st century B.C.: a sanctuary of Apollo with temples, halls, treasuries, portals, and a

Delos The Lion Terrace along the Processional Way

ceremonial way; a temple of Leto with a processional way flanked by a terrace with nine monumental marble lions (7th century B.C.); a stadium; and numerous pieces of monumental marble statuary from the 7th and 6th centuries B.C.

Delphi The cult place of a mother goddess already familiar in the Mycenaean period, situated in the province of Phocis on the southern slope of Mount Parnassus. Later it became the most important Greek temple and oracle site: a sanctuary of Athena but foremost of *Apollo and then also of Dionysus, whose cult lost its orgiastic content at Delphi. Through the *Pythia, Apollo prophesied at Delphi in response to queries; sometimes his oracular sayings were spontaneous. The oracles had to be interpreted by priests since they were often extraordinarily cryptic and metaphorical. The Apollonian spirit, which shaped religious legislation, acquired great significance for Greek ethics and politics. The Delphic oracles in particular gained general validity for all of Greece and even beyond.— After its liberation ca. 590 B.C. from domination by the city of Crisa, Delphi became an autonomous state and, with the help of the Delphic amphictyony, was able to preserve its independence during the Holy Wars and on into the 3rd century A.D. The end came when the sanctuary was plundered by the emperor Constantine and subsequently closed by Theodosius.— From 1892 to 1911, French excavators exposed the walled sanctuary of Apollo, including the sacred way, numerous monuments, votive offerings (e.g., the "charioteer"), treasuries with relief decoration and sculptural pieces (the Athenian treasury was reconstructed in 1903–1906), a bouleuterion, the sphinx of the Naxians on a column, and the stoa of the Athenians with its many historically significant inscriptions. At the center of the main sanctuary are the (mostly destroyed) altar and temple of Apollo (4th century B.C.). Also within the sacred precinct of Apollo are a theater and the Lesche, or clubhouse, of the Cnidians, decorated with (destroyed) wall paintings by Polygnotus; a stadium lies to the northwest. Outside the precinct are additional sanctuaries and the fountain house of the Castalian spring.

Delphinios Epithet of Apollo. *Dolphin.

Delphos A legendary son of Apollo, after whom *Delphi is supposed to have been named.

Delphyne In Greek mythology, a monster, half-serpent, half-woman, who guarded the tendons from the hands and feet of Zeus, which the Typhon had cut out of him during a fight. Aegipan and Hermes stole them back again, however. Delphyne was killed by Apollo.

Demaratus A banished Corinthian and the father of *Tarquinius Priscus.

Demeter One of the most popular Greek divinities, a goddess of fertility and growth, and the object of great veneration. She was highly esteemed in her capacity as a mother but even more so as a goddess of women. Homer seldom mentions her because aristocratic society took little interest in rural vegetation deities. In mythology, Demeter was a daughter of Kronos and Rhea, and by Zeus the mother of *Persephone, who is often referred to in the tradition as the "corn maiden" or "Kore." The bond between mother and daughter was so strong that when Hades abducted Persephone, Demeter out of rage inflicted barrenness on the earth. Searching all over the world for her daughter, she ar-

Demeter of Cnidos

85

Demeter Sacrifice of a
pig to the fertility god-
dess Demeter; after a
depiction on an Attic
vase

rived at the court of King *Celeus of Eleusis.
There, assigned to the care of his youngest son,
*Demophon (2), she tried to make him immortal.
When she finally learned that Hades had abducted her daughter, Demeter reconciled herself
with him and agreed to let Persephone live for
part of the year in the underworld; the remain-
der she would spend with her mother—clearly
an image of the alternation between flowering
and withering in nature. When Demeter had
won Persephone back, the earth again brought
forth its fruits.—Out of gratitude for the hospitality that she had received at the court of his father, the Eleusinian king, during her search for
her daughter, Demeter instructed Triptolemus in
agriculture. Together with Persephone, the goddess was worshiped at the Thesmophoria, a fertility festival for women, at the harvest festival of
the Thalysians, and in the *Eleusinian mysteries. Her cult also extended to Magna Graecia.—
In Rome, Demeter was identified with *Ceres.

Demodike According to one strand of the tradition, as the wife of Cretheus of Iolcus, she tried
to seduce Phrixus.

Demodocus In the *Odyssey,* he appears as a
famous blind singer, whose song delighted the
guests at the court of the Phaeacian king Alcinous. When Odysseus stayed with Alcinous, he
was deeply moved as he heard Demodocus
sing of various episodes from the Trojan War.

Demoleon A son of *Antenor and Theano who,
like his many brothers (except for Glaucus), was
killed in the Trojan War.

Demophon 1. The son of *Theseus and Phaedra or Antiope (in another version), and brother
of Acamas. A participant in the Trojan War, he
was among those who hid inside the wooden
horse. At the fall of Troy, he fell in love with
Laodice but then forgot her on his way home
when he stopped in Thrace. There he succeeded in wooing the king's daughter Phyllis
and either betrothed himself to her or married
her. Proceeding on to Athens, he stayed in that
city for so long that Phyllis despaired and killed
herself, believing that she had lost her beloved.

She was turned into a leafless almond tree, which put forth leaves when Demophon finally returned and embraced the tree. Later he became king of Athens. 2. The infant son of the Eleusinian king Celeus and Metanira. At night *Doso (Demeter) laid him in the embers of the hearth, wishing to immortalize him. But he died when his mother, fearing for her child's life, failed to understand the meaning of this ceremony and put a stop to it. 3. A companion of Aeneas on the latter's voyage to Italy, who was killed by Camilla.

Despoina An Arcadian fertility goddess, identified as a daughter of Demeter. Her name, meaning "mistress," could also be the epithet of any goddess.

Deucalion 1. In Greek mythology, he was king of Pherae in Thessaly, son of Prometheus, and husband of *Pyrrha (1). Around him one of the oldest flood legends developed: because of their many crimes, Zeus planned to destroy the human race by means of an immense flood. On the advice of his father, Deucalion constructed a wooden chest, which he supplied with every necessity. He and his wife floated on the water for nine days and nights in this ark. They landed on Mount Parnassus and, after making an offering of thanks to Zeus, Deucalion prayed to the god for permission to create a new human race. Zeus granted his prayer, instructing him and his wife to throw stones behind them as they walked; from the stones men and women were generated.—The great flood that Deucalion and his wife survived is also called the Deucalion flood. 2. Son of Minos and Pasiphae who took part in the Argonautic expedition and the Calydonian boar hunt.

Deucalion flood *Deucalion (1).

Dexamene One of the *Nereids.

Dia 1. In Greek legend, another name for *Naxos, the island on which Theseus abandoned Ariadne. 2. An island in the Black Sea, also called the "island of Ares." There the Stymphalian birds, banished by Heracles, took refuge and posed a danger to the Argonauts.

Diana

Diana of Versailles (4th century B.C.)

Diana An ancient Italian divinity, venerated as goddess of the moon, of women, of slaves, of forests, and (from the imperial period) also of hunting. She had sanctuaries on Mount Tifata near Capua and one in Aricia. A temple erected to Diana on the Aventine in Rome as the sanctuary of the Latin League was supposed to have stood under the special protection of King *Servius Tullius. Diana's main festival occurred on August 13. From an early date, she was equated with the Greek goddess *Artemis.

Diasia A festival of Zeus celebrated at Athens, outside the city walls, in January and February. The god it referred to was benevolent on the one hand, and severe on the other hand. Likewise, some of its rites were melancholy and some were cheerful.

Dictynna A Cretan goddess who is often connected or identified with *Britomartis.

Dido (Phoenician, *Elissa) A legendary princess of Tyre, who fled from her brother Pygmalion after he had killed her husband. She succeeded in reaching Africa, where she founded Carthage. When King Iarbas of Libya threatened her because she refused to marry him, she killed herself.—According to another version, presented in Virgil's *Aeneid*, Dido committed suicide after Aeneas set sail from Carthage, where he had landed on his eventful journey to Italy and succeeded in winning her love.

Dii (*Di*) The collective Roman designation for the twelve foremost Greek gods, who also play a significant role in Roman mythology.

Dike Daughter of Zeus and Themis (one of the *Horae), and sister of Eunomia and Eirene. She personified justice in early Greek mythology. In general, Dike is also a concept for the right apportionment to each according to status.

Dikte A mountain on Crete, which may be identical with the mountain range called Lasithi today. In some sources, it is said to be the homeland of the Harpies and perhaps the birthplace of Zeus (another conjectural birthplace of Zeus is Mount Ida).

Diktys In Greek legend, he was the son of
Magnes and a Nereid, and the brother of Polydectes. As a fisherman on the island of Seriphus, he fished up Danae and her son *Perseus
from the sea. They had been put out to sea in a
chest by Danae's father, *Acrisius. Perseus later
elevated Diktys to be king of Seriphus.

Dindymene An epithet of the goddess Cybele
that derived from the cult places she had on
several mountain ranges in Asia Minor bearing
the ancient name of Dindymon.

Dino One of the *Graiae, attendants of the Gorgons, she was the daughter of Phorcys and
Ceto, and the sister of Enyo and Pemphredo.

Diomede 1. Daughter of *Xuthus and Creusa,
and the wife of Deion, to whom she bore several children. 2. The wife of Amyclas and mother
of various children, including *Hyacinthus.

Diomedes 1. Legendary king of the Bistonians
in Thrace, he was the son of Aias and the
nymph Cyrene. He possessed horses which
were fed on human flesh until *Heracles tamed
them by killing Diomedes and feeding him to his
own horses as fodder. After that they could be
brought without any risk to Argos, where Heracles dedicated them to the goddess Hera.—As
a horse-guarding hero, the original Diomedes
was probably honored with human sacrifices. 2.
Legendary king of Argos, and son of Tydeus
and Deipyle (daughter of Adrastus), he was one
of the most famous Greek heroes. With his father-in-law, Adrastus, he took part in the expedition of the Epigoni against Thebes as well as
the Trojan War, commanding a fleet of eighty
ships at the latter. His heroic deeds are re-
counted in the fifth book of the *Iliad*. At Troy,
Diomedes fought side by side with Odysseus
and killed many Trojan warriors. After he stole
the Trojan *Palladium, it was prophesied to the
Greeks that without the Palladium in their possession, the capture of Troy would be impossi-
ble. Diomedes was the special favorite of Pallas
Athena, who rushed to his aid on numerous occasions when he was in dire distress. He himself did not shrink from assaulting the god Ares

and wounding the goddess Aphrodite as she stood by her son Aeneas.—After the destruction of Troy, Diomedes first returned home but left Argos again without delay when he ascertained to his chagrin that his wife had become unfaithful to him and even appeared to be plotting against his life. Various wanderings brought him finally to Italy, where he founded several cities, among them Canusium and Sipontum. His remaining destiny is lost in obscurity. According to one tradition, reported by Pindar, Athena made him immortal.—Diomedes was worshiped at several cult places in Italy.—Whether at an early stage Diomedes (who probably originated as a god of war) was identical with the Thracian hero of the same name cannot be determined with certainty.

Dion King of Sparta who had three daughters with his wife, Iphiteia, on whom Apollo bestowed the gift of prophecy.

Dione A Greek goddess, she was the daughter of Oceanus and Tethys or (following another version) of Uranus and Gaia. Revered as the wife of Zeus, especially at Dodona, she was thought to be the mother of Aphrodite.

Dionysia The general designation for the festivals held in honor of *Dionysus, but particularly for the four great Dionysian festivals that were celebrated annually in Athens.

Dionysus (Latin, *Bacchus*) A Greek nature divinity, specifically god of wine and more broadly of vegetation, who played an exceptionally important role among the Greeks. His separate characteristics are so iridescent that they can be combined to produce a composite picture only with great difficulty. Where Dionysus originated and when his cult was disseminated in Greece are questions to which no firm answer has been found. In any case, though, the first part of his name points to the genitive of the name of Zeus, and it is as the son of Zeus and Semele that he entered the mythological record. According to the myth, at the instigation of Zeus's jealous wife Hera, Semele expressed the wish to see her lover in embodied form. When Zeus

Dionysus Priest

Dionysus riding on an ass

then appeared to her as thunder and lightning, she was consumed by fire. Zeus carried to term the fruit of their union (born as Dionysus) in one of his thighs and gave the infant first to the wet nurse Ino and then to the nymphs of Nysa to raise. Later, on Naxos, Dionysus was wedded to Ariadne.—In the imagination of antiquity, Dionysus's cult came either from Thrace, Lydia (the name *Bakchos* is probably of Lydian derivation), or Phrygia (at all events from a foreign land) to Greece about the 8th century B.C. It was marked by a type of ecstasy and enthusiasm hitherto foreign to the Greeks. For this reason the veneration of the god first established itself against much resistance, especially from the Ionian aristocracy. Significantly, Homer does not yet know Dionysus as a great Olympian god. At the festivals held in his honor, which were mainly spring and wine celebrations, the god in the form of a bull would often lead a train of noisy Maenads, Bacchantes, Thyiades, Satyrs, Nymphs, or other disguised figures through the

Dionysus His mysteries and dances

woods. They danced, dismembered animals, ate the latter raw, and reached a state of ecstasy that originally had nothing to do with wine. Only gradually were the licentious and even phallic components of the cult moderated, so that Dionysus came to occupy a secure place in the religion of the Greeks. It is significant for this process that Dionysus was venerated from a particular historical moment, even at Delphi, the chief sanctuary of Apollo.—At the Dionysian festivals, especially in Athens, dramatic performances were routinely staged; thus the cult of Dionysus can also be viewed in relation to the genesis of drama.—Among the Romans, Dionysus was identified at an early date with the god Liber and eventually accepted under the name Bacchus. As the *Bacchanalia celebrated in his honor degenerated, the state intervened to regulate them, but without prohibiting practice of the cult as such.—Early artistic representations of Dionysus show him as a bearded old man, whereas later ones portray him as a handsome youth.

Diores A friend of Aeneas, who was killed by *Turnus.

Dioscuri

Perieres ⊤ Gorgophone

Tyndareos ⊤ Leda
Aphareus |
Leucippus |
    Castor
    Polydeuces*

*Polydeuces is chiefly identified as the son of Zeus

Dioscuri (Greek for "sons of Zeus") In Greek mythology, they were the twin brothers Castor and Polydeuces (Castor and Pollux, in Latin). Conflicting reports named Leda and Zeus as their parents or, alternatively, Leda and the Spartan king Tyndareos, for which reason they were also called Tyndarides. According to another tradition, Castor was the mortal son of Tyndareos, and Polydeuces the immortal son of Zeus. Their sisters were Helen and Clytemnestra. Castor was famed as a horse tamer, and Polydeuces excelled as a boxer. The Dioscuri delivered their sister Helen from the hand of *Theseus, took part in the Argonautic expedition, accompanied Heracles against the Amazons, and were present at the Calydonian boar hunt. When they abducted the brides on the occasion of the wedding of their cousins Idas and *Lynceus (2), a quarrel ensued (in another version the quarrel was over a captured herd of cattle) during which Idas killed Castor and Polydeuces killed Lynceus. Zeus then struck Idas with one of his thunderbolts. Because of the close bond between the twin brothers, Zeus allowed them to remain together, dividing their time between Olympus and the underworld. In this way Polydeuces shared his immortality with the mortal Castor.—The cult of the Dioscuri spread over the whole of Greece and Italy. In Rome they were venerated at a temple in the Forum, which gave rise to the legend that, at the battle of the Romans with the Latins in 499 B.C. by Lake Regillus, the Dioscuri had come to the aid of the Romans and had themselves carried the news of victory to Rome.—The Dioscuri were especially important to sailors, serving them as navigational guides via the constellation of the Twins; and in battle they were invoked as helpers in need.

Dioscuri Castor and Polydeuces

Dirae (from the Latin *dirus*, meaning "horrible," "frightful") Another name for the *Erinyes, known in Latin as the Furies, referring in particular to Alecto, Megaira, and Tisiphone.

Dirce Wife of the Thessalian king Lycus, she treated her kinswoman *Antiope, mother of the twins *Amphion and Zethus, like a slave, inflicting so much suffering on her that Amphion and Zethus finally avenged their mother by killing Dirce.

Discordia Goddess of conflict and discord, she was the daughter of Zeus and Hera and the twin sister of Ares.

Dis Pater Roman god of the underworld, equivalent to the Greek Pluto (Hades). Together with his wife Proserpina (the Greek Persephone), he ruled over the kingdom of the dead. From the middle of the 3rd century B.C., there was a Roman cult of Dis Pater and Proserpina.

Dithyramb A cult song in honor of *Dionysus and later also of other gods. Although probably the seed of tragedy, the connections of the dithyramb with tragedy can no longer be reconstructed in detail. It was sung and danced to flute accompaniment; either the choral leader gave the keynote, followed by the choral performance, or the chorus performed antiphonally.

From the time of Arion of Lesbos (7th–6th century B.C.), the dithyramb was elevated to an art form. Perfected by Pindar, Simonides, and Bacchylides of Ceos (6th–5th century B.C.), it developed in the direction of greater and greater refinement thereafter.

Dius Fidius A Roman divinity who guaranteed oaths. The linguistic connection of Dius with Jupiter is obvious; and Fidius, derived from *fides*, was one of his epithets. Together with Semo, Dius Fidius had a temple on the Quirinal with a roof that was not completely closed but let parts of the sky remain visible. The reason for this was the injunction that one should swear only in the open air, as though in the presence of the god of heaven.

Dodona A very old and famous oracular seat of Zeus in Epirus, mentioned already in Homer, it was a sanctuary with the most varied sacred structures in addition to other structures, for example, a huge theater from the Hellenistic period.—Nothing is precisely known about the origins of the oracle. At first the oracular sayings were inferred from the murmuring of a sacred oak, and later from the clang of a brass cymbal; prophets interpreted the sayings. The details of how the oracle was consulted are obscure, although small lead tablets with questions and answers written on them have been found. Dodona suffered extensive destruction in 219 B.C. and at other times but retained its importance as an oracular seat into the Christian era.

Dodona Dodonian Zeus; Dodona was a very ancient oracular site of the god

Doliones A people resident at Cyzicus, whose king received the Argonauts hospitably.

Dolios A faithful old servant of Odysseus and Penelope who had also served Laertes for twenty years. He and his numerous sons greeted Odysseus joyfully when the latter returned home. Dolios had helped Penelope to ward off the suitors.

Dolon A Trojan spy and son of the herald *Eumedes (1). When he snuck into the Greek camp at night in disguise, he was detected, captured, and killed by Odysseus and Diomedes.

Dolphin A sea mammal that played a prominent role in the mythology of antiquity. Its great intelligence, benevolence toward human beings, and mobility gave rise among many peoples connected with the sea to various legends. Cretan-Minoan civilization, as well as that of Greece and Rome, regarded the dolphin as divine. In Greece it was sacred above all to Apollo but also to Dionysus, guardian of seafaring, to Aphrodite, who was born from the sea, and to Poseidon as god of the sea. There are numerous accounts of dolphins rescuing human beings from danger at sea by carrying them on their backs to land. The dolphin was given the further role of psychopomp, accompanying the souls of the dead safely to the kingdom of the dead.

Dolphin Sea voyage of Dionysus; his ship is surrounded by dolphins, which were sacred to him; from a Greek bowl (ca. 350 B.C.)

Dorians An ancient Greek tribe, which in the course of the Doric migration from northern Greece pushed southward across the region of Doris and came to occupy the Peloponnesus (except for Achaea and Arcadia), the southern Cyclades, Crete, Rhodes, and the southwest coast of Asia Minor. In legend the Dorians were the descendants of *Dorus.

Doris 1. A sea goddess and daughter of Oceanus and Tethys, she married *Nereus, to whom she bore the *Nereids. 2. One of the Nereids.

Dorus One of the three sons of Hellen, the brother of Aeolus and Xuthus, and the legendary ancestor of the *Dorians.

Doso The nurse of *Demophon (2), one of Metanira's sons, and the wife of Celeus, king of Eleusis. Actually she was Demeter in disguise.

Doto One of the *Nereids.

Dolphin Various dolphin representations on ancient coins

Dryads In Greek mythology, *nymphs who lived in trees. The fate of each was closely tied to that of her respective tree; when her tree died, so did the nymph.

Dryas A frequently occurring name in Greek legend. 1. A son of Ares who took part in the *Calydonian boar hunt. 2. A centaur who was present at the wedding of *Pirithous. 3. One of the fifty sons of Aegyptus, who was murdered by his wife Eurydice, a *Danaid, on their wedding night. 4. The father of *Lycurgus (1).

Dryope Daughter of *Dryops (1). She bore a son, Amphissus, to Apollo, who had made love to her in the form of a serpent or tortoise. When she plucked the blossoms from a lotus tree, she herself was turned into a lotus tree or poplar. According to another version, the Hamadryades abducted her and turned her into a nymph.

Dryops 1. The father of *Dryope. 2. A son of Priam. 3. A son of Apollo. 4. A companion of Aeneas in Italy, who was killed by Clausus.

Dymas 1. A Trojan in the Trojan War who, having disguised himself as a Greek, was discovered and killed by the Trojans. 2. A Phrygian king, and the father of Hecuba, who was killed by the Dorians when he invaded the Peloponnesus.

Dynamene One of the *Nereids.

Eagle A commonly symbolic bird, which also played a role in Greek and Roman mythology. Seen as notably symbolic features were its strength, its endurance, and its heavenward flight. Especially considered to be the holy bird of Zeus, the eagle often served as the god's messenger, proclaiming his will to mortals.

Earth divinities These were chthonic gods. Particularly in the older Greek religions, they were mythical divine beings of a lower order who held sway under the earth or within it, ruling over life and death, blossoming and decay.

Echidna In Greek mythology, a monster with a woman's body whose underside merged into a serpent. Traditionally her parents could have been Phorcys and Ceto, Tartarus and Gaia, or Chrysaor and Styx, among others. Her husband was *Typhon, to whom she bore various other monsters, including Cerberus, the Chimaera, the Sphinx, and the Nemean lion. Mortal but unaging, she lived in a cave in Cilicia or the Peloponnesus, and plundered passersby. Echidna was finally brought down by *Argos Panoptes.

Echion 1. An Argonaut and the son of Hermes and Antianeira. Unsurpassed in dexterity, he was supposed to have shot off the first lance in the *Calydonian boar hunt. At Troy he was among the heroes who hid inside the wooden horse. 2. One of the *Spartoi and a companion of *Cadmus, he married Agave (1), daughter of Cadmus. Agave bore him a son, *Pentheus.

Echo A nymph in Greek mythology whose fate is narrated variously by different traditions. A daughter of Gaia and companion of Hera, she was pursued by Pan, according to one tradition, but did not return his love. The enraged god induced some mad shepherds to tear her to pieces, and only her voice was preserved. In another version, Hera deprived her of her voice because she was supposed to have promoted the love affairs of other nymphs with Zeus. She retained only the capacity from time to time to repeat the last words spoken by another person.—According to a further tradition, Echo fell passionately in love with *Narcissus, who failed to respond to her. Out of sorrow she wasted away to such a degree that only her voice remained.

Edonos Possibly a son of Poseidon and Helle. His legendary people inhabited part of Thrace.

Egeria A Roman water nymph. In legend she was first the lover and later the second wife of Numa Pompilius, whose kingship she supported by her wise counsels. She was venerated in Rome and Aricia. When her husband died, she mourned him so deeply that she dissolved into tears and Diana turned her into a spring. As a goddess, Egeria was thought to protect unborn children.

Eidothea 1. Daughter of the old man of the sea, *Proteus, who lived on the island of Pharos. 2. A nymph who was involved in the rearing of Zeus.

Eidyia A daughter of Oceanus and Tethys, the wife of Aeetes, and the mother of *Medea and Apsyrtus.

Eirene with the infant Pluto (ca. 370 B.C.; copy)

Eileithyia Daughter of Zeus and Hera, she was the goddess of women and childbirth, identified by the Romans with Lucina.

Eirene (Latin, *Irene*) Greek goddess of peace, daughter of Zeus and Themis, and one of the *Horae. She was venerated in Athens from 374 B.C., when the Athenians made peace with Sparta; otherwise her cult was not widespread. The artistic representation of her with the boy Pluto on her arm is famous.—Her Roman counterpart is the goddess *Pax.

Elato Another name for *Baton, the charioteer of Amphiaraus.

Electra 1. Daughter of *Agamemnon and Clytemnestra, she was the sister of Orestes, Iphigenia, and Chrysothemis. Electra does not appear in Homer, unless she is to be identified with *Laodice (1), one of the daughters of Agamemnon mentioned by the poet. She does, however, figure in the works of Aeschylus, Sophocles, and Euripides with certain variations. After the treacherous murder of her father by Clytemnestra and Aegisthus, Electra remained at Mycenae, where she was exposed to many dangers; but she sent her brother Orestes to an uncle in Phocis so that he would have a carefree youth. Later when Orestes returned home, spurred on by her implacable hatred, she drove him to avenge the death of their father, which he did by killing their mother and Aegisthus. Eventually Electra married Pylades, her cousin and the closest friend of her brother (for Orestes had been raised in the parental home of Pylades). 2. One of the *Pleiades, she was the daughter of Atlas and Pleione, and by Zeus the mother of Dardanus and Jason. She lived on the island of Samothrace.—According to another version, the Etruscan king Corythus was the father of her children. Because Electra had rejected Zeus, the god in his burning anger hurled down from heaven the *Palladium, from which Electra had sought aid. 3. One of the *Oceanids, she married Thaumas and became the mother of Iris and the *Harpies.

Electryon King of Mycenae, and the son of Perseus and Andromeda, he married Anaxo, with whom he had six sons and a daughter, Alcmene. Electryon was inadvertently killed by Alcmene's husband, *Amphitryon, when the latter threw a club after a runaway cow, striking his father-in-law in the process.

Elephenor King of the Abantes on the island of Euboea. After he had received Acamas and Demophon at his court, all three set out for Troy, where Elephenor was killed.

Eleusinian mysteries In legend, these mysteries were founded by Eumolpus and Celeus. In antiquity their celebration occurred annually, every September, mainly to honor Demeter, with a splendid procession along the sacred way from Athens to Eleusis. The return of Persephone from the underworld was commemorated in the initiation hall (*telesterion*). The mysteries were open only to initiates, who hoped to gain from them a happy life in the hereafter. The celebration of the Eleusinian mysteries involved the use of specially directed flashes of light.

Eleusis A Greek city in Attica located about 12 miles northwest of Athens. Vestiges of the city are still extant, together with the sacred precinct, including the *telesterion* encircled by terraces and featuring ascending stepped seats on three (originally four) sides.

Elgin marbles The ancient sculptures acquired chiefly at Athens by Lord Elgin, the English ambassador to the Ottoman court, which came into the possession of the British Museum in London in 1816. Taken from the Parthenon, the Erechtheion, and elsewhere, they have been enormously significant for the knowledge of Greek art in Europe.

Elis A coastal area in the northwestern Peloponnesus, having from 471 B.C. a capital city of the same name. Olympia, site of the *Olympian Games, is also located there in the valley of the Alpheus.

Elissa Another name for *Dido, the foundress of Carthage.

Elpenor In the *Odyssey,* the youngest of Odysseus's companions. Asleep in a drunken stupor, he fell from the roof of Circe's palace and so met his death. When Odysseus encountered him in the underworld, Elpenor asked Odysseus for a worthy burial, which the legend reports he received.

Elysium (Elysian fields) In Greek mythology, the land of the blessed at the western edge of the world. Those whom Zeus loved were taken there to lead a happy existence. Elysium is to be identified with the Isles of the Blessed and distinguished from *Hades, where the dead continued a shadowy existence. Either Rhadamanthys or Kronos is named as the lord of Elysium.

Emathion According to one strand of tradition, he was king of Arabia. The son of Tithonus and Eos, and brother of Memnon, Emathion tried to prevent Heracles from picking the apples in the garden of the Hesperides but was killed by the latter in the attempt.

Empusa In Greek mythology, a female phantom who frequently appeared in the company of Hecate. She often had the foot of a donkey and could transform herself into various animals, but also occasionally took the form of a beautiful maiden. Characteristically, Empusa was sent out by Hecate to fill wayfaring strangers with anxiety and terror.

Endeis The wife of *Aeacus.

Endymion In Greek mythology, the son of Aethlios (according to another tradition, of Zeus) and *Calyce. He was beloved by the moon goddess Selene, who visited him in his sleep and bore him fifty daughters. Endymion prayed to Zeus for everlasting sleep and eternal youth.

Enodia ("goddess of the ways") An epithet of *Hecate.

Entellus The winner of the boxing contest at the funeral games for *Anchises.

Enyalios In Greek mythology, a secondary god of war and companion of Ares. No myth worth mentioning is told of him. One strand of tradition views Enyalios as no more than an epithet of Ares. To the extent that he was understood as a deity in his own right, Enyalios was identified with the Roman god Quirinus.

Enyo A Greek war goddess, she was the daughter of Ares and his companion in battle. The Romans usually identified her with their goddess *Bellona.

Eos (Latin, *Aurora*) Goddess of the dawn, sister of Helios and Selene, and wife of *Tithonus, she was generally regarded as the daughter of the Titan Hyperion and Theia. When she entreated Zeus to grant her husband immortality, she forgot to ask that he be given eternal youth as well. Both with her ever more drastically aging husband and with other lovers, she had a number of children. Every morning she announced the arrival of her brother Helios and accompanied him on his journey across the heavens.

Eos holding the corpse of her son Memnon; red-figure vase painting (1st half of the 5th century)

Eos

Epaphus An Egyptian king, and son of Zeus and *Io, who married Memphis and became the father of Libya. Epaphus was also credited with founding the city of Memphis. The Greeks identified him with the Egyptian god Apis.

Epeios Leader of the Phocians at Troy, where he took part in the war with a fleet of thirty ships. Epeios was thought to have been responsible for designing and erecting the wooden horse.— At the boxing match on the occasion of the funeral games for Patroclus, he emerged victorious. A later tradition also saw him as the founder of Pisa possibly in addition to Metapontos and other cities, too.

Ephialtes 1. One of the *Aloades. Like his brother *Otus, with whom he battled against the gods, Ephialtes was colossal in size. 2. The Greek who allegedly informed the Persians of the Greek position at the battle of Thermopylae in 480 B.C.

Ephyra One of the *Oceanids and the first legendary inhabitant of the city of Ephyra on the isthmus of Corinth.

Epicaste Another name, used especially by Homer, for *Iocasta.

Epidaurus An Argolid city on the Saronic Gulf, it was the site of one of the famous *Asclepieia, where patients sought healing by means of oracles and medical treatment. Among the sanctuary's extensive ruins of temples, baths, gymnasia, sleeping quarters, and other structures, the theater is particularly noteworthy, being one of the best-preserved Greek theaters anywhere.

Epigoni (Greek for "posthumous") The legendary sons of the *Seven against Thebes who, ten years after the futile attempt of their fathers to take Thebes, succeeded in conquering and destroying the city under the leadership of Alcmaeon and with the help of *Adrastus (1).

Epimelios An epithet of Hermes in his role as protector of flocks.

Epimenides A Greek seer, poet, and scholar from Crete, who should probably be regarded as a historical figure of the 7th century B.C., although the works attributed to him are certainly not by him. Epimenides is surrounded by legends. Among the best known is the story of his falling asleep for fifty-seven years in a cave. He is supposed to have lived to an extraordinarily advanced age.

Epimetheus (Greek for "he who considers too late") The son of Iapetus and brother of Prometheus, Epimetheus married *Pandora against his brother's urgent counsel. Pandora bore him a daughter, *Pyrrha (1).

Epione The daughter of King Merops, according to one tradition, she married *Aesculapius and bore him several children.

Epiphany (*Epiphaneia*, Greek for "appearance") In antiquity generally, the manifestation of a divinity. In the context of the Roman ruler cult in the provinces, Epiphany referred to the appearance of the (divinized) emperor.

Epona A Celtic goddess who protected horses, donkeys, and mules as well as riders and grooms. She was especially popular among soldiers and received worship also from the Romans. Regarded as the daughter of a man and a mare, in artistic representations Epona was usually seated on a mare, surrounded by horses and mules to which she offered food.

Epopeus King of Sicyon and son of Poseidon, he married *Antiope, who was pregnant by Zeus. Epopeus was killed in battle by Lycus, Antiope's uncle.

Erato 1. One of the *Danaids. 2. Among the nine Muses, the Muse of love poetry.

Erato One of the Muses

Erebus In Greek mythology, the darkness of the underworld, personified by Hesiod as the son of Chaos. The union of Erebus and Nyx gave rise to *Aether and *Hemera.

Erechtheus A mythical king of Athens, he was engendered by the Athenian earth, perhaps from the seed of Pandion, and brought up by Athena. According to another tradition, though, he may have been identical with *Erichthonius. In a battle against the Eleusinians and Eumolpus, Erechtheus triumphed because he had sacrificed one of his daughters after being instructed to do so by an oracle; his other daughters then killed themselves. A different tradition reports that only the one daughter died but Poseidon later destroyed Erechtheus and his family because she had been sacrificed.

Ergane An epithet of Athena in her capacity as helper of men and women engaged in handicrafts.

Erginos King of Orchomenus, son of *Clymenus (2), and father of Agamedes. After a war against Thebes from which he emerged victorious, Erginos imposed on the Thebans the onerous annual tribute of one hundred bulls for the following twenty years. Heracles freed the Thebans from this obligation by mounting a campaign against Erginos; he either killed the king or made peace with him. Another tradition reports that Heracles demanded two hundred bulls per year as tribute from his worsted adversary.

Erichthonius An earthborn king of Athens, he sprang from the seed of Hephaestus, who had tried to seduce the virginal Athena. After his birth, Athena put the infant Erichthonius in a closed chest, entrusting the latter to the daughters of Cecrops (*Aglauros). Despite the stern prohibition of the goddess, they opened the chest and at the sight of the serpent-shaped child were driven mad. Erichthonius succeeded Cecrops as king of Athens.—*Erechtheus.

Erichthonius Birth of Erichthonius; Greek vase painting

Eridanus God of a mythical river, he was the son of Oceanus and Tethys. The river was the same one into which *Phaethon plunged with the sun chariot of his father Helios; according to the tradition, it could have been the Po.

Erigone Her father, Icarius of Athens, spread the art of viticulture (which he had learned from Dionysus) throughout his native land. But thinking he had poisoned them, the peasants murdered him. Erigone then searched for her father's body with her faithful dog Maira; when she found it, she hanged herself from a tree at the spot. She and her father were translated to the heavens among the stars. In another version, the so-called swinging festival (Aiora) was introduced at the place of Erigone's suicide in order to absolve her.

Erinyes (Latin, *Furiae*) In Greek mythology, the Erinyes were sinister, subterranean avenging goddesses with serpent-covered heads, who mercilessly persecuted transgressors and wrong-doers, seeking to drive them to insanity or death (as, for example, in the case of the matricide Orestes). According to Hesiod, they were chil-dren of Gaia generated from the blood that flowed when Uranus was mutilated. Another ver-sion identifies them as daughters of Night. Indi-vidually attested from an early date, they usually appeared as a trinity bearing the names Alecto ("the unremitting one"), Megaira ("the envious one"), and Tisiphone ("the avenger of murder"). Sometimes they were also designated as the Semnai ("venerable") or Eumenides ("well-dis-posed"). Whether the latter titles were merely eu-phemisms designed to incline the goddesses to-ward mercy or whether the goddesses had gradually been transformed into friendly chthonic deities who no longer needed to exercise their avenging function (because it had been assumed by the state) cannot be determined with certainty.

Eriphyle The daughter of Talaus of Argos and Lysimache, she was the sister of *Adrastus (1) and the wife of the seer *Amphiaraus. When Amphiaraus foresaw that only Adrastus would survive the campaign of the *Seven against Thebes, he hid himself but was betrayed by his wife, who had let Polynices bribe her with the necklace of Harmonia. Alcmaeon, son of Am-phiaraus, avenged the death of his father at Thebes by killing Eriphyle.

Eris (Greek for "strife") In Greek mythology, the goddess of discord and strife, as well as the sis-ter and companion of *Ares. Unlike all the other gods and goddesses, Eris was not invited to at-tend the wedding of Peleus and Thetis. She avenged herself by tossing a golden apple, in-scribed with the words "the fairest," among the guests. The goddesses Hera, Athena, and Aphrodite were thereby drawn into a vehement conflict (*Paris), which led indirectly to the Tro-jan War.—In Virgil's *Aeneid*, Eris appears under the name Discordia.

Eros

Eros (Latin, *Amor*; also Cupid) The Greek god of love, Eros was not yet named by Homer. In Hesiod, together with Gaia and Tartarus, he followed Chaos, thus being associated with the oldest gods. Later he figured as the son of Aphrodite and Ares, frequently accompanied by Himeros (desire) and Pothos (longing). Although his exceptional beauty was highly valued by the Greeks, the cult of Eros remained of slight importance. At Thespiae in Boeotia, one of his few cult places, Eros was worshiped in the form of a rough stone, indicating his connection with the origin of the world. Later a statue carved by Praxiteles replaced this stone.—Early artistic representations of Eros show him as a handsome, boyish youth who was often naked, winged, and equipped with bow and arrow. Eventually he assumed the character of a merely playful boy, shooting his arrows at gods and humans while gradually losing his divine rank. At the same time, a tendency developed in favor of representing him in the plural form of little winged Erotes rather than as a single figure, and of banishing him from the realm of mythology to that of art. The Erotes were revived in the Renaissance as putti.

Eros Winged Eros; from Myrina, Hellenistic period

Eros with bow and arrow; after a painting by Franceschini (detail)

Eros with a plough drawn by butterflies; the god of love is presented here in the diminutive form of one of the winged Erotes; from a gem, 18th century

Eros

Erulus (*Erylus*) A king of Italy and son of Feronia, goddess of the grain harvest. She gave him three lives, but he lost all of them in one day at the hands of Evander.

Erymanthian boar A powerful boar that lived on Mount Erymanthus in Arcadia. One of the labors assigned to *Heracles was to bring it alive to his master Eurystheus at Mycenae. After pursuing the boar across a snowy field until it collapsed from exhaustion, he carried it on his shoulders to Eurystheus, who was terrified at the sight of the huge beast.

Erysichthon Son of the Thessalian king Triopas, and one who despised the gods. Despite severe warnings, he cut down a tree in one of the groves of Demeter and was punished with a hunger that could not be satisfied, ending up as a beggar. According to another version, Erysichthon finally devoured himself.

Erytheia One of the Hesperides, she was a guardian of the garden in which the tree that bore the golden apples grew. Zeus and Hera had received it as a wedding gift.

Eryx 1. A mountain at the northwest edge of Sicily, which was sacred to the fertility goddess Astarte and later consecrated to Aphrodite. 2. A legendary Sicilian king, who was the son of Poseidon and Aphrodite and the half-brother of Aeneas. Renowned as a wrestler, he did away with all his opponents until Heracles conquered and killed him.

Esquiline (Latin, *Esquilinus mons*) One of the seven hills of Rome. The tradition records that it was originally the place of execution for criminals. In early Roman times, it also served as a cemetery and as a residential area for the poor. Later, especially from the Augustan era onward, the character of the Esquiline changed; it became the site of Maecenas's gardens, Nero's Golden House, and the baths of Trajan and Titus in addition to luxurious private homes.

Eteocles One of the sons of Oedipus and Iocasta, he was the mortal enemy of his brother *Polynices, with whom he was supposed to share the rulership of Thebes on an annually alternating basis. When Eteocles would not surrender his office at the appointed time, Polynices induced his father-in-law Adrastus to organize the expedition of the *Seven against Thebes. Eteocles fell as defender of Thebes in combat with his brother Polynices. He was given an honorable burial, but Creon (2) prohibited the burial of Polynices. *Antigone disregarded the prohibition.

Eteoclus An Argonaut and the brother of *Evadne (2). He was a man of great integrity, who met his death as one of the *Seven against Thebes.

Euboea The second-largest Greek island, with its capital at Chalcis. Because the Abantes settled there, the island was also named Abantis. In the historical period, only one phyle of Chalcis was still called Abantis.

Eubuleus A swineherd at Eleusis, who witnessed the abduction of *Persephone (Kore).

Eudora 1. One of the *Hyades. 2. One of the *Nereids.

Eudorus Son of Hermes and friend of Achilles, he was one of the five commanding officers over the *Myrmidones in the Trojan War.

Euenus Son of Ares and husband of Alcippe, with whom he had several children. When *Idas carried off his daughter *Marpessa in a winged chariot that Poseidon had given to him, Euenus pursued the pair as far as the river Lykormas. Realizing at that point the hopelessness of his undertaking, he killed his horses and then drowned himself in the river, which was later named Euenus in memory of him.

Eumaeus Swineherd of Laertes and later of Odysseus, he was a slave of royal lineage who served his masters with great loyalty. When Odysseus returned home to Ithaca disguised as a beggar, Eumaeus took him in; and after Odysseus had revealed his identity to Eumaeus, the latter supported him in his struggle against the suitors of Penelope.

Eumedes 1. A Trojan herald and the father of Dolon, who met his death in the Trojan War. 2. Son of Dolon who accompanied Aeneas to Italy, where he was killed by Turnus.

Eumelus Son of *Admetus and Alcestis, he brought eleven ships to Troy and possessed the fastest Greek troops in the Trojan War. Eumelus won the war chariot race in the funeral games for Achilles.

Eumenides (Greek for "the well-intentioned") The *Erinyes, or Furies, euphemistically characterized as benevolent deities.

Eumolpus A Thracian hero from Eleusis, he was the son of Poseidon and *Chione (2). He and Celeus were credited with founding the Eleusinian mysteries. In the war between Eumolpus and Athens, the Eleusinians were defeated; Eumolpus was killed by *Erechtheus after the latter had sacrificed his daughter to ensure victory, at the behest of the Delphic oracle.

Eunomia The Greek ideal of political order and of the life of the individual in the context of that order. It also referred to the conduct of citizens in accordance with such an order. Eunomia was later personified as one of the *Horae.

Euphemus One of the Argonauts and son of Poseidon, he could move across water without getting his feet wet. On the Argonauts' homeward journey, Euphemus received from the sea god Triton a clod of earth which he let fall into the sea. At the spot where it fell, the island of Thera rose up. The descendants of Euphemus settled on this island. As Medea prophesied, colonizers from Thera later founded Cyrene in North Africa.

Euphorbos Son of Panthoos, he was known in the tradition as the Trojan warrior besides Hector who killed *Protesilaus, the first Greek to disembark at the beginning of the Trojan War. He was also the first Trojan to wound Patroclus. Euphorbus himself was slain by Menelaus.

Euphrosyne One of the *Charites and the personification of joy.

Euripides A Greek poet and playwright who was born ca. 480 B.C. on Salamis and died in 407 or 406 at the court of the Macedonian king Archelaus. He was the youngest of the three great Attic tragedians. To Euripides the world appeared to be governed by irrational forces, and the real substance of conflict behind events resided in the individual. His plots are thus psychologically motivated, borne along by passions, and frequently linked to a critique of the traditional portraits of the gods. Euripides is sup-

Euripides: of the 92 dramas attributed to him (the numbers vary), the following have survived:

Alcestis
Medea
Heracleidae
Andromache
Hippolytus
Hecuba
Suppliants
Electra
Heracles
Troades
Helen
Iphigenia in Tauris
Ion
Phoenissae
Orestes
Iphigenia in Aulis
Bacchae

The *Rhesus,* originally attributed to Euripides, is no longer considered genuine. The *Cyclops* is the only fully preserved satyric play of Euripides.

Euripides

109

posed to have written 92 plays, of which quite a few are known by title but only 18 or 19 have survived intact.

Europa (*Europe*) 1. Daughter of Phoenix, or the Phoenician king Agenor, and of Telephassa. As she was playing with her girlfriends on the seashore, Zeus approached her lustfully in the form of a handsome bull and carried her off across the sea to Crete. Europa bore him two sons, *Rhadamanthys and *Minos, in addition to *Sarpedon (1), according to one strand of the tradition. Later she married Asterius. The continent of Europe may have been named after her.—Especially with reference to her rape by Zeus, the figure of Europa was a favorite theme among the artists of antiquity. 2. An *Oceanid.

Agenor—Telephassa

Europa—Zeus
Cadmus
Phoenix
Cilix

    Minos
    Rhadamanthys
    Sarpedon

Europa with Zeus in the form of a bull

Euros (Latin, *Volturnus*) The designation given by the ancient Greeks to the southeast wind. Like all the *Winds, Euros was understood to be a son of Astraeus and Eos.

Euryale One of the *Gorgons, she was the daughter of Phorcys and his wife Ceto (who was also his sister).

Euryalus An Argonaut and probably one of the *Epigoni, he was the son of Mecisteus, whom the tradition occasionally counted among the *Seven against Thebes. Euryalus led the Argives in the Trojan War. At the funeral games for Patroclus, Epeios defeated him in the boxing match.

Eurybatos The son of Euphemus, he was said to have killed the monster *Lamia.

Eurybia Daughter of the Titan Oceanus and of Gaia.

Eurycleia The faithful nurse of Odysseus, she recognized him by a scar as she was washing his feet after his return from his wanderings.

Eurydice 1. The wife of *Orpheus. As she was fleeing from *Aristaeus, who desired her and sought to win her for himself, Eurydice died from a snake bite and descended into Hades. Orpheus went down to try to free her. 2. The wife of *Acrisius and mother of Danae.

Euryganeia According to a very early tradition, she was the wife of Oedipus and the mother of Antigone, Eteocles, Ismene, and Polynices.

Eurylochos A companion of Odysseus. On the homeward voyage, Odysseus sent Eurylochos with half of his men to the sorceress Circe on the island of Aeaea. It was her habit to turn her visitors into animals. This time she turned her guests into swine—all except Eurylochos, who had not drunk any of her magic potion. Eurylochos married a sister of Odysseus. Zeus killed him when he and others stole some cattle from Helios and slaughtered them because they did not have enough to eat.

Eurymachos An aristocrat on the island of Ithaca and the son of Polybus, he was a suitor of *Penelope who behaved with particular insolence toward Odysseus.

Eurymede Also called Eurynome, she was the daughter of Nisus, king at Megara. Eurymede married Glaucus of Corinth and became the mother of *Bellerophon.

Eurynome An Oceanid and the mother, by Zeus, of the *Charites. As a goddess, according to Apollonius Rhodius, she ruled Olympus together with Ophion until they were forced to yield to Kronos and Rhea, who hurled them either into the sea or down to Tartarus.

Eurypylus 1. In Greek mythology, a hero who fought in the Trojan War. Counted among those who hid inside the wooden horse, he was wounded by Paris after he had killed a son of Priam. As Troy was falling, Eurypylus discovered a sacred chest containing an image of Dionysus, at the sight of which he went mad. He proceeded to Patrae (today Patras), where human sacrifice to Artemis was still practiced. There, instructed by an oracle, he founded the cult of Dionysus. Eurypylus himself was thus healed, and the local inhabitants released from their onerous obligation to practice human sacrifice; for they had received the prophecy that, whenever someone should arrive at Patrae and should introduce a new cult there, they would no longer be compelled to practice human sacrifice. 2. A Trojan ally and the son of Telephus and Astyoche (daughter of Laomedon), he led the Mysian contingent in the Trojan War. Having killed Machaon and the Boeotian Peneleos, Eurypylus was himself killed by Neoptolemus as he prepared to set the Greek ships on fire. 3. The Trojan beloved by Cassandra, he was killed by Pyrrhus.

Eurystheus King of Mycenae and Tiryns, he was the son of Sthenelus and Nikippe, and the grandson of Perseus. Reacting to Zeus's announcement to the gods on Olympus, before the birth of Eurystheus, that the next-born descendant of Perseus would rule over Mycenae, Hera in her jealousy delayed the birth pangs of Alcmene and had Nikippe delivered of the sickly Eurystheus after only seven months of pregnancy. Alcmene gave birth afterward to Heracles, who became Eurystheus's vassal and was charged with the performance of twelve labors by his master. Eurystheus tried to keep both Heracles and his offspring from gaining power, but was finally defeated and killed by the *Heraclids.

Eurytion A Centaur who got drunk at the wedding of the Thessalian prince of the Lapiths, *Pirithous, and made off with the bride. Later Eurytion, or another centaur by the same name, forced *Mnesimache to marry him, but when he appeared to claim his bride he was killed by Heracles.

Eurytus 1. King of Oichalia and grandson of Apollo, he was a renowned archer who reputedly taught Heracles the art of archery. But when Eurytus had the audacity to challenge his grandfather to an archery competition, the latter killed him.—According to another version, Eurytus promised his beautiful daughter *Iole to the man who should surpass him and his sons in an archery contest. Heracles emerged the winner but was cheated of his prize because he had hurled one of Eurytus's sons, *Iphitos, down from a fortress tower at Tiryns in a fit of madness. 2. One of the *Moliones and the twin brother of *Cteatus.

Euterpe The Muse of lyric poetry accompanied with the flute; her symbol was the flute.— *Muses.

Euterpe One of the Muses

Evadne 1. Daughter of Poseidon and *Pitane, she became the mother by Apollo of Iamus, and so the ancestral mother of the prophetic line of the Iamidae at Olympia. 2. The sister of Eteoclus, she married *Capaneus and gave birth to *Sthenelus (2), one of the *Epigoni. Evadne committed suicide by throwing herself on the funeral pyre of her dead husband.

Evander An Arcadian hero and son of *Carmenta, who went to Rome as an exile (perhaps for killing his father). According to the legend, he founded a settlement on the Palatine and transmitted Greek traditions and cultural values to Italy. He was an ally of Aeneas, on whose behalf his son Pallas fell in battle against the Rutulians, enemies of Aeneas.

Fama *Pheme.

Fates *Parcae. *Moirai.

Faun *Faunus.

Fauna An ancient Roman goddess of field, forest, and livestock, she was the feminine counterpart of *Faunus, whose daughter, wife, or sister she was held to be. Occasionally identified with *Bona Dea, she was worshiped by the Romans under this name.

Faunus Faun playing an aulos; from a black-figure vase painting

Faunus Barberini Faun (Barberini Satyr); a faun sleeps off his intoxication on a boulder; important work of the Hellenistic period

Faunus An ancient Roman prophetic god of field and forest, he functioned as guardian of farmers and shepherds in addition to livestock and arable land. Son of Picus, he was the companion of *Fauna; tradition variously named him as her father, husband, or brother. Although the Romans derived his name (using a folk etymology) from *favere*, meaning "propitious," Faunus had in fact the character of a threatening wolf god whose propitiousness needed to be elicited so that he would bestow fertility on the herds. From an early date, Faunus was identified with the Greek god *Pan. At his chief festival, the *Lupercalia*, celebrated in February, he was venerated as the "repulser of the wolf." Besides this state festival, a peasant celebration took place on December 5 with exuberant, rustic rites.— Comparable to the Satyrs and Pans, the lustful Fauns (regarded in legend as the children of Faunus) resembled their progenitor and like him were usually represented as bowlegged creatures.

Faustulus A legendary Roman shepherd, he was the husband of *Acca Larentia. Faustulus discovered the twins *Romulus and Remus, who had been exposed by *Amulius, and according to the tradition became their foster father.

Favonius The Roman name for the west wind, called *Zephyrus by the Greeks.

Felicitas Among the Romans she personified happiness, was understood to be divine, and was the goddess of happiness between persons and peoples. At the close of the republic and during the imperial period, she played an important role.

Feronia An ancient Italian goddess of agriculture and healing, whose provenance is uncertain, although she may have been Sabine or Etruscan, Feronia was worshiped principally in central Italy. Considered to be the guardian of slaves and freedmen, she was the object of their special devotion. Her main sanctuary was situated on Mount Soracte. Among her other cult places were the temple at Tarracina and a sanctuary on the Campus Martius at Rome.

Fetiales An ancient Roman priesthood of twenty members who exercised constitutional functions. They were involved in the drawing up of treaties with other peoples as ambassadors and advisers. Especially in connection with declarations of war and peace, they had complicated rites to perform. During the later republic, they lost their importance but won it back temporarily under Augustus.

Fides Among the Romans the highly valued concept of reliability, good faith, and fidelity, it already received mention in the XII Tables. Fides included the relationship of loyalty between patron and client, but also laid the foundations for Rome's international relations.—In Roman state religion, Fides was the goddess of oaths and of loyalty, with interlaced hands as her chief symbol. Her cult, introduced according to legend by *Numa Pompilius, was the duty of the *Flamines. From the middle of the third century B.C., she had a temple in Rome.

Flamines These Roman priests stood in the service of certain divinities. They were divided into the three *Flamines maiores*, responsible for the divine triad consisting of Jupiter, Mars, and Quirinus, and the twelve *Flamines minores*, responsible for the cults of the other gods.—In their conduct, the Flamines had to observe a great number of taboos.

Flora An Italian goddess of flowers and gardens who possessed a temple in Rome on the Circus Maximus, she was analogous to Ceres and Demeter. Her main festival was the Floralia, celebrated annually from the end of April to the beginning of May as a joyful folk holiday with unrestrained exuberance.—In one strand of the tradition, Flora also appears as a goddess of love.

Floralia The feast days of the Italian goddess *Flora.

Fontinalia The festival of the Roman god of springs *Fontus.

Fortuna by V. Solis the Elder

Fortuna

Fontus, Fons (Latin for "spring") Son of Janus and Iuturna, he was the Roman god of springs at whose festival, the *Fontinalia*, celebrated on October 13, the Romans covered their fountains with garlands and threw blossoms into the spring water.

Fortuna Italian goddess of fate later venerated only as a goddess of good fortune. She had both a public aspect (as *Fortuna populi Romani*) and a private aspect (as *Fortuna privata*). During the classical period of Rome, she was identified with the Greek *Tyche. Fortuna possessed important cult places in Antium and Praeneste, and as *Fortuna populi Romani* a temple on the Quirinal in Rome. She is frequently encountered in the art of the Renaissance. The personification of random, fluctuating good fortune, she often appears in artistic representations standing on a wheel or sphere. One of her characterizing attributes was the cornucopia.

Fratres Arvales The Roman association of the Arval Brethren, whose tradition was very old but for the republican period poorly developed. The twelve members, legendary sons of *Acca Larentia, comprised a kind of priestly college. Augustus revived the college, and until the third century A.D. it had great significance for the complicated fertility rites that had to be performed annually, especially in honor of the goddess Dea Dia. Already in the historical period, though, the text of the cult song of the Arval Brethren, composed in archaic Latin, could no longer be readily understood by Romans.—The Fratres Arvales also played a role in the imperial cult in that they took vows to the emperor and his family.

Fulgora Roman goddess of lightning, she protected people against thunderstorms and inclement weather.

Furies (*Furiae*) The Roman goddesses of revenge analogous to the Greek *Erinyes.

Furrina An old Roman goddess whose significance had already fallen into oblivion in the time of Varro and is equally unknown today. Because of her name, she was occasionally taken for one of the Furies, but this interpretation is very questionable. Furrina had a sacred grove on the Janiculum, one of the seven hills of Rome, where a festival was celebrated in her honor at the end of July.

Gadfly *Io.

Gaia (Greek for "earth") One of the most ancient Greek goddesses and understood as Mother Earth. In the *Theogony* of Hesiod, she was counted among the primordial principles. In and of herself, Gaia procreated Uranus (the heavens) and Pontus (the sea). By Pontus she became the mother of a great line of sea gods as well as the mother of the Titans, the Cyclopes, the Hecatoncheires, the Erinyes, the Giants, the Melian nymphs, and others.—Gaia brought about the downfall of Uranus by Kronos and supported the Titans and Giants in their struggle against Zeus, but finally she had to recognize Zeus as the most powerful of all the Olympian gods. She was never strongly personified and possessed proportionally few cult places, which were concentrated in Attica. On the other hand, she figured importantly in philosophical and cosmological literature. Like Helios, she was also invoked as a witness to oaths. A very ancient tradition made her the first incumbent of the Delphic oracle.

Galatea (Greek for "she who is milk white") One of the *Nereids, she was courted in vain by *Polyphemus. According to a more unusual version, Galatea eventually submitted to Polyphemus and bore him a son.—The story of Galatea, with distinct variations, was a popular subject in Hellenistic literature.

Ganymedes The son of *Tros (1) and his wife Callirhoe, Ganymedes was considered the most beautiful of all mortals. For this reason, Zeus abducted him and made him cupbearer at the gods' table on Mount Olympus. As compensation for the loss of his son, Ganymedes' father

Ganymedes The beautiful Ganymedes with eagle

received immortal horses or a golden vine.— The abduction of Ganymedes was variously narrated in the tradition as having been effected either by Zeus directly, or by an eagle, or by Zeus in the form of an eagle.—Roman accounts also speak of Ganymedes being set in the heavens as the constellation Aquarius.— *Hebe.

Garden of the Hesperides Heracles takes the golden apples

Garden of the Hesperides In Greek mythology, the garden of the gods in which the *Hesperides, together with the dragon *Ladon, guarded the golden apples that Gaia had given to Zeus and Hera as a wedding present. It was one of the labors of *Heracles to break into this garden and take the golden apples.

Gardens of Adonis The pots, jars, and baskets filled with the fast-growing and quickly withering plants and flowers designated for the Adonis festival.—*Adonia.

Gasterocheires The seven Cyclopes, who built the "Cyclopean walls" of Tiryns and Mycenae.

Gate of ivory In the ancient Greek imagination, the gate through which unpleasant dreams from *Hypnos made their way to dreaming human beings.

Ge (*Gaea*) The Greek goddess *Gaia.

Gemini The constellation of the Twins, namely the Dioscuri, who guided seafarers on their voyages.

Genius In Roman religion a kind of invisible spirit watching over the individual male, it was imagined as the quintessence of his effective powers, especially his virility. It corresponded to Juno as the child-bearing capacity of women. A man's genius accompanied him from birth to death, so that his birthday was its chief festal day. On that day a sacrifice was made to it. The genius of the pater familias played a special role, and the slaves of the household were called upon to venerate it, too. Under Augustus the concept of the genius was broadened; the *Genius Augusti* was elevated above those of other men and given a cult identity within the framework of the evolving emperor cult with its divinization of the sovereign. From the time of Augustus, it was also customary to swear by the genius of the emperor.—Gradually these guardian spirits were no longer associated only with single individuals but also with groups of men such as the legions, with places (*genius loci*), with Rome and the Roman people (*genius populi Romani*), and so on. Thus the content of the concept changed in the direction of a less-specific protective spirit.

Geryon A monster with three bodies or three heads, he was the son of *Chrysaor and Callirhoe. He lived with his herdsman Eurytion and the prodigious hound Orthros (or Orthos) on the legendary island of Erytheia. One of the labors assigned to *Heracles was to plunder the vast herds of cattle owned by Geryon. Heracles killed herdsman and hound first, then did away with Geryon, and finally returned with the cattle on a journey traditionally represented as extraordinarily arduous.

Giants An earthborn race of superhuman beings in Greek legend who, although often identified with the *Titans, in contrast to the latter were not immortal. They issued from the drops of blood that *Gaia absorbed when Uranus was mutilated. The Giants were bitter enemies of the Olympian gods, who defeated them in the so-called Gigantomachy, burying them under volcanoes and islands. The battle took place on the Phlegraean Fields, the location of which is uncertain. The Giants, with their half-dragon, half-human bodies and their armaments of clubs, torches, and boulders, would never have succumbed to the Olympians if *Heracles had not rushed to the aid of the gods. His action ful-

Giants Artemis and Hecate do battle with the Giants

filled the prerequisite condition that the gods could only achieve victory with the help of a mortal.—The theme of the Gigantomachy was treated in Greek art from the first half of the 6th century B.C., for example, in vase paintings and architectural sculpture. At first represented as purely human figures (e.g., on the metopes of the Parthenon at Athens), the Giants were later portrayed as fantastic hybrid creatures (e.g., on the frieze of the altar at Pergamum).

Gigantomachy *Giants.

Girdle of Venus In Roman mythology, a girdle named after Venus, the goddess of love, which endowed mortal as well as immortal women with heightened sexual appeal.

Glaucus Among the numerous bearers of this name in Greek mythology and legend are the following: 1. A sea god who was worshiped especially by fishermen and sailors because of his favorable disposition toward them. According to the tradition, Glaucus himself was originally a fisherman in Boeotian Anthedon but was transformed into a god when he leapt into the sea after consuming a magic herb, which he had been using to bring dead fish back to life. Like most sea gods and daimons, Glaucus possessed the gift of prophecy and the power of metamorphosis. 2. Son of the Lycian king Hippolochus and grandson of Bellerophon. An ally of the Trojans and one of the two commanders-in-chief of the Lycian contingent in the Trojan War, he showed exceptional courage and valor. In view of the friendship between their families, he exchanged weapons with *Diomedes (2) rather than fighting with him. Later he was slain by Aias the Great. 3. Son of Minos and Pasiphae. As a small child he fell into a vat of honey and suffocated but was restored to life by a seer named Polyeidus (in another version, by Aesculapius) with a magic herb. 4. Son of Sisyphus and Merope. After suffering defeat in a chariot race, he was torn to pieces by his own horses and became a daimon terrifying to horses.

Glauke Also called Creusa, she was the daughter of King Creon of Corinth. When Jason fell passionately in love with her and wanted to marry her, his wife Medea wreaked a terrible revenge. She sent Glauke a precious wedding garment, which went up in flames when the bride put it on, fatally burning Glauke, her father, and numerous wedding guests.

Glaukippe She may have been the mother of Hecuba by Dymas.

Golden Age In Greek mythology, the first completely happy human era, analogous to the biblical paradise. It was marked by the dominion of Kronos or Saturn.—In antiquity, particularly splendid historical epochs were understood as recurrences of the Golden Age, for example, the Periclean and Augustan periods.

Golden apples *Hesperides. *Garden of the Hesperides.

Golden bough A bough sacred to Persephone, which grew on a tree in the vicinity of Cumae. Aeneas found it with the help of the gods. It served him as a token of permission, signifying that he could set foot in the underworld. Legitimated by the golden bough, Aeneas was conveyed by *Charon across the river *Styx.

Golden fleece In Greek legend, the golden hide of a ram on which Phrixus and Helle once fled to Colchis. After overcoming many obstacles and receiving assistance from *Medea, Jason and the other *Argonauts succeeded in stealing the golden fleece from King *Aeetes, who had it guarded by a fire-breathing dragon.

Gordian knot An artistically intertwined knot on the shaft of a war chariot, allegedly tied by *Gordius and kept in his castle or in a temple. Legend connected the untying of the knot with mastery of Asia. In 334–333 B.C., Alexander the Great is supposed to have cut through the Gordian knot, either with his sword or by some other means.

Gordium *Gordius.

Gordius The legendary founder of the Phrygian royal dynasty and the father of *Midas. The capital of the kingdom of Phrygia was Gordium in northwest Asia Minor, where the *Gordian knot, allegedly tied by Gordius, was kept.

Gorgo Usually a name for *Medusa, the mortal among the *Gorgons.—*Gorgoneion.

Gorgoneion The head of the Gorgon *Medusa. It had a grotesquely hideous appearance, with a muzzlelike mouth that showed its teeth and let its tongue hang out. Although the Gorgoneion was understood as an emblem of terrifying divine powers, a primarily apotropaic function was attributed to it.

Gorgons Gorgo from the west pediment of the temple of Artemis on Corfu

Gorgons Gorgo on a Greek amphora (500–490 B.C.)

Gorgons In Greek mythology, three of the daughters of *Phorcys (1) and Ceto: Euryale, Sthenno, and *Medusa. They were pictured as ghastly monsters, generally winged, with snakes in their hair and around their waists, and with huge teeth. Their horrifying appearance caused anyone who looked at them to petrify into stone. The Gorgons were often interpreted as symbolic embodiments of the awful aspects of the numinous. Their older sisters, the *Graiae, served as their guardians.

Gorgophone Daughter of Perseus and Andromeda, she was married first to *Perieres and then after his death to *Oebalus. She bore several children to both husbands.

Graces In Roman mythology, the three goddesses of grace and charm equivalent to the Greek *Charites.

Graiae Daughters of Phorcys and Ceto, they were the sisters and guardians of the *Gorgons. Usually mentioned as a group of three bearing the names Pemphredo, Enyo, and Dino, the Graiae came into the world already gray-haired. Even as children, they acted like old women (hence their designation "the gray ones"). Between them the three had only one eye and one tooth, which they rotated. Perseus robbed them of both, thus compelling them to show him the way to the nymphs.

Graces The three Graces (one of them is hidden from view) with the urn containing the heart of King Heinrich II (Paris; work of Germain Pilon, 1535–1590)

Granicus A river god, and son of Oceanus and Tethys.—Also the name of a small river in northwestern Asia Minor, where in 334 B.C. Alexander the Great won a significant victory over the Persians, and where in 74 B.C. the Romans expelled Mithridates VI from Pontus.

Gravidus One of the epithets of *Mars.

Great Bear The constellation otherwise known as the Big Dipper and in Latin as Ursa Major, to which the bear goddess *Callisto was transposed, while her son Arcas entered Ursa Minor.

Great Mother *Magna Mater. *Cybele.

Griffin A fabulous animal customarily endowed with the head of an eagle, the body of a lion, and wings. The griffin symbolized majesty, authority, strength, and vigilance (because of its piercing gaze). Among the Greeks it was sacred to Apollo and Artemis. In legend, griffins were renowned as custodians of gold, especially against the Arimaspeans, a one-eyed people in the Scythian part of northern Greece.

Griffin Symbol of majesty, authority, strength, and vigilance; copperplate engraving by M. Schongauer

Gyes 1. One of the *Hecatoncheires, and son of Uranus and Gaia. 2. A king of Lydia and historical figure of the 7th century B.C., who was the subject of many legendary tales. He overthrew King *Candaules (according to Plato, with the help of a ring that could make him invisible), winning both the king's throne and his wife for himself.—Herodotus reports that Candaules, whose wife was extraordinarily beautiful, showed her naked either bathing or in her bedroom to his friend Gyes. When she discovered her husband's treachery, feeling that her honor had been compromised, she demanded that Gyes either kill Candaules and marry her or allow her to die on account of this outrage. Gyes killed his friend, married the widow, and became king of Lydia. 3. A king of Lydia who was said by an oracle to be less fortunate than *Aglaos, the poorest man in Arcadia.

Hades Greek god of the underworld, son of Kronos and Rhea, and husband of *Persephone. The Greeks generally interpreted his name to mean "the invisible." With his brothers, Zeus and Poseidon, Hades divided the government of the universe. He ruled over the souls of the dead and from his house there was no return journey. Hades was also identified with Plutus or Pluton (in Latin, Orcus). Later the name Hades served to designate the underworld itself as well.—*Cerberus.

Haemon Son of Creon (2), he was killed by the Sphinx, according to an ancient tradition. Another version (found in Sophocles) made him the fiancé of *Antigone, and he committed suicide over her corpse. A third variant recounts that Haemon and Antigone in fact married but Antigone left her husband to follow her father into exile.

Haemonides Italian priest of Apollo who was killed by Aeneas.

Haimos The son of Boreas and husband of *Rhodope (1). When the couple presumptuously passed themselves off as Zeus and Hera, they were turned into the Balkan mountain massif called Haimos.

Halirrhothius Son of Poseidon and Euryte, he abducted and assaulted Alcippe, daughter of Ares. Ares avenged his daughter by killing Halirrhothius but was sentenced to a term of servitude as punishment for the murder by the Areopagus (which convened for the first time on this occasion, according to the tradition). In another version, Halirrhothius killed himself as he was trying to cut down the olive tree of Athena on the Areopagus.

Halitherses A seer from Ithaca, skilled in augury, who was a friend of Odysseus and Penelope. He warned Penelope's importunate suitors of Odysseus's imminent return.

Halys A Greek river god, and son of Oceanus and Tethys, he courted *Sinope in vain.

Hamadryades Wood nymphs, who died together with the trees in which they lived. The designation Hamadryades occurs frequently as a synonym for *Dryad.

Harmonia In Greek mythology, the daughter of Ares and Aphrodite (according to another version, of Zeus and Electra). She married *Cadmus of Thebes, to whom she bore several children. For her wedding the bride received a costly peplos and a necklace fashioned by *Hephaestus. This so-called necklace of Harmonia brought misfortune to anyone who possessed it.

Harpalyce 1. Daughter of *Harpalycus, king of the Thracians. Her father, who raised her, taught her how to use weapons; as a result, she gained a reputation as a huntress and could also take part in military expeditions. When Harpalycus had to flee into the woods after the Getae revolted, his daughter fed him with her bounty until she was captured and killed by other hunters. 2. The daughter of *Clymenus (1), who made her his lover even though he had married her to another man. In revenge Harpalyce served her father a child from their incestuous union at a meal, whereupon he killed her. One strand of the tradition reports that Harpalyce was turned into an owl.

Harpalycus 1. A friend of Aeneas, who was killed by *Camilla. 2. The son of Hermes and father of *Harpalyce (1), who taught Heracles boxing.

Harpies In Greek mythology, two, or more often three, daughters of Thaumas and Electra, who took the form of fabulous creatures and had various names (although the names Aello, Ocypete, Podarge, and Celaeno predominated). The Harpies were identified as storm daimons, and Podarge as the mother of the windswift horses *Balios and Xanthus. Originally represented as beautiful winged goddesses, they were later pictured as hideous, gigantic birds with female heads. A famous scene in the legend of the Argonauts narrates an incident in which the Harpies, portrayed as "snatchers," stole part of his meal from the blind old seer Phineus and then soiled the rest of it.

Hebe

Hebe carrying a pitcher of nectar and a bowl of ambrosia

Hebe Greek goddess of youthful beauty, she was the daughter of Zeus and Hera, and the wife of Heracles. She served nectar to the gods on Mount Olympus until *Ganymedes assumed the cupbearer's office.—Hebe was equated with the Roman Iuventas.

Hecale An old woman who extended hospitality to *Theseus and fed him before he captured the Marathonian bull. On his return journey, he made a sacrifice to her when he discovered that she had died in the meantime.

Hecate A Greek goddess who probably originated in Asia Minor. In Homer she is not yet named, whereas in Hesiod she is noted as daughter of the Titan *Perses (2) and Asteria. At first Hecate was worshiped primarily as a generalized goddess. From the 5th century B.C., her characteristic features and particular functions emerged more clearly: as a ghostlike, magical goddess as well as a goddess of witchcraft, brandishing her torch and whip, she wandered here and there terrifying people. In her capacity as goddess of the ways, she had the epithet Enodia ("guardian of the ways"), especially with reference to places where roads forked (hence her epithet Trioditis). For this reason she was often represented with a triple form. When identified with Artemis, she was venerated as a goddess of women who assisted them during labor; in connection with Persephone, she was seen as a goddess of the underworld; and she also appeared in the tradition as a moon goddess. If she received little attention in the official cult of the Greek motherland, her importance for private worship was all the greater. Offerings of food and dogs were presented to her in her private cult.

Hecate as guardian of forks in the road, hence this triple representation; Greek, 4th century

Hecatomb In ancient Greece, a sacrifice of 100 animals, and later any large-scale sacrifice accompanied with a sacrificial meal.

Hecatoncheires (Greek for "the hundred-handed") In Greek mythology, the sons of Uranus and Gaia—giants with 100 arms and 50 heads. Briareos (called Aegaeon in another version), Cottus, and Gyes were banished to Tartarus by their father but then freed by Zeus and reinvigorated on Mount Olympus by means of nectar and ambrosia. Out of gratitude, they came to the aid of the Olympians in the battle of the latter against the Titans.

Hector In Greek legend, the oldest son of *Priam and Hecuba, the husband of *Andromache, and the father of Astyanax. After a deeply moving farewell to his wife (originally narrated in the *Iliad*, the scene was repeated many times over in literature and art), Hector became the foremost Trojan adversary of the Greeks. He distinguished himself with numerous acts of heroism, killing *Patroclus among others. Following the death of Patroclus, Achilles challenged Hector to a duel in which Hector finally suffered defeat. His corpse was dragged around the walls of Troy into the Greek camp, but Priam succeeded in ransoming it.

Hecuba In Greek legend, the daughter of King Dymas of Phrygia (in another version, of Kisseus). To her husband, *Priam of Troy, she bore nineteen children, including Paris, Hector, Deiphobos, Helenus, Polydorus, Cassandra, and Polyxena. After the fall of Troy, she became the slave of *Odysseus and accompanied him on his homeward journey to Greece. En route, she discovered the corpse of her son *Polydorus (2), whom Priam had richly endowed as a boy and entrusted to the care of King Polymestor. Wishing to acquire the wealth of Polydorus for himself, Polymestor had murdered Priam's son. Hecuba took vengeance on him by luring him to her tent, where she blinded him and (with the aid of other Trojan women) killed his children. After her death, Hecuba was turned into a bitch, which could point to an association with *Hecate derived from their similar-sounding names. In antiquity her tomb was imagined to be on the promontory of Cynos Sema ("dog's grave") overlooking the Hellespont.

Hekateros Father of the Curetes, the mountain nymphs, and the Satyrs, possibly through a daughter of Phroneus.

Helen Originally, in Greek mythology, she was probably a vegetation goddess venerated in the tree cult practiced in several places in Greece. Later she achieved prominence as a heroine considered to be the most beautiful woman of her time; it is in this guise that she appears in the *Iliad* and the *Odyssey*. The daughter of Zeus and *Leda, she was the sister or half-sister of the *Dioscuri and Clytemnestra. Attic legend reports that at quite a young age she was abducted by Theseus and Pirithous but released from her captivity in the underworld by her brothers and brought back to Sparta. Her second abduction was more significant, providing the legendary occasion for the *Trojan War: because of her extraordinary beauty, many suitors sought her hand. Helen chose Menelaus and married him after her stepfather Tyndareos (on the advice of Odysseus) made all the other suitors swear to accept his stepdaughter's choice and to come to the aid of her husband should Helen be overtaken by any misfortune. The suitors had to honor this oath when Helen was abducted by Paris (*Judgment of Paris) to Troy. With the fall of Troy, she was taken captive; despite the fact that she had given herself to Deiphobos after the death of Paris, Menelaus brought her back home to Sparta with him.— The traditional evaluation of Helen varies. On the one hand, she was charged with complicity in the genesis of the Trojan War, during which her attitude toward the two parties was depicted as inconstant, for example, by Homer. On the other hand, an attempt was made to demonstrate her fidelity and innocence with respect to her husband, Menelaus, and his people. The second tendency is most obvious in a story in which it was a second Helen, created by Zeus, a nebulous phantom, who was abducted to Troy by Paris while the real Helen as a virtuous wife in Egypt awaited the end of the war and the return of her husband. Among the versions of this story that have been handed down is Euripides' dramatization in *Helen*.

Helenor A Lydian prince who accompanied Aeneas to Italy, he was killed by the Rutulians.

Helenus The son of Priam and Hecuba, like his twin sister *Cassandra he was endowed with the gift of prophecy. Taken prisoner by Odysseus during the Trojan War, he revealed to the Greeks, under compulsion, that the conquest of Troy was tied to possession of the *Palladium. Another version made the subject of Helenus's words *Philoctetes, who held in his possession the arrows of Heracles (*Hydra of Lerna); in order to take the city, the Greeks would have to bring Philoctetes to Troy.—After the death of *Neoptolemus, Helenus married Andromache.

Heliades The sons and daughters of the Greek sun god *Helios.

Helikaon The son of *Antenor and Theano, he was wounded in the Trojan War by the Greeks but saved by Odysseus, who felt obligated to Antenor.

Helios The Greek sun god, son of *Hyperion and Theia, brother of Selene and Eos, and husband of Perse (also Perseis; in another version his sister Selene was his wife), he was usually represented with solar disks or a crown of solar rays. As the ancients imagined it, Helios drove in his chariot up across the heavens by day from east to west and returned by night in a golden cup (which served as a boat) over the stream of Oceanus back to his starting point. Since he saw everything that happened in the world on his travels, he could, for example, tell Hephaestus about the adultery of the latter's wife, Aphrodite.—The sacred herds of the sun god grazed on Thrinakie (in antiquity usually understood to be Sicily); as punishment for the slaughter of some of them by Odysseus's companions, the entire crew of Odysseus's ship drowned.—Helios was regarded as the god of truth and was called upon to witness oaths (as were some other divine beings). At the same time, he also had the power as a god of light to heal blindness or to punish offenders by blinding them. Apart from cult places in the Peloponnesus and on Rhodes, where the famous Colossus was consecrated to him, Helios was the object of little official veneration. However,

Helios The Greek sun god on a Rhodian coin; 3rd century

129

he did play an important role in the theology of the sun. His legitimate children were Aeetes, Circe, Pasiphae, and Perses. In addition, his liaisons with numerous other women produced many offspring.—The Roman god corresponding to Helios, *Sol, was also associated with the imperial cult.

Helle A figure of Greek legend, she was the daughter of Athamas of Thebes and *Nephele, and the sister of *Phrixus. At the instigation of her stepmother, Ino, Helle was supposed to be sacrificed together with her brother. In an effort to save her children, Nephele gave them the *Golden fleece as a means of transportation through the air to Colchis. Phrixus reached their destination unharmed, but Helle fell into the Dardanelles, which then received the name *Hellespont after her.

Hellen King of Phthia, son of Deucalion, and father of *Aeolus, *Dorus, and *Xuthus. Hellen was the eponym of the Hellenes.

Hellespont In antiquity and the Middle Ages, the name for the Dardanelles, separating Europe and Asia. According to legend, they were named after *Helle, who plunged into the sea there.

Hemera The daughter of *Erebus and *Nyx, she personified day.

Hephaestus The Greek god of fire, then of the forge and artisans, and finally also of the arts and craftsmanship itself. His provenance was probably Asia Minor, Lemnos being his most important cult center. From the 6th century B.C., he was venerated in Athens, too. There a temple was erected to him, the so-called Theseum, which served as the focus of his main festival, the *Hephaestia*. Otherwise his cult on the Greek mainland is scarcely attested.—In Greek mythology, Hephaestus was the son of Zeus and Hera. His lameness gave rise to a number of legends, the most common of them telling of his mother's anger when she discovered that he had been born with crippled legs which led her to throw him into the sea. Thetis and Eurynome saved him and cared for him, and he was again

Hephaestus Greek god of fire, smith and artisan; Attic statuette of bronze, 5th century B.C.

received on Mount Olympus. The beauty of Aphrodite, his wife in the *Odyssey*, and of Charis, his wife in the *Iliad*, matched the beauty of the artifacts created by Hephaestus. In their imagination the ancients situated the workshop of the god under the earth or on Mount Aetna, where his masterpieces were produced with the help of the Cyclopes. These included the scepter of Agamemnon, the armor of Achilles, the chariot of Helios, the necklace of Harmonia, and many others. To avenge himself on his mother, Hephaestus made a throne for her which held her fast when she sat on it. Dionysus intervened by getting Hephaestus drunk and escorting him to Olympus to release the goddess. When Aphrodite had a clandestine affair with Ares, Hephaestus caught her in a net, thus exposing her to the laughter of the Olympians. Apart from his legitimate children, Hephaestus had various other offspring with his numerous mistresses.—The Roman god analogous to the Greek Hephaestus was *Vulcan.

Hera A Greek goddess, she was the daughter of Kronos and Rhea, both the sister and wife of Zeus, and the mother of *Ares, *Hephaestus, *Hebe, and *Eileithyia. Whether all the children assigned to her were really hers remains questionable. Eileithyia ("midwife") was also one of her epithets.—As the wife of the highest Olympian god, Hera (whose name denotes "a female ruler") was considered to be the queen of heaven and played a prominent role in legend and myth. She received veneration at many cult places, but especially at Argos (hence her epi-

Heracles

The order of the labors fluctuates in the tradition, and there are also variant accounts of individual labors.

Perseus⌐Andromeda
⌐
Alcaeus
Sthenelus
Electryon⌐Anaxo
⌐
Zeus⌐Alcmene
⌐
Heracles—Megara

Heracles The infant Heracles in combat with the serpents intended to kill him and his brother

thet "Argeia") and Olympia.—Hera functioned as the guardian of marriage and childbirth in addition to the whole course of a woman's life. She bore the honorary title Teleia (referring to the goddess who brings fulfillment).—Greek mythology also portrayed her in an entirely different light. This Hera frequently suffered from the infidelity of her husband, Zeus. His numerous love affairs aroused her anger and her wild jealousy (the latter often assuming grotesque proportions), which became a favorite theme of Greek burlesques of the gods. Her hatred could be implacable. For example, in the Trojan War, because of the Judgment of Paris, she sided with the Greeks and opposed the Trojans with bitter enmity.—The Roman counterpart of Hera was *Juno.

Heracles (Latin, *Hercules*) One of the most important and most beloved of Greek legendary heroes, he came from the line of Alcaeus, hence his epithet "Alcides." The name Heracles itself cannot be explained with absolute certainty. The many connections with Hera suggest that it may mean "he who is made famous by Hera." Heracles was the son of Zeus and *Alcmene, wife of *Amphitryon. Zeus made love to Alcmene disguised as Amphitryon as he would have appeared on the battlefield. As the day approached for the birth of his son, Zeus announced to the Olympians that the next child born from the house of Perseus would become lord of Mycenae. Tormented by jealousy, Hera delayed the labor pains of Alcmene and plotted to have *Eurystheus, son of Sthenelus and Nikippe, born first. Only afterward did Alcmene give birth to Heracles and to his twin brother, *Iphicles, whose father was not Zeus but rather Amphitryon.—Even as an infant, Heracles distinguished himself by his extraordinary physical strength. Thus he destroyed the serpents that had been commissioned by Hera to kill him and his half-brother. Heracles was instructed in all the arts but when he struck his music teacher Linus (3) dead with his lyre for criticizing him, Heracles' stepfather sent him to Mount Cithaeron, where he was compelled to watch over the herds and where he killed the Cithaeronian lion.

To this period also belongs the parable told by the Sophist Prodicus about "Heracles at the crossroads," in which the hero had to choose between virtue and enervation (personified by two female forms) and chose virtue.—After Heracles had liberated the Thebans from the onerous tribute imposed on them by Orchomenus, the Theban king Creon gave him his daughter Megara to wed. Then Hera, in her ongoing desire for revenge, interfered in his life again: suffering an attack of madness sent by the god-

Heracles learns archery

Heracles Received among the immortals on Mount Olympus after his death, Heracles is reconciled with Hera

dess, Heracles murdered the children who had been born to him and Megara. To expiate this act, he was pressed into the service of Eurystheus for twelve years, during which he had twelve difficult tasks to perform. Although these "labors of Heracles" are traditionally not ordered in a strict sequence, they form the nucleus of the legend of Heracles. By no means, however, do they comprise the entire list of his accomplishments. He survived many other adventures, but the sources give very contradictory reports about them.—When he had completed the twelve labors, Heracles separated from Megara, giving her in marriage to his relative and comrade *Iolaus. After an intense rivalry with the river god *Achelous, Heracles himself married *Deianira, who bore him *Hyllus. When the Centaur *Nessus tried to insult Deianira, Heracles killed him. Seeking revenge before he died, the Centaur advised Deianira, who was afraid of losing her husband's love, to save his blood as a love charm. She applied this blood to a shirt (the so-called Nessus shirt) that Heracles was to wear at a sacrificial ceremony. The satu-

Heracles Depiction of Heracles; from a vase painting by the Kleophrades painter

Heracles Night-sea journey of Heracles with club, in the cup of the sun; from the interior of an Attic vase, 5th century B.C.—Part of the cycle of Heracles' labors is known to us only through artistic representations

rated garment inflicted such severe wounds and intense pains on Heracles that he had himself cremated on a funeral pyre kindled by *Philoctetes, who responded to his fervent entreaties. Amid thunder and lightning the dying hero was taken up to Olympus to be among the immortals. Even Hera became reconciled with him, and Zeus gave him Hebe as his wife.—In antiquity Heracles was venerated throughout Greece. He was received into the state cult at Rome in 312 B.C., after a private cult had already developed.—Heracles figured as the subject of numerous poems expounding the full range of his attributes, from those of the radiant hero who has chosen the way of virtue to those of the coarse and vigorous warrior. In the fine arts, too, he has played a significant role since antiquity. His deeds are often known to us only from artistic representations, especially vase paintings.

Heraclids The very numerous mythological descendants of *Heracles were given this designation. After various turns of fortune, they reconquered the Peloponnesus, which they regarded as their rightful inheritance.

Hercules The Latin name for the Greek hero *Heracles.

Herm *Hermes.

Hermanubis *Anubis.

Hermaphroditus A hybrid divinity and the son of Hermes and Aphrodite, he was distinguished

Hermaphroditus

by his exceptional beauty. Because he did not return the passionate love of the water nymph *Salmacis, she begged the gods to unite her body forever with his, and the gods fulfilled her request.—The Greeks believed that anyone who bathed in the spring of Salmacis would turn into a hermaphrodite. The idea of divine hybrid beings probably derived from the East.

Hermes A very old Greek god with a widespread cult, he served as the messenger of the gods. Zeus and the nymph Maia were his parents. Functioning as the patron of travelers, merchants, shepherds, and scoundrels, he began his life with some mischievous activities. Thus according to legend, on the very day of his birth in a cave on Mount Cyllene in Arcadia, he invented the lyre, creating it from a tortoise, and stole a herd of cattle from his brother Apollo. Then he drove the cattle backward, obliterating his own footprints by means of his reversed sandals. When he should have been called to account, he lay peacefully slumbering in his cradle. In one version, Hermes finally had to return the cattle to his brother; in another he was allowed to keep them and presented the lyre to Apollo in exchange. Apollo gave him a magic wand which, together with his winged traveler's hat and winged shoes, became characteristic of him. With this wand he could put people to sleep and wake them up again. Later the wand was understood more as a herald's staff (*Caduceus), i.e., as an attribute of the god's messenger.—Etymologically the name Hermes is connected with the Greek word *hermaion,* meaning "pile of stones." The piles of stones that were set up to orient travelers were sacred to Hermes, as were the herms placed in front of houses. These were pillar-shaped monuments carved with the bearded head of Hermes, incipient arms, and a phallus, which served as route and boundary markers but were also supposed to protect people's homes.—Aside from the particular tasks entrusted to him on occasion by the Olympian gods and his role as a travel companion, Hermes led the souls of the dead to the other world in his capacity as *psychopomp* (conductor of souls). In connection with this last

Hermes with the infant Dionysus, whom he brought to the nymphs of Nysa to raise; a work of Praxiteles

Hermes with winged cap and *kerykeion*

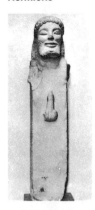

Hermes Pillar-shaped monument called a herm; from Siphos—Such herms were consecrated to the cult of Hermes from an early date

function, on the third day of the Anthesteria, a spring festival celebrated for the dead, pots containing food were put out for him as offerings while prayers were said for the dead.—As god of shepherds, who had the ability to multiply the herds, Hermes was sometimes represented by a ram. Since as an infant he had successfully robbed his brother, he also functioned as god of the "lucky find." As such, he was named Hermaion and given authority over robbery and theft. Because of his enormous cunning, all sorts of inventions were ascribed to him, but he was also seen as a helper in the spiritual realm and venerated as the patron of orators, for example. Mindful of the god's own youthfulness and swiftness, youths entering athletic competitions put themselves under his protection.—The image of Hermes changed under the impact of Egyptian influence during the Hellenistic age. As Trismegistus (the Thrice Great) Hermes assumed the features of a mystical god of the universe.—Among the Romans, *Mercurius corresponded to the Greek Hermes.

Hermione A legendary Greek figure, she was the daughter of *Menelaus and Helen. Her first husband was *Neoptolemus. Later she married *Orestes, who had killed Neoptolemus (probably at Delphi).

Hero and Leander One of the most famous couples of Greek legend. Hero was a priestess of Aphrodite at Sestos, and Leander lived in Abydos. From there he would swim across the Hellespont at night to visit his beloved, whom he could not marry because both sets of parents objected. One stormy night, the light used by Hero to show him the way went out, and Leander drowned in the swelling water. When she saw his corpse, the grief-stricken Hero threw herself into the sea and drowned.—The story of Hero and Leander has often been treated in literature, for example, by Ovid and Schiller.

Herodotus A Greek historian (ca. 490-425 B.C.) from Halicarnassus, he was the father of Western historiography. The overarching theme of his *Histories* (which comprise nine books) is the confrontation between Greece and the East;

they present detailed descriptions of people and places in the eastern Mediterranean. The work is sustained by belief in the divine guidance of destinies.

Herse Daughter of King *Cecrops (1). Together with her sisters, she opened the chest containing *Erichthonius, against the will of Athena.— Another version tells of her becoming the mother of Cephalus and Ceryx by Hermes.

Hersilia A Sabine and daughter of Hersilius. Abducted by the Romans, she mediated between the Sabines and the Romans. Her first husband was *Hostilius, to whom she bore Hostus Hostilius. After Hostilius died, she may have married Romulus. When he died, Hersilia was divinized.

Hersilius A Sabine and the father of *Hersilia.

Hesiod A Greek poet who lived ca. 700 B.C., he is the first Western poet whose personality comes through to us. Hesiod came from Ascra in Boeotia, where he lived as a farmer like his father. According to his own statement, he was called to be a poet by the Muses. His *Theogony* attempts to provide a history of the gods as well as a genealogical classification of myths. Hesiod addressed his later poem, *Works and Days*, to his younger brother Perses, who had withheld his inheritance from Hesiod. It combines teaching about the five ages of the world with rules of conduct and a kind of almanac. The *Theogony* is one of our most important sources for information on Greek mythology and religion.

Hesione Daughter of the Trojan king *Laomedon. When Laomedon cheated Apollo and Poseidon of their previously agreed upon wages after they had built a wall around Troy, Apollo afflicted the city with the plague and Poseidon unloosed a man-eating sea monster on it. An oracle decreed that, in order to avert disaster from Troy, Laomedon would have to feed his daughter to the monster. Whoever succeeded in saving Hesione would receive as his reward the divine horses once bestowed by Zeus on Laomedon's grandfather Tros. Although Heracles saved Hesione, Laomedon did not keep his word; Heracles then attacked Troy and killed most of the king's sons. He gave Hesione, whom he had taken captive, to his companion *Telamon in marriage.

Hesperides In Greek legend the daughters of Nyx or of Atlas and Hesperis (other versions name Phorcys and Ceto or Zeus and Themis as the parents). There were usually said to be three of them, but occasionally seven are mentioned. Together with *Ladon they watched over the *Garden of the Hesperides and its golden apples. One of the labors of *Heracles was to pluck some of the apples.

Hesperis Daughter of Hesperus, she was often regarded as the mother of the *Hesperides.

Hestia Greek goddess of the hearth, she was the daughter of Kronos and Rhea. Counted among the twelve great Olympian gods, she always remained a virgin. Offerings were made to her at the domestic hearth as the focal point of the family, but also in public buildings like the Athenian *prytaneion* and at Delphi, where the hearth of Hestia was thought to represent all the hearths of Greece.—The Roman counterpart of the Greek Hestia, *Vesta, was worshiped as a state goddess.

Hilaira A daughter of Leucippus, the husband of Philodike. She and her sister Phoebe were abducted by Castor and Polydeuces (*Dioscuri).

Himeros Among the Greeks, the divinized personification of desire and longing. A companion of *Eros, he often appeared in the entourage of Aphrodite.

Hind of Ceryneia *Ceryneia.

Hippe Daughter of Chiron and beloved of Aeolus, son of Hellen.

Hippocoon 1. In Greek legend, king of Sparta, son of Oebalus, and brother or half-brother of *Tyndareos (among others), whom he drove from power. Heracles made war on him and was wounded, but after Asclepius had healed Heracles, he defeated Hippocoon and restored Tyndareos to the throne. 2. A companion of Aeneas on the voyage to Italy, he distinguished himself at the funeral games for Anchises by his exceptional accomplishments. 3. An ally of the Trojans, he warned *Rhesus that Diomedes and Odysseus intended to steal his famous horses.

Hippocrene (Greek for "spring of horses") According to legend, the hoof beat of *Pegasus gave rise to this spring on Mount Helicon, which was sacred to the Muses and a source of poetic inspiration.

Hippodameia In Greek legend, the daughter of *Oenomaus of Pisa in Elis, and the wife of *Pelops, to whom she bore many children. It was prophesied to Oenomaus that his daughter's marriage would bring him death. For this reason, every suitor first had to compete with him in a chariot race and suffer death at his hands after Oenomaus had won the race with his swift horses. Nevertheless, Pelops managed to win and carry off Hippodameia.—According to another tradition, by promising to share the sovereignty with him, Pelops bribed *Myrtilus to replace the linchpins in the wheels of the king's chariot with wax. As a result, during the competition the chariot broke and Oenomaus was thrown to his death. Hippodameia was then free to marry Pelops.

Hippolyte Queen of the Amazons, she was the daughter of Ares and Otrera (Otrere) and possibly the mother of Hippolytus by Theseus. In the course of Heracles' combat with the Amazons, Hippolyte met her death when Heracles assaulted her and robbed her of a girdle that Ares had given her.—According to another, rarer version, Hippolyte died of a broken heart because Heracles had stolen the girdle presented to her by Ares.

Hippolytus 1. Son of *Theseus and Hippolyte (or alternatively of the Amazon Antiope). After the death of his first wife, Theseus married *Phaedra, a daughter of Minos, who fell passionately in love with her stepson and tried to seduce him. When Hippolytus rejected her advances, she slandered him (posthumously) because she was afraid of being discovered by her husband. Theseus believed his wife and had

Hippolytus dragged to death. 2. A giant, he was a son of Gaia and the brother of the other giants. Wearing a cloak of invisibility, Hermes killed him in the battle between the gods and the giants.

Hippomenes Son of the Boeotian king Megareus. According to one strand of the tradition, it was he rather than Melanion who defeated the renowned huntress *Atalanta in a footrace and so won her as his bride.

Hippothoe The daughter of *Mestor (1) and Lysidice, she was the mother of Taphius by Poseidon.

Hippothoon (Hippothous) 1. King of Eleusis and son of Poseidon and *Alope. Exposed as an infant, he was nursed by a mare (according to one version). 2. An illegitimate son of *Priam. 3. Leader of the Pelasgians, allies of the Trojans in the Trojan War. He was killed by *Aias the Great when he came seeking the body of Patroclus.

Hiskilla Wife of the Thessalian king *Triopas (1), she was the mother of several children, including *Erysichthon.

Hodios Epithet of *Hermes in his capacity as god of travelers.

Homer Traditionally the oldest and most significant epic poet of antiquity, he was regarded by most Greeks as the author of the *Iliad* and the *Odyssey*. Although he was once thought to be fictional, his historicity is no longer seriously doubted. However, biographical information about him is extremely scant. He probably lived in the 8th century B.C. Seven cities claimed the honor of being his birthplace, but the most cogent arguments attach to Smyrna in Asia Minor. From the 5th century B.C. there are references to his blindness, poverty, and extensive travel as a rhapsode, which may be purely legendary. The numerous busts of the poet are ideal, predominantly Hellenistic portraits, revealing nothing about the actual appearance of Homer.—The historical background of the two great epics ascribed to him, the *Iliad* and the *Odyssey*, has been verified by Schliemann's excavations and

Homer This idealizing bust of Homer reveals nothing about the actual appearance of the poet. Only in the Hellenistic period did Greek idealizing busts take on portraitlike features

the research connected with them. The poems were composed in the Aeolian-Ionian dialect in hexameters. Their highly figurative language had an enormous influence on all succeeding Greek literature and indeed on Western literature altogether.—The leitmotif of the *Iliad* is the wrath of Achilles at Agamemnon's appropriation of the royal princess Briseis, who had been awarded to Achilles. Despite the fact that the poem covers only about fifty days out of the ten-year Trojan War, it paints a splendid picture of a heroic age in which gods and humans played roles of equal importance. The underlying mood is tragic: faced with the alternatives of a long life or early death and eternal glory, Achilles chooses the latter. In his wrath over his wounded honor, he brings the Greek army to the edge of doom and loses his best friend, Patroclus, on the battlefield. His revenge on Hector, the greatest hero on the Trojan side, is terrible. Yet the epic concludes with a reconciliation between Achilles and the aging king Priam, who ransoms his fallen son from the hands of the enemy.—In the *Odyssey,* the lesser prominence of the gods leaves more room for the presentation of simpler folk. This work narrates the wanderings of Odysseus; for ten years he must endure all the hardships of the sea and distant lands until he finally arrives home in Ithaca. There he takes revenge on the enemies of his son Telemachus, who has been searching for him. As the suitors of his faithful wife Penelope, these same enemies have been squandering his estate. The *Odyssey* was composed after the *Iliad*. Scholars have not established with certainty whether the two epics actually derive from the same poet. Many diverse theories have been developed under the heading of the so-called Homeric question.

Hope In the ancient imagination, hope is what remained in Pandora's box after it was opened; at that moment every evil escaped from the box and took possession of mankind.

Hopladamas As one of the giants, he protected Rhea from her husband, *Kronos.

Horace (*Quintus Horatius Flaccus*) A Roman poet who lived from 65 to 8 B.C. The son of a freedman, his importance as a poet of the Augustan Age was second only to that of Virgil. His foremost compositions are odes written in the tradition of Alcaeus and Sappho, with either political or specifically lyrical themes. Among the contents of his two books of *Epistulae*, the *Ars Poetica* (a didactic poem about art) acquired particular renown and influence.

Horae In Greek mythology, the three goddesses of the seasons and of the powers of nature: Thallo (goddess of blossoms), Auxo (goddess of growth), and Karpo (goddess of ripe fruit). Identified as daughters of Zeus and Themis, they often appeared in the retinue of Apollo, Aphrodite, and Dionysus. In Hesiod their frame of reference shifted from the natural to the ethical. Their names then became *Dike (justice), *Eunomia (good order), and *Eirene (peace), and they functioned as guardians of the social order.

Hora Quirini Roman goddess of beauty, she was the divinized version of Hersilia, wife of Romulus.

Horatii This old Roman patrician clan had already died out in the 5th century B.C. According to the legend, three Horatii brothers fought with three Curiatii from Alba Longa over the issue of ascendancy between Rome and Alba Longa. After the death of two Horatii, the third is supposed to have defeated the three Curiatii and then to have killed his own sister because she had been in love with one of the Curiatii and had mourned his death. The outcome of the struggle confirmed the ascendancy of Rome.

Hostilius The husband of *Hersilia and father of Hostius Hostilius, he fell in combat against the Sabines.

Hubris From Homer onward a frequently occurring concept in Greek ethics, which signified a proud and haughty attitude on the part of a human being toward the gods and the laws.—In front of the Areopagus in Athens stood the so-called stone of Hubris, onto which the accused person in a lawsuit had to step.

Hyacinthus A handsome youth in Greek legend, he was the son of Amyclas and Diomedes and beloved of Apollo. Apollo inadvertently killed him while throwing the discus, because Zephyrus (the west wind), who was plagued by jealousy, blew the discus toward Hyacinthus's head. From the blood of the slain youth Apollo caused the hyacinth to sprout.—Hyacinthus likely originated as a vegetation god whose death and transformation were believed to symbolize the annual dying and reawakening of nature.

Hyades Daughters of Atlas and Pleione or Oceanus and Tethys, their number was usually given as five or seven. Sisters of the Hesperides and the Pleiades, they were occasionally mentioned (among others) as nurses of the infant Dionysus. Grief over the death of their brother *Hyas drove them to commit suicide, after which Zeus turned them into stars.

Hyas Son of Atlas and Pleione, he was the brother of the *Hyades, the Hesperides, and the Pleiades. When he was killed by a bull, a lion, a serpent, or a wild boar in Libya, the Hyades felt his loss acutely.

Hydra of Lerna This serpentlike monster from Greek mythology, who lived in the marshes of Lerna, tormented the inhabitants of the Argolid. The Hydra had nine heads and whenever one of them was cut off, two new ones sprang up in its place. Together with his nephew Iolaus, *Heracles succeeded in overcoming the Hydra by cutting off all of the heads and scorching the necks with a burning log. He smeared his arrows with the monster's spleen, which rendered them poisonous. Thereafter the arrows inflicted incurable wounds on whomever they pierced.

Hydra of Lerna
Heracles subdues the Lernaean hydra

Hydra of Lerna
Heracles struggling with the hydra; Greek vase painting

Hygieia

Hygieia Greek goddess of health and daughter (in another version, wife) of *Asclepius, she was worshiped together with him at Epidaurus and other places.

Hyginus (*Gaius Julius*) A freedman and librarian of Augustus, who died around A.D. 10, he authored mythological, religious, and geographical works. The very informative mythological handbook entitled *Fabulae* is, probably incorrectly, attributed to him.

Hylas Son of Theiomenes or Theiodamas, he was an Argonaut and the special favorite of *Heracles. When Hylas was abducted at Cios in Mysia by the water nymphs, Heracles left his companions to search for him, but Hylas's wailing cries were of no avail. According to legend, this event was reenacted every year by the local residents as part of a cult.

Hyllus In Greek mythology, the son of Heracles and Deianira, and the husband of Iole, whose dying father had entrusted her to him. Hyllus was the leader of the *Heraclids who, even after the death of *Heracles, were persecuted by the hate-filled *Eurystheus until he and his sons fell in battle. In spite of several attempts, Hyllus and the Heraclids did not succeed in winning back their patrimony, the Peloponnesus. Only after the death of Hyllus were his followers able to do this.

Hylonome Daughter of Ixion and Nephele. Her love for *Kyllaros was so great that, when he died at the hands of the Lapiths, she committed suicide.

Hymenaeus Greek god of marriage

Hymenaeus (or *Hymen*) Greek god of marriage, he was represented as a handsome youth with a bridal torch and a garland in his hand. His parents were Dionysus and Aphrodite, or Apollo and a Muse; occasionally others are named. At weddings he was invoked with a solemn hymn, the Hymenaeus. Thus presumably Hymenaeus was regarded as the divine personification of the wedding hymn.

Hyperbios One of the fifty sons of *Aegyptus, he helped Thebes to defend itself in combat with the *Seven against Thebes. Later he was killed on his wedding night by his wife, one of the *Danaids.

Hyperboreans In antiquity these legendary people were reputed to live in northernmost Greece (on the far side of the north wind, *Boreas). Whether they had a historical origin has not been determined by scholars. The Hyperboreans were portrayed as a people of light, peace, and perpetual bliss, dwelling in a fertile and temperate land to which Apollo would occasionally retire. Political utopias were later localized there.

Hyperion One of the *Titans, he married his sister Theia, who bore him Helios, Selene, Eos, and (according to one tradition) Aurora. Either Hyperion was identified with Helios or Helios carried the epithet Hyperion.

Hyperippe Daughter of the Arcadian king Arcas and the Dryad Erato.

Hypermestra 1. One of the fifty daughters of Danaus, she showed herself unique among them in not stabbing to death her husband (Lynceus) on their wedding night. Traditionally, Hypermestra was supposed to have been buried in a common grave in Argos with her husband and their son Abas. 2. Daughter of Thestius and Eurythemis, she married *Oecles and became the mother of *Amphiaraus.

Hypnos Greek god of sleep, he was the son of *Nyx, the brother of Thanatos, and (in a later tradition) the father of Morpheus. Hypnos could put anyone, even Zeus, to sleep against their will. In Greek cult, he was of minor importance. Artistic representations frequently depicted him as a winged youth.

Hypsipyle Daughter of King Thoas of Lemnos, she secretly saved her father from the clutches of the Lemnian women when out of jealousy they killed all the men on the island in a single night. Hypsipyle herself became queen of Lemnos and the beloved of Jason, who stopped there with the *Argo* and remained for a year. She bore him sons named Thoas and Euenos. When it became known later that Hypsipyle had saved her father, pirates sold her as a slave to King Lycurgus of Argos, who entrusted to her the care of his young son Opheltes. Hypsipyle proved willing to show the *Seven against Thebes to a spring when these strangers arrived in desperate need of water. On their way to the spring, Opheltes, who had been set down to sleep in the grass, was fatally bitten by a snake. *Amphiaraus saved Hypsipyle from the child's vengeful parents. The Seven against Thebes killed the dragon and instituted the *Nemean Games in connection with the funeral for the child, as a memorial to him.—Later Hypsipyle's sons found their mother again and brought her back to Lemnos.—The story of Hypsipyle, with its extraordinary richness of detail, was repeatedly treated by ancient authors, among them Euripides, Apollonius Rhodius, Valerius Flaccus, and Publius Papinius Statius.

Iacchus God of the Eleusinian mysteries, he was frequently identified as the son of Demeter or Persephone and sometimes also as the husband of Persephone. Because of the similarity between the two names, poets in particular often equated him with Bacchus-Dionysus. In fact, Iacchus probably originated from a personification of the joyful cry "*iakche*," sounded during the Eleusinian procession. The cult of Iacchus was very likely confined to Athens and the surrounding area; in any case its presence elsewhere in Greece cannot be proved.

Ialmenus Co-regent of Orchomenus, a son of Ares, and one of the Argonauts. As a suitor of Helen, together with his brothers he furnished a contingent of thirty ships for the Trojan War.

Ialysus Son of Kerkaphos and Kydippe, and grandson of Helios and Rhodos, he cofounded the city of Ialysus. The name of the city was later changed to Rhodos, after his grandmother.

Iambe Servant of *Celeus and Metanira, Iambe was the figure impersonated by Demeter in her despairing search for her daughter. With their jokes, the daughters of Celeus and Metanira succeeded in making her laugh.

Iamus Son of Apollo and Evadne, he possessed the gift of prophecy and became the ancestral head of a line of prophets.

Ianassa One of the Nereids.

Ianeira One of the Nereids.

Ianthe A Cretan maiden, she was betrothed to *Iphis, who though female had been brought up as a boy. Just before the wedding, Isis changed Iphis into a real boy.

Iapetus One of the Titans in Greek mythology, and the son of Uranus and Gaia, he married Asia, Clymene, or Themis, and became the father of Atlas, Epimetheus, and Prometheus. Occasionally he was also characterized as the father of humankind. According to one strand of tradition, Zeus hurled him into Tartarus during the combat with the Titans, after which an island colonized by humans rose up over him.

Iapis A Trojan whom Apollo instructed in the use of healing herbs, so that he was able to restore many persons to good health.

Iarbas A North African king who was prepared to give Dido as much land as she could cover with an ox hide. By cutting the ox hide into thin strips, she encompassed the area on which she founded Carthage.

Iardanus The father of Omphale and a king of Lydia.

Iasion Son of Zeus and *Electra (2). Demeter fell in love with him and as a result of their union gave birth to Plutus and Philomelus. Iasion perfected the mysteries of Samothrace and was worshiped as a god by the Arcadians.—According to another version, Zeus struck him with lightning because of his union with Demeter.— He may have derived from a pre-Greek god of agriculture.

Iaso A goddess of healing, she was the daughter of *Asclepius and Epione. She had various siblings, who were similarly known for their proficiency in the art of healing.

Iasus In Greek legend the name of several figures, including: 1. One of the *Dactyls and son of Rhea. 2. The son of Lycurgus and father of Atalanta by Clymene—to protect his daughter's virginity, he devised a race which the suitors of Atalanta had to win in order to gain her hand. 3. King of Argos and possibly a son of *Argos Panoptes. 4. A Greek who was killed in the Trojan War by Aeneas.

Icarius This name was borne by several legendary Greek figures, including the father of *Erigone, to whom Dionysus taught the art of vine growing.

Icarus The son of *Daedalus, he plunged to his death wearing the wings made by his father out of feathers and wax, because he flew too close to the sun. Daedalus constructed the wings in order to liberate himself and his son from their captivity under Minos.

Ida 1. The karstic mountain range in the interior of Crete, which today is called Psiloritis. According to Greek legend, it was the birthplace of Zeus. 2. A mountain range in the southern Troad (Asia Minor) and the locale of numerous Greek legends. Here Paris is reputed to have delivered his judgment in the beauty contest between Aphrodite, Athena, and Hera. This range gives rise to many rivers, which also play a role in mythology.

Idaeus The Trojan herald who pulled the chariot in which Priam brought back the body of his son Hector, recovered from Achilles.

Idaia A daughter of *Dardanus who lived as a nymph on Mount Ida in Phrygia. She became the mother of Teucer by Scamander and thereby the progenitress of the Trojan royal line.

Idas 1. Son of Aphareus of Messene (or Poseidon) and Arene, he was the twin brother of *Lynceus (2). Both brothers took part in the voyage of the Argonauts and the Calydonian boar hunt. The legend reports that Idas first married his cousin Phoebe, who was then stolen from him by the *Dioscuri. When Apollo attempted to rob him of his next love, Marpessa, Idas approached him with his bow drawn; combat was averted only by the intervention of Zeus, who let Marpessa decide between the two suitors. She chose Idas and bore him a daughter named Cleopatra.—Because of the conflict with the Dioscuri, Idas and Lynceus took up arms against them. Idas killed Castor and was himself destroyed by a lightning flash sent by Zeus. Lynceus met his death at the hands of Polydeuces. 2. One of the *Dactyls, he was the son of Rhea or Anchiale and the brother of many siblings.

Idmon 1. One of the fifty sons of Aegyptus, he was murdered by his wife on their wedding night. 2. The son of Abas (or Apollo) and Asteria (or Cyrene), he joined the Argonauts as a prophet, even though he foresaw his own death on the expedition; he died while hunting.

Idomeneus Son of Deucalion and king of Crete, he took part in the campaign against Troy and returned home without injury. According to one strand of tradition, he vowed to sacrifice to Poseidon as an offering of thanks whatever he encountered first after landing on Crete. Despite the fact that his son turned out to be the victim, he kept his promise. A later legend reports that he was driven from his homeland and fled to Italy.

Ikelos Also called *Phobetor*, he was one of the numerous sons of Somnus, brother of Hypnos, and possessed the ability to assume animal forms.

Ilia Another name for the Roman vestal virgin *Rhea Silvia.

Iliad One of the two epic poems of *Homer, which portrays about fifty days in the ten-year Trojan War.

Iliona In Greek mythology, the oldest daughter of Priam and Hecuba. She raised her youngest brother, Polydorus, whom Priam had chosen to inherit the kingdom of Troy, as her own child in order to protect him from attempts on his life. Iliona married Polymestor and bore him a son, *Deipylos, who was passed off as Polydorus. After the Trojan War, Priam caused his son-in-law to have Deipylos murdered. When Polydorus subsequently discovered the truth, he induced Iliona to kill her husband.

Ilioneus 1. A companion of Aeneas on his journey from Troy to Italy. 2. According to Ovid, one of the children of Amphion and *Niobe.

Ilissus A river in Attica where legend tells that *Boreas abducted Oreithyia.

Ilium This was the ancient name for Troy, taken from Ilus, the founder of the city. Later it was also used to designate the region around Troy.

Illyrius Son of Cadmus and Harmonia. Cadmus, who came from the west, was made king of the Illyrians, named after his son Illyrius

Ilus In Greek legend, a son of Tros and *Callirhoe (2) and the husband of Eurydice. According to one tradition, he won a dappled cow at a wrestling match. An oracle then commanded him to found a city wherever the cow should lie down, which turned out to be on one of the hills sacred to Ate. This city received the name Ilium, later changed to Troy. Ilus received the Palladium from Zeus.

Imbrios Son of *Mentor, he married a daughter of Priam. In the Trojan War he was killed by *Teucer (2).

Inachus A river god, he was the son of Oceanus and Tethys and father of *Io. The first king of Argos, he appears in Greek legend as the progenitor of the Argive princely house.

Indigetes Already in antiquity this was a disputed term for a group of gods who could not be more precisely defined. Hypotheses and theories of various kinds have not led to any definitive explanation of them. Perhaps they were originally mortal heroes who were subsequently divinized, like Heracles or Aeneas, for example.

Ino In Greek legend, a daughter of Cadmus and *Harmonia. She raised the youthful Dionysus. After marrying the Theban king Athamas, she became the mother of Learchus and Melicertes, and the stepmother of Helle and Phrixus. She conspired to do away with her stepchildren. When Athamas in a fit of madness killed

1.
Athamas—Nephele
Phrixus Helle

2.
Cadmus—Harmonia

Athamas—Ino
          Semele
Learchus Agave
Melicertes Autonoe

Learchus, Ino leapt into the sea with Melicertes, where she was elevated to the status of sea goddess, receiving the name Leucothea.— *Mater Matuta.

Io Priestess of Hera at Argos, she was the daughter of *Inachus and Melia. Zeus fell in love with her and turned her into a white cow, which the jealous Hera requested as a present and

then had guarded by *Argos Panoptes. When Hermes freed Io, Hera caused her to be pursued by a huge gadfly all over Europe. In Egypt her human form was restored to her and she bore Zeus a son, Epaphus, who later as king of Egypt built the city of Memphis. The strait between Europe and Asia where Io crossed over took the name Bosporus ("cattle ford") from her.

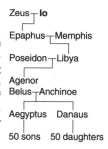

Io guarded by Argos Panoptes (shown here with only two eyes)

Zeus ⊤ Io

Epaphus ⊤ Memphis

Poseidon ⊤ Libya

Agenor

Belus ⊤ Anchinoe

Aegyptus Danaus

50 sons 50 daughters

Iobates King of Lycia, he was the father of Stheneboea, wife of Proetus of Tiryns, who fell in love with *Bellerophon. Iobates underwent many adventures, including the conquest of the *Chimaera.

Iocasta (Also *Epicaste*, her Homeric name) Daughter of Menoikeus, sister of Creon and Hipponome, wife of *Laius, and mother of *Oedipus, who was exposed in infancy by his father. As an adult Oedipus struck his father dead, not knowing him by sight, and married his mother. According to one strand of tradition, this union produced Antigone, Eteocles, Ismene, and Polynices. When Iocasta realized that her husband was in fact her son, she committed suicide in her despair.

Iolaus Originally a Boeotian hero venerated at Thebes, he is later identified as the charioteer and battle companion of Heracles. Son of Iphicles, he was the husband of Megara, who had been Heracles' first wife. A participant in the

Argonautic expedition and the Calydonian boar hunt, Iolaus helped Heracles with some of his labors. In legend he is also mentioned as the winner of a chariot race at the Olympic Games.

Iolcus This ancient site in the Thessalian region of Magnesia on the gulf of Pagasae was the birthplace of Jason. Under his leadership the *Argonauts embarked on their voyage to Colchis.

Iole Daughter of *Eurytus. Eurytus broke his word to Heracles when he refused him the hand of the beautiful Iole even though the hero had fulfilled the precondition for marriage to her, namely, victory in an archery contest with the king. Heracles responded by forcibly possessing Iole as his wife. After his death, Iole married *Hyllus, leader of the *Heraclids.

Ion He was the son of Apollo and Creusa, daughter of Erechtheus. She gave birth to him secretly and then exposed him. Hermes brought Ion to Delphi, where he grew up as a servant in the temple of Apollo. Meanwhile Creusa had been married to Xuthus; when the marriage produced no children, the couple came to consult the Delphic oracle. The oracle reunited and reconciled Ion with his mother.—Among the Greeks, Ion functioned as the eponymous hero of the Ionians.—The story of Ion and Creusa underwent several poetic adaptations, including those of Sophocles and Euripides.

Ionia In antiquity the area comprising the west coast of Asia Minor with its outlying islands.

Iphianassa 1. Another name, used especially by Homer, for *Iphigenia. 2. Daughter of *Proetus of Tiryns and Stheneboea.

Iphicles Son of *Amphitryon and *Alcmene, he was both the half-brother and the twin brother of Heracles. His wife, Automedusa, bore him a son, Iolaus. Iphicles took part in the Calydonian boar hunt and assisted Heracles with some of his labors.

Iphiclus A famous Argonaut, he distinguished himself with his exceptional swiftness. After *Melampus cured him of his inability to beget children, he became the father of two sons by Diomedeia.

Iphidamas One of the numerous sons of Antenor and Theano, he was killed by Agamemnon in the Trojan War.

Iphigenia Legendary daughter of the Mycenaean king *Agamemnon and Clytemnestra, she was the sister of Orestes, Electra, and Chrysothemis. When the Greek fleet bound for Troy was becalmed at Aulis, the offended goddess Artemis required of Agamemnon that he sacrifice Iphigenia to atone either for having slaughtered an animal sacred to her or for having claimed to be as excellent a hunter as she; without this sacrifice the fleet would be unable to sail. However, at the last moment (according to one version) Artemis carried Iphigenia off to Taurus, where she had to officiate at the human sacrifices that were customary there. *Orestes arrived at Taurus and was supposed to be sacrificed, but the siblings recognized each other and fled to Attica, taking with them the cult image of Artemis that had once been removed from Attica. The story of Iphigenia has often been treated in world literature.

Iphimedeia Daughter of Triopas and *Hiskilla, she was the wife of Aloeus, the mother of the colossal *Aloades, and beloved of Poseidon. One strand of the tradition reports that she and her daughters were kidnapped by Thracian pirates but then rescued by the Aloades.

Iphis 1. Daughter of Ligdos and Telethusa. Being poor, her parents feared that their newborn child would be killed when it became known that it was a girl. For this reason they dressed her as a boy until her thirteenth year, at which time Isis turned her into an actual boy so that Iphis could marry *Ianthe. 2. A Cypriot youth who hanged himself because Anaxarete rejected his love. Aphrodite punished the girl by turning her into a stone.

Iphitos 1. Son of *Eurytus and Oichalia, he was killed by Heracles when the latter suffered a fit of madness. 2. According to legend, as king of Elis he renewed the Olympic Games because

Iris

Isis Horus, the son of
Isis and Osiris

Isis with her son Horus
(ca. 1300 B.C.)

the Delphic oracle had announced to him that
this was the only way to end the plague rav-
aging his land. Iphitos aided the Heraclids
against the peoples of the Peloponnesus.

Iris Daughter of Thaumas and Electra, she was
a sister of the *Harpies. Equipped with golden
wings, she hurried down to earth and into the
sea from Mount Olympus, delivering messages
from Zeus and Hera. Later Hermes replaced her
in this role. Iris was also regarded as the personification of the rainbow, at first still severed
from her character as messenger of the gods
but then identical with it.

Iros Actually named Arnaios, he was a beggar
servant to the suitors of Penelope. When he
learned of the return of the man disguised as a
beggar whose identity yet remained hidden
(Odysseus), Iros mocked his ostensible rival
and was slain by him in a boxing match (according to another version, he was severely
wounded).

Isandros Son of *Bellerophon, and brother of
Hippolochus and Laodameia, he died in combat
against the *Solymi, a savage mountain folk.

Ischys Son of Elatus of Arcadia, and lover of
*Coronis (1).

Isis An ancient Egyptian goddess whose original home was probably in the Nile delta, Isis
was worshiped as a ruler goddess and a mother
goddess. Both the sister and the wife of Osiris
(who had been murdered by Seth), she conceived by him posthumously and gave birth to
Horus. Searching for her beloved husband in
her grief, Isis became a symbol of unswerving
conjugal fidelity and maternal love. Her chief
place of worship was at Philae in Egypt, but her
cult also penetrated into other areas of the
Mediterranean. In Greece, where she was associated with Io and Demeter, she was known at
least from the time of Herodotus. By way of
Magna Graecia, the cult of Isis spread to Rome
and the Roman provinces, where she developed more and more into a universal goddess.—Isis was usually represented with the infant Horus at her breast and the hieroglyph of

the throne on her head, often too with cow horns and solar disk.

Isle of the Blessed *Elysium.

Ismene This name applies to several figures in Greek legend, including: 1. A daughter of Oedipus and Iocasta (in another version, Euryganeia), whom one strand of the tradition designates as the sister of Antigone, Eteocles, and Polynices. 2. A daughter of *Asopos.

Ismenos The eldest son of Amphion and *Niobe.

Issedonians A legendary people who lived even farther north than the *Hyperboreans.

Isthmian games One of the four great series of Panhellenic games, they were celebrated every two years in honor of Poseidon at the Isthmus of Corinth. From the 3rd century B.C. onward, these games were supplemented with musical competitions.

Italus The king of Sicily after whom Italy was named. He was the son of Telegonus and Penelope.

Ithaca One of the Ionian islands of Greece and situated north of Cephalonia, it was the homeland of Odysseus, according to Homer.

Itylus 1. Son of Aedon and Zethus. 2. *Itys in one strand of the tradition.

Itys His parents were the Thracian king *Tereus and *Procne. When Procne discovered that her husband had raped her sister Philomela, and then had cut out Philomela's tongue to avoid being found out, she took her revenge by killing her son Itys and serving him to the hated Tereus for dinner.—The king, Philomela, and Procne were all turned into birds.

Iulus (*Julus*) Originally named *Ascanius, he was the son of Aeneas and Creusa. After accompanying his father to Italy, Ascanius was renamed Iulus and became the progenitor of the patrician line of the Julians.

Iuppiter The Roman god *Jupiter.

155

Iustitia seated on a globe (detail); woodcut by a German master of the 16th century

Iustitia (*Justitia*) The Roman personification of justice corresponding to the Greek *Dike, she was worshiped by the Romans as a divinity. Her cult acquired importance particularly in the Augustan Age after Augustus had dedicated a sanctuary to her. *Iustitia Augusta* counted among the virtues that were officially attributed to the emperor.—Iustitia also appeared on Roman coins.

Iuturna The Roman goddess *Juturna.

Ixion King of the Lapiths in Thessaly, he was the son of Phlegyas (in another version, of Ares), the husband of Dia, and through her the father of Pirithous. As his father-in-law was about to depart with the bride-price owed to him, Ixion treacherously murdered him by thrusting him into a red-hot coal pit. This action made Ixion the first murderer. Initially no one would purify him, but then Zeus absolved him of his crimes and even invited him to the gods' table. There Ixion presumptuously approached Hera, intending to seduce her, but was unaware that Zeus had discerned his intrigues and substituted *Nephele for Hera. She bore Ixion the *Centaurs. Ixion was punished for his outrages by being bound to a constantly turning wheel of fire. According to one strand of the tradition, he was thrown into Tartarus and doomed to be an eternal penitent.

Ixion on the wheel as a penitent in the underworld

Janiculum (Latin, *mons Ianiculus*) One of the seven hills of ancient Rome, it was situated on the right bank of the Tiber River opposite the Field of Mars. Because of its military importance, bridges linked the Janiculum to the city. In the 3rd century A.D. it was enclosed within the city walls.

Janus A very old Roman deity with many enigmatic features, he functioned as a god of portals but also of entering and exiting, in both the literal and the figurative senses. The month of January bore his name, and New Year's Day was sacred to him as were the Calends of every month. His main feast day, called the *Agonium*, fell on the 9th of January. Before important undertakings by private or public persons, Janus was called upon for protection and help. In the hymn of the Salii, he was praised as the highest of the gods. The temple of Janus in the Forum stood open during times of war, being closed only when Rome was at peace. Augustus extolled himself in his *Res gestae* for the fact that, under his rule, the temple doors were closed three times whereas throughout the entire previous history of Rome they had been closed just twice.—Janus was generally represented with a "double" head, consisting of two profiles: one on the right and one on the left.

Janus on a Roman copper coin; as usual he is represented with two faces, i.e., with both right and left profiles

Jason A legendary Greek hero, he was the son of *Aeson and Alkimede (in another version, Polymede). After the death or banishment of Jason's father by his uncle *Pelias, Jason was turned over to the centaur *Chiron to be educated. But he demanded that his father's kingdom be returned to him when he reached maturity. In an effort to postpone this eventuality and in the hope that his nephew would not survive the commission, Pelias dispatched him to fetch the *Golden fleece from Colchis. On their journey Jason made himself the leader of the *Argonauts and obtained the desired booty with the help of *Medea, whom he married. When he later proved unfaithful to her and proposed to take *Glauke as his new wife, Medea wreaked a terrible revenge. There are varying accounts of Jason's further fortunes. According to one wide-

Janus

spread version, death came to him from a wooden plank that broke loose from the Argo and fell on him.

Judgment of Paris The judgment provoked by *Eris, who tossed an apple among the wedding guests at the marriage of Peleus and Thetis bearing the inscription "the most beautiful." It fell to Paris to choose the recipient. Compelled to decide between Aphrodite, Hera, and Athena, he awarded the prize to Aphrodite, who had promised him *Helen in exchange. Paris abducted Helen and so gave the occasion for the Trojan War. In Homer the Judgment of Paris is not yet mentioned as a reason for the outbreak of war.

Juno The name of this ancient Italian goddess probably derives from *iuvenis*, referring to the vitality of a young woman. In the imagination of antiquity, Juno corresponded to the masculine

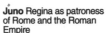

Juno Regina as patroness of Rome and the Roman Empire

Juno

Juno Juno Ludovisi (Rome)

*Genius, serving as the companion of feminine nature from birth to death. Jupiter, Minerva, and Juno were worshiped together on the Roman Capitol as the Capitoline triad. Although some of her epithets (e.g., *Juno Regina*, guardian of the city of Rome and the Roman Empire) point in another direction, she was in the first instance a goddess of women and the whole life cycle of women, especially of childbirth (as *Juno Opi-*

gena and *Juno Lucina*—she who brings children into the light of the world). The animal sacred to Juno was the goat, and her sacred fruit was the fig. All the Calends were consecrated to her. Her feast day, the Matronalia, was celebrated on March 1.

Jupiter (*Iuppiter*, from the Latin *Diespater* meaning "father of light") The Latin name of the Indo-European god of heaven corresponding to the Greek Zeus, from whom he "inherited" many characteristics. Jupiter played an extraordinarily important role in the life of the Romans as weather god on the one hand, and preserver of the established social order and protector of the state on the other.—As god of weather he sent lightning (*Jupiter Fulgur*), thunder (*Jupiter Tonans*), and rain (*Jupiter Pluvius*). As preserver of law and order, he safeguarded marriage and oaths in particular, functioning himself as god of oaths (*Dius Fidius*). He was worshiped on the Roman Capitol (together with *Juno and *Minerva) under the epithets *Optimus Maximus* and *Jupiter Capitolinus*, as the embodiment of the Roman idea of the state. The temple of the Capitoline triad served as the setting for various state activities: the declaration of war by the Senate, the publication of international treaties, the termination of triumphal processions led by victorious returning generals, etc.—All days of the full moon were sacred to Jupiter. The *Ludi Romani* were celebrated in his honor in September, as were the *Ludi plebeii* in November.

Jupiter

Justitia *Iustitia.

Juturna This Roman goddess of springs, whose origins were probably Etruscan, was the sister of Turnus and the mother of *Fontus. The water from her springs was reputed to have healing powers. She possessed several sanctuaries in Rome. On January 11, her festal day, in an unknown year a temple was dedicated to her.

Juventas (also *Iuventas*) Roman goddess of eternal youth, which she personified. The special guardian of Roman youths, she was identified with the Greek *Hebe.

Kaikinos A river god, he was the son of Oceanus and Tethys and the brother of the other river gods.

Kaletor A Trojan nobleman and descendant of Dardanus, he was a cousin of Hector. Kaletor died in the Trojan War at the hands of Aias the Great.

Kallianassa One of the *Nereids.

Kallidike Queen of the Thesproti, she married Odysseus after the Trojan War and bore him *Polypoites (1), who succeeded her on the throne.

Kandalos One of the *Heliades; together with some of his brothers he murdered *Tenages and went into exile along with his accomplices. Kandalos is supposed to have been the first person to offer sacrifices to Athena.

Kardys The father of *Clymenus (3) and king of Olympia.

Karme A nymph from the retinue of Artemis, she became the mother of *Britomartis by Zeus.

Karnabon King of the Getae in Thrace. When he killed one of the serpents of Triptolemus, the goddess punished him by translating him to the constellation of the serpent-holder.

Karpo As one of the *Horae, she was the goddess of ripe fruit.

Kebriones An illegitimate son of Priam, he served his half-brother Hector as charioteer and was killed by Patroclus.

Kedalion A legendary Greek journeyman smith, he was bestowed as a companion by Hephaestus on the blinded *Orion as the latter made his way toward Helios to have his sight restored.

Kelmos A boyhood playmate of Zeus, he was turned into a lodestone because he declared that Zeus would be mortal.

Ker (plural, *Keres*) Among the ancient Greeks an ambiguous concept with two principal meanings: in the abstract it was understood as doom, disaster, death, and so on; in the concrete, it was a demon of destruction, especially the destruction caused by death.

Kerkaphos One of the sons of Helios and Rhodos, he was the father of Ialysus, Camirus, and Lindus, after whom the main towns on the island of Rhodes were named. Kerkaphos and his brothers (one of them being *Macar) were among the first humans to offer sacrifices to Athena.

Kerkopes In Greek mythology, they were playful imps whom Heracles first bound in fetters but then released because he was amused by their antics.

Kerykon This legendary Greek figure, who challenged all passersby to a duel and proceeded to kill them, was finally defeated by *Theseus.

Keuthonymos The father of Menoites, shepherd of Hades.

Kilissa The nurse of Orestes, she sacrificed her own son in order to save Orestes' life.

Kisseus 1. One of the fifty sons of Aegyptus, he married one of the fifty daughters of his father's brother *Danaus. 2. A son of Melampus (companion to Heracles), he was an ally of Turnus who died at the hands of Aeneas. 3. King of Thrace and the father of Theano. 4. A river god, he is named in one strand of the tradition as a possible father of Hecuba.

Kleodora 1. A *Danaid who married one of the sons of Aegyptus. 2. A nymph.

Kleodoxa One of the daughters of Amphion and *Niobe, she was killed by Artemis and Apollo.

Kleostratos A youth who was saved by his lover, Menestratos, from the fangs of the dragon that attacked the city of Thespiae every year.

Klonia A nymph and the wife of Hyrieus (or Chthonios, according to another version), she was the mother of Lycus and Nycteus.

Klytia One of the Oceanids and beloved of Helios (or Apollo, according to another tradition), she was changed into a sunflower when the god left her.

Knossia A nymph who became the mother of Xenodamos by Menelaus.

Kolontas The father of *Chthonia (1), he burned to death in his own house, according to legend, when he refused to extend hospitality to Demeter.

Kometes Son of Sthenelus, Kometes was commissioned by his friend *Diomedes (2) to take care of the latter's wife, *Aegialeia, during his absence at the Trojan War. Kometes and Aegialeia committed adultery, and when Diomedes arrived back home, they drove him out of the country.

Konobos One of the four horses of Ares.

Koon The oldest of the numerous sons of *Antenor, he was killed by Agamemnon in the Trojan War.

Kopreus Son of *Pelops and Hippodameia, he was the herald of *Eurystheus. Kopreus had to convey a message to Heracles, who killed him. According to another tradition, the Athenians killed him.

Korax Legendary king of Sicyon, son of Coronis, and brother of Lamedon. He was deposed by Epopeus (*Antiope), who succeeded him on the throne.

Kore Daughter of the grain goddess *Demeter. Her real name was *Persephone, but in certain contexts she was referred to as the Kore ("corn maiden").

Koronides Designation for Metioche and Menippe, two daughters of Orion. Aphrodite granted them beauty, and Athena endowed them with dexterity in the art of weaving. The Koronides killed themselves in order to bring an end to an epidemic in Orchomenus.—The legend has a number of variants, among which the best known relates that Orion fell in love with the mother of the Koronides, Pleione, and pursued her. Taking her daughters with her, she fled. The three were subsequently immortalized and placed among the stars.

Kranaos This king of Athens was driven from the throne by his son-in-law Amphiktyon. According to legend, the Deucalion flood occurred during his reign.

Kratos 1. A *Titan, about whom one strand of tradition relates that he blinded Prometheus by order of Hephaestus. 2. According to Hesiod, the son of Pallas and Styx, whose various children included Bia, personifying power and might.

Kriasos Son of Argos, a Peloponnesian ruler, and of Evadne.

Krino Daughter of *Antenor and Theano, she emigrated from her homeland with her parents after the death of most of her numerous brothers and the destruction of Troy.

Krokos A handsome youth who loved a nymph. Because of his impatience, both of them were changed into flowers or yew trees.

Kronia A summer festival celebrated in Attica in honor of *Kronos, the Kronia united masters and slaves at a joyful banquet. It was comparable to the Roman Saturnalia.

Kronos The youngest and most important of the *Titans, he was a son of Uranus and Gaia. Because she was angry with her husband for banishing the Cyclopes and Hecatoncheires, Gaia persuaded Kronos to castrate his father with a sickle and seize world dominion for himself. To spare himself a fate like his father's, Kronos swallowed all of his own children (born to him from his sister and spouse Rhea) except Zeus, who escaped him through Rhea's trickery: instead of the infant, she handed Kronos a stone wrapped in swaddling clothes. Zeus was raised by nymphs in a secret place and upon reaching maturity forced his father to vomit up his siblings. At that point the struggle began for world dominion, which Zeus finally won. Uranus and all who had taken his side, especially the Titans, were locked up in Tartarus but later pardoned. Zeus delegated sovereignty over the Isles of the Blessed to his father.—The idea of one generation of gods being superseded by another is not Greek but very likely Eastern in origin.—Another version interprets this myth of supersession as concerning the transition from one historical period to the next in a downward direction, beginning with the Golden Age, when

Kronos gripping the sickle with which he castrated his father

Kronos exercised a benevolent rule and human beings enjoyed a paradisal existence.

Krotopos King of Argos, he was the father of Psamathe ("sand maiden"), who was probably the mother of *Linus (1).

Krotos Son of Pan, he was transformed into the archer constellation (Sagittarius).

Ktesios An ancient spirit who watched over storerooms. His name was also an epithet of Zeus (*Zeus Ktesios*).

Ktesippos 1. A suitor of *Penelope, he was killed by the swineherd Eumaeus, who had remained faithful to his master, Odysseus. 2. A son of Heracles and *Deianira.

Ktimene Daughter of King Laertes of Ithaca and Anticlea, she was the sister of Odysseus and wife of *Eurylochos.

Kydippe 1. A priestess of Hera, and the mother of *Biton and Cleobis. 2. The daughter of rich parents, she married Akontios, whose family was poor but honorable.—*Akontios and Kydippe.

Kyllaros In Greek legend, he was a *Centaur and son of Ixion and Nephele. Distinguished for his exceptional beauty, he fell passionately in love with *Hylonome, who killed herself after his death.

Kymodoke One of the *Nereids.

Kymothoe One of the *Nereids.

Kynortas Son of Amyclas and *Diomede (2), he succeeded his brother Argalos on the throne as king of Sparta.

Kynosura A nymph from Mount Ida on Crete who cared for the infant Zeus, she was placed among the stars.

Kytissoros Son of Phrixus and Chalciope, he helped the Argonauts to obtain the *Golden fleece and escape from Colchis. The legend has a series of variants.

Labdakos King of Thebes, son of *Polydorus (1), grandson of Cadmus, and father of *Laius, he was killed in the war with Pandion.

Labyrinth 1. Among the Greeks this term referred to Amenemhet's temple of the dead at Hawara in Egypt. 2. The structure built by the famous architect *Daedalus, comprising many tortuous passageways, in which King Minos of Crete kept the *Minotaur prisoner.

Lacedaemon The legendary ancestor of the Lacedaemonians, he was probably a son of Zeus and Taygete.

Lachesis One of the *Moirai, she was a daughter of Zeus and Themis and the sister of Clotho and Atropos. To each person she allotted his or her fate.

Labyrinth Floor pattern from the church of San Vitale in Ravenna; 6th century. It conveys an impression of the tortuousness of the passages in the structure where King Minos detained the Minotaur

Laconia In antiquity this region of the southern Peloponnesus was called Lacedaemon; Sparta was its capital.

Ladon 1. A many-headed dragon, sprung from Phorcys and Ceto, which helped to guard the *Garden of the Hesperides. One version of the legend reports that Heracles killed Ladon just before he took the golden apples. 2. A particularly charming Greek river and also the name of its god. 3. A companion of Aeneas on his journey from Troy to Italy.

Laertes In Greek mythology, king of Ithaca and the father of *Odysseus. He participated in the Calydonian boar hunt and the Argonautic expedition.

Laestrygones In Greek mythology, they were man-eating giants, traditionally located near Formiae in Italy but occasionally also in Sicily. They posed a particular danger to *Odysseus on his homeward journey from Troy by demolishing his fleet with boulders and devouring the crew. Odysseus succeeded in saving only himself and his own ship, escaping over the high sea from the destructive rage of the Laestrygones.

Laius King of Thebes, son of *Labdakos, and father of Oedipus. At the death of Labdakos, Lycus first assumed power; he was followed by

Amphion, since Laius was still a minor. Laius lived at the court of King Pelops in the Peloponnesus, where he fell in love with Chrysippus, the king's son. When Laius abducted Chrysippus, the latter committed suicide. Cursed by Pelops, Laius returned to Thebes and acceded to his father's throne after the death of Amphion. His wife was *Iocasta. Their son Oedipus later struck down his father, not recognizing him, and unwittingly married his mother, Iocasta.—Labdakos was regarded as the founding father of the house of Labdakos.

Lamia Daughter of Belus and *Libya, she was originally a beautiful young woman with whom Zeus fell in love. Hera in her jealousy inflicted madness on Lamia, with the result that she swallowed her own children. According to the legend, Lamia became a horrible ghost who stole the children of other mothers and sucked out their blood. From Zeus she acquired the faculty of metamorphosis. She had certain features in common with the Roman *Lemures.

Lampetia One of the *Heliades, she tended the cattle that were sacred to Apollo. After the death of her brother *Phaethon, she was turned into a poplar tree.

Laodamas King of Thebes and son of Eteocles; during his childhood Creon acted as regent. Laodamas led the Thebans against the Epigoni. Either he was killed by them or he fled to Illyria.

Laodameia 1. Daughter of Acastus and wife of *Protesilaus. Her husband was the first of the Greeks who sailed against Troy to touch Trojan soil, on which he immediately perished at the hands of Hector. Laodameia was inconsolable over his death and prayed to the gods to let Protesilaus return to earth from the underworld at least for one day. When the allotted time had elapsed, she returned with him to the realm of shadows. According to another version, Laodameia had an image of her husband, the constant sight of which tormented her. But when her father burned the image, she threw herself into the flames.—The story is preserved in a fragmentary tragedy of Euripides. 2. The daughter of *Bellerophon, she married *Sarpedon (2) (another version makes her his mother by Zeus) and was later killed by the arrows of Artemis.

Laodice 1. Daughter of Agamemnon and Clytemnestra, she was also known as Electra. 2. The most beautiful daughter of Priam and Hecuba, she was swallowed up by the earth after the fall of Troy.

Laokoon A priest of Apollo and Poseidon at Troy, he was the son of Antenor (or Capys, in another version); occasionally Priam and Hecuba are also named as his parents. When

Laokoon Discovered in 1506 on the Esquiline, this statue group is now in the Vatican—After the 18th century Laokoon's right arm and that of his younger son, as well as the right hand and forearm of the elder son, were incorrectly restored, but they have since been amended

the Greeks made a pretense of leaving Troy in their ships, Laokoon warned his compatriots against the wooden horse, which had been left behind by their adversaries. Opinions about what should be done were divided, but finally Laokoon was chosen by lot to make a sacrifice on the shore with his sons to Poseidon. Suddenly two serpents emerged from the sea; they killed Laokoon and his sons and then crawled to the temple of Athena. The Trojans interpreted all of this as a sign that the horse should be dragged into the city.—The death of Laokoon found various explanations in legend. Traditionally it was often viewed as a punishment, because priests of Apollo were strictly forbidden to marry and have children, a prohibition that Laokoon had violated.

Laomedon King of Troy and son of *Ilus and Eurydice, he was the father of Priam, Astyoche, and Hesione, among others. As retribution for having conspired against Zeus, Poseidon and Apollo were forced to build the walls of Troy at a rate of payment previously agreed upon with the king. When Laomedon refused them their wages, Apollo struck the city with plague and Poseidon sent a man- and beast-devouring monster against it. Heracles finally appeared as the savior of the situation. He killed the monster and freed Hesione, the king's daughter, who in obedience to an oracle had been exposed to it. Laomedon then refused to give Heracles his recompense, namely the immortal horses that Zeus had once presented to his grandfather. In retaliation, Heracles marched against Troy with an armed force, conquered the city, and killed the king. He married Hesione to his friend Telamon. Priam, the only son of Laomedon to survive, rebuilt the city.

Laothoe Through Priam the mother of a son, Lycaon, and perhaps also the mother of Polydorus.

Lapiths In Greek mythology, a Thessalian people whose leading members were drawn into a fight with the *Centaurs at the wedding of Pirithous. The Lapiths also took part in the Calydonian boar hunt and the Trojan War.

Lar A Roman tutelary god. *Lares.

Lara (also *Lala*, meaning "chatterer") Daughter of the river god Almon, she was the wife of Hermes, to whom she bore the *Lares. According to another version, she was a particularly loquacious Roman nymph who talked to everyone about Jupiter's love affair with Juturna. Greatly angered, Jupiter ripped out her tongue and induced Mercury to escort her to the underworld. After Mercury made love to Lara, she gave birth to the Lares.

Lararium A small chapel or niche near the domestic hearth in ancient Roman homes, where the images of the *Lares were venerated.

Larentalia The chief festival of the *Lares, it was celebrated on December 23.

Larentia An ancient, little-known Roman goddess to whom a sacrifice was made at the Larentalia on December 23. From early times, the Romans believed that she was *Acca Larentia, the legendary foster-mother of Romulus and Remus.

Lares (singular, *Lar*) Ancient Roman tutelary deities of the family (*Lar familiaris*), their images were venerated in a small chapel or niche near the domestic hearth (Lararium). Beyond the domestic realm they functioned as guardians of the crossroads (*Lares compitales*) and of travelers (*Lares viales*). Their main festival (the Larentalia) was celebrated on December 23. The Lares were related to the *Penates. They probably originated as rural deities whose sphere of influence gradually expanded. During the Roman imperial period, the cult of the Lares became associated with the imperial cult.

Lares compitales Guardians of the crossroads, whose festival was celebrated on January 5.—*Lares.

Lares viales Tutelary gods of travelers.—*Lares.

Latinus King of Latium. According to Roman tradition, his father was Heracles; according to Greek tradition, his parents were Circe and Odysseus. Other persons, e.g., Faunus and Marcia, are also named as Latinus's parents. He extended hospitality to Aeneas and gave him his daughter *Lavinia in marriage. In one strand of the tradition, Aeneas succeeded Latinus as king of Latium.

Latium The area originally settled by the Latini.

Latmos A mountain in Asia Minor where Endymion slept his eternal sleep and was visited at night by Selene.

Lares Anonymous Lar

Lares Anonymous Lar

Latona Another designation for *Leto, the mother of Apollo and Artemis.

Laurel tree The tree sacred preeminently to the god Apollo.

Lausus 1. Son of *Numitor, he was killed by his uncle Amulius. 2. Son of Mezentius and ally of Turnus, he was killed by Aeneas.

Laverna Roman goddess of thieves and vagabonds.

Lavinia Daughter of *Latinus, king of Latium, she became the second wife of Aeneas. He won her after engaging in strenuous combat with Turnus, king of the Rutulians, who likewise sought the hand of Lavinia. The city of Lavinium, founded by Aeneas, was named after her.

Leades Son of Astacus of Thebes, he defended the city against the *Seven against Thebes.

Leander The lover of Hero, he lived in Abydos. *Hero and Leander.

Learchus Son of *Athamas and *Ino, and brother of Melicertes, he was slain by his father when the latter suffered an attack of madness.

Leda Daughter of King Thestius of Aetolia and Eurythemis, she was the wife of *Tyndareos and the mother of several children. According to legend, the father of these children was in some cases her husband and in others Zeus, who made love to her in the form of a swan. After such a union Leda gave birth to two eggs, from which Helen and the Dioscuri emerged. Another

Leda with the swan

tradition mentions only Helen and Polydeuces as children of Zeus.—Even in antiquity, artists were attracted by the motif of Leda and the swan.

Leimoniads A designation for flower and meadow nymphs.

Leiodes One of Penelope's suitors, and the only one whom she truly loved, Leiodes was killed by Odysseus when the latter returned from Troy.

Leipephile Daughter of *Iolaus and Megara.

Leitos A Boeotian leader and Argonaut, he was one of Helen's suitors. Together with Peneleos, he contributed fifty ships to the Trojan War effort. Although wounded by Hector, he was the only Boeotian leader to survive the war.

Leleges A mythical people who were supposed to have inhabited central and southern Greece, parts of Asia Minor, and the Aegean islands. In the Homeric epics they are localized in the region around Troy. Their historical classification remains obscure; they may have been a pre-Greek people indigenous to some area in the Aegean basin.

Lemnos A Greek island in the northern Aegean, it was subjugated ca. 510 B.C. by Miltiades for Athens. The legendary cult center of the Cabiri and Hephaestus, it also figures in several mythological stories.

Lemures (also called *Larvae*) Injurious Roman spirits, possibly daimons of death, they were greatly feared in contrast to the Lares and Penates. Their festival, the *Lemuria*, was celebrated on May 9, 11, and 13, when the pater familias drove them out of the house with elaborate rites designed to conciliate them.

Lenaea The Greek winter festival of *Dionysus, it was marked by the performance of new literary productions, such as tragedies and comedies, as well as by other events.

Leodokos An Argonaut, he was the son of *Bias (1) and Pero.

Lernaean hydra *Hydra of Lerna.

171

Lesbos A Greek island in the Aegean Sea situated off the west coast of Asia Minor, it was the homeland of many lyric poets. Here, according to legend, Aphrodite gave *Phaon the oil that made him beautiful.

Lethe In the Greek imagination, the underworld stream of oblivion and one of the five rivers of Hades. It encircled Elysium, where the dead lived in eternal bliss. Whoever drank from this river lost the memory of his or her earthly existence.

Leto (Latin, *Latona*) Daughter of the Titan Coeus and of Phoebe, she became the mother of Apollo and Artemis by Zeus. When Leto was pregnant with these twins, Zeus's jealous wife, Hera, brought it about that no one would afford her shelter for her confinement. Consequently, Leto wandered over the whole earth until she finally found refuge on the island that was later named Delos, where she gave birth to her children. Leto had a tender and enduring relationship with Apollo and Artemis. The two defended her against the giant *Tityus, who persecuted her, and against the mockery of *Niobe. For this reason, mother and children were often worshiped together.

Leto flees with her children from Python

Leucippe Daughter of Minyas and Orchomenus, she was the sister of Alcithoe and Arsippe. Because the three sisters refused to take part in a celebration for Dionysus, the offended god drove them to insanity. In that state they killed the son of Leucippe and were changed into bats. Leucippe was also a sister of *Clymene (2) and Periclymene.

Leucippus 1. Son of Oenomaus and brother of Hippodameia, he tried to win Daphne by disguising himself as a girl, but her friends killed him with Apollo's arrows. 2. Son of *Perieres and *Gorgophone, he was the legendary founder of Leuktra.

Leucothea Wife of King Athamas, and originally called *Ino, she received the name Leucothea after being transformed into a sea goddess. She was often identified with *Mater Matuta.

Leukos 1. A Cretan usurper, he seduced Medea, the wife of Idomeneus. Then he proceeded to kill her and her daughters, overthrow the king, and create a kingdom out of ten of the city-states of Idomeneus. 2. A companion of Odysseus in the Trojan War, he was slain by Antiphos, a son of Priam.

Leukosia Daughter of *Achelous, and one of the *Sirens, she was the sister of Ligeia and Parthenope. The Sirens lured sailors to their island by means of their lovely song and then killed them. To escape this fate, Odysseus had his companions stop their ears with wax and bind him to the mast of his ship.

Liber An ancient Roman fertility god and the husband (or brother, in another version) of *Libera, he was worshiped together with her and Ceres as a triad. Their main festival was celebrated on March 17. Liber was identified with Bacchus and frequently confused by the Greeks with *Iacchus, god of the Eleusinian mysteries.

Libera An ancient Roman fertility goddess and the wife (or sister) of *Liber, she was worshiped at Rome together with Liber and Ceres.

Libertas The personified freedom of the Roman people, venerated in ancient Rome as a goddess. She had a temple on the Aventine, built by Tiberius Sempronius Gracchus, consul for the year 238 B.C. Libertas was also a favorite motif on Roman coins of the imperial period.

Libitina Roman goddess of burial, she possessed a sacred grove in Rome where undertakers stored their equipment. In poetic terms, she was also understood as death itself and, because of the resemblance of her name to *libido* (according to popular etymology), was sometimes erroneously identified with Venus, goddess of love and desire.

Libra The seventh sign of the zodiac: a pair of scales.

Libya Daughter of *Epaphus and Memphis, she was the wife of Triton, to whom she bore several children. In addition, she became the mother by Poseidon of *Agenor and *Belus, and perhaps also the mother of *Lamia. Her homeland, Libya, took its name from her; in antiquity it was equated with Egypt.

Lichas According to one version of the legend, *Deianira commanded this herald of Heracles to deliver to his master the shirt of Nessus, which was destined to destroy him (Heracles). When Heracles realized what was happening, he overwhelmed Lichas and threw him into the sea. In the ancient imagination, this incident occurred on the reefs (called the Lichades) of the promontory at the western tip of Euboea; so it was assumed that the Lichades had been named after Lichas. But in reality the process was reversed: Lichas was named after the Lichades.

Licymnius A son of *Electryon, he was the only son to survive his father's battle with the Taphii. Because Licymnius was still a child, Electryon conferred the rulership on Amphitryon, a son of Alcaeus, who was promised to his daughter Alcmene. After Amphitryon killed Electryon through an unlucky accident, he fled to Thebes. Closely connected with Heracles and the Heraclids, he was probably killed by Tlepolemus during an attack by the Heraclids on Argos.

Ligeia Daughter of *Achelous and one of the *Sirens, she was the sister of Parthenope and Leukosia.

Limnoreia One of the *Nereids.

Lindus Grandson of Helios and Rhodos, he was a cofounder of the city on Rhodes that was named for his grandmother.

Linus 1. Son of Apollo and *Psamathe (2), he was torn to pieces by the dogs of *Krotopos. 2. Probably the son of Amphimarus and the Muse Urania, he was a poet and musician. 3. Son of Ismenos, he taught Heracles, Orpheus, and others to play the lyre. When he rebuked Heracles, the latter killed him in a fit of anger.—Possibly (2) and (3) represent the same person.

Linus Heracles being instructed in music by Linus

Lion The fifth sign of the zodiac. The Greeks conceived of it as the *Nemean lion, which was killed by Heracles and then set in the heavens by Hera.

Liriope A nymph who became the mother of *Narcissus by the river god Cephisus.

Literses A poet who lost a poetry contest with Daphnis. One of his daughters then married the victor.

Lityerses Son or bastard son of Midas, he challenged all newcomers at the royal court to a reaping competition after which he killed the defeated opponent. Finally he himself was defeated, perhaps by Heracles.

Lock of Berenice (*Coma Berenices*) A small, not very noticeable northern constellation, named after *Berenice. It illustrates the ancient custom of paying homage to significant persons by placing them, after death, in the heavens as stars or constellations (*katasterismos*).

Locris Two areas in central Greece inhabited by the Locrians: 1. The coastal region west of the Gulf of Euboea. 2. The coastal region along the Gulf of Corinth.

Lotis A daughter of Poseidon who, when she was pursued by *Priapus, turned into a lotus (or laurel) tree. According to another version, Priapus tried to surprise Lotis in her sleep, but his attempt was foiled by the noisy braying of a donkey.

Lotus-eaters The lotus-eaters of North Africa (according to another version they lived in a fictional land) whom Odysseus visited on his way home from Troy. Receiving him graciously, they gave him and his companions lotus fruit to eat. The effect of the fruit was to make whoever ate it forget his native land and wish only to remain in the land of the lotus-eaters.

Loxias An epithet of Apollo, the meaning of which may suggest someone who can decipher the will of Zeus.

Lua A little-known Roman goddess who supervised religious purification. Her frequent identification with Rhea brought her into hypothetical connection with Saturn as his wife.

Lucina Latin goddess of birth, she was worshiped at Rome in combination with *Juno as Juno Lucina. She corresponded to the Greek *Eileithyia, a daughter of Zeus and Hera.

Lucius Son of Tarquinius Superbus and Tanaquil, he married Tullia, a daughter of Servius Tullius. In contrast to his wife, who was kind and courteous, Lucius was ambitious and self-seeking. Eventually he killed her and married her sister.—The legend has several variants.

Lucretia In Roman legend, the wife of King Lucius Tarquinius Collatinus. Dishonored by Sextus Tarquinius, she committed suicide and so supposedly caused the fall of the Roman kings.—The story of Lucretia was frequently referred to by poets and artists.

Luna The moon goddess Luna; detail from the great rose window in the cathedral at Lausanne (beginning of the 13th century)

Luna Roman moon goddess, she may originally have been Sabine. Identified with the Greek Selene, she was also associated with Diana and Hecate. Her main temple on the Aventine in Rome was said to have been built under Servius Tullius; in any case it was already standing in 182 B.C.

Luperca Roman goddess of herds and fruitfulness.

Lupercal A cave on the Palatine in Rome, where according to legend a she-wolf nursed Romulus and Remus.

Lupercalia One of the most ancient Roman festivals, it was celebrated on February 15 in honor either of the god Lupercus or of Faunus.

The festivities included the sacrifice of a dog and a goat and were connected with purification and fertility rites. Originally the celebration was probably pastoral, with cult observances for the protection of herds against wolves.

Lupercus Roman god of herds and fertility.

Lycaon King of Arcadia, he was the son of Pelasgus and Meliboea. His fifty sons shared his notoriety for cruelty. When Zeus visited him, Lycaon served the god a dismembered boy to eat. This angered Zeus so much that he annihilated Lycaon and his family with a lightning flash.—According to another version, Zeus transformed Lycaon into a wolf and sent a flood (*Deucalion flood) that destroyed most of the human race.

Lycia In antiquity a country on the southwest coast of Asia Minor inhabited by (presumably Indo-European) Lycians. Conquered in 545 B.C. by Persia, it was later contested among the Diadochi. Together with Pamphylia, Lycia became a Roman province in A.D. 43.—According to legend, in her flight from Hera, *Leto sought refuge there.

Lycomedes King of Scyros, he was the son of Apollo and Parthenope and the father of Deidameia, the lover or wife of Achilles. Lycomedes hid Achilles to protect him from having to take part in the Trojan War by dressing him as a girl; but Achilles betrayed himself by his intense interest in weapons.—One strand of the tradition names Lycomedes as the murderer of *Theseus.

Lycurgus 1. King of the Edonians in Thrace, and son of Dryas. Because of the orgiastic nature of the cult of Dionysus, he opposed that god, whom he banished from his land. Dionysus jumped into the sea and was received by Thetis. He punished the king with madness, inducing him to kill his own son while believing that he was felling vines. In another version, Lycurgus cut off both of his legs in his madness. The legend further relates that Zeus blinded him. Dionysus also made the land barren, which caused the people to rebel against their ruler. The crowd dragged him up onto the Pangaeus mountain ridge, where he was torn apart by horses.—The myth shows that the imported cult of Dionysus with its orgiastic features could be introduced into Greece only against strong resistance. 2. King of Nemea, father of *Opheltes, and one of the *Seven against Thebes. According to one strand of the tradition, he is supposed to have awakened Asclepius from death. 3. A legendary Spartan lawgiver and friend of the gods, who probably originated as a god himself. He is credited with implementing reforms decisive for the development of Spartan social organization. Even in antiquity, the period of his activity was disputed; the evidence suggests a time between the 11th and 7th centuries B.C.

Lycus This name, common to many Greek heroes, was shared by the following: 1. King of the Mariandynoi, who supported Heracles in his struggle with the Bebryces. 2. Son of Pandion and Pylia, who was one of the few mortals able to speak in oracles. 3. King of Thebes, husband of Dirce, and brother of the Theban king Nycteus, who when dying conferred his sovereignty on the latter and commissioned him to bring his daughter *Antiope back to Thebes. Later he was killed by *Amphion and Zethus. 4. King of Thebes who, having seized power forcibly, was killed by Heracles. 5. A companion of Aeneas on his journey from Troy to Italy. 6. One of the fifty sons of Aegyptus (*Danaids). 7. A son of Ares. 8. A king of Boeotia. 9. A Centaur and son of Ixion and Nephele. 10. A son of Priam.

Lydia In antiquity a country situated in the middle of the west coast of Asia Minor. According to legend, it was named after Lydos, the mythical son of Attis, whose mother was *Nana.

Lykaste A daughter of Priam, she married *Polydamas (1), a son of Antenor.

Lyke A daughter of *Literses, she may have married Daphnis (according to one strand of the tradition).

Lykeios Epithet of Apollo meaning "wolf-god." Its interpretation is disputed, but it may point to the origin of the god: the Lycian, i.e., the god from Lycia.

Lyko A daughter of *Dion. She and her two sisters possessed the gift of prophecy.

Lykotherses King of Illyria, he was murdered by his second wife, *Agave (1). Her motive was to have *Cadmus succeed him on the throne.

Lynceus 1. Son of Aegyptus and the only one of the fifty brothers who was not killed by his wife on their wedding night (*Danaids); his wife was Hypermestra. He was the father of Abas. Some sources report that Lynceus killed *Danaus and his family in order to avenge the death of his brothers. 2. Son of Aphareus and Arene, and brother of *Idas (1). He took part in the Calydonian boar hunt and the Argonautic expedition, distinguishing himself by his unusually keen vision, which penetrated every object. In a conflict with the *Dioscuri, Idas killed Castor and Polydeuces killed Lynceus. Zeus then brought down Idas with one of his lightning flashes. 3. A companion of Aeneas on his journey from Troy to Italy, who was killed by Turnus.

Lysander A Trojan ally who was wounded in the Trojan War by *Aias the Great.

Lysianassa Daughter of *Epaphus and Memphis, she was the sister of Libya and became the mother of *Busiris by Poseidon.

Lysimache The wife of Talaus, she gave birth to several children, including *Adrastus and *Eriphyle.

Lysippe 1. Daughter of *Proetus and Stheneboea or Anteia, she married *Melampus after he had cured her of her madness. 2. One of the fifty daughters of *Thespius.

M

Maenads Maenad with a leopard; from a bowl by the Brygos painter (ca. 490 B.C.)

Maenads Maenad on a pointed amphora; from a work by the Kleophrades painter (ca. 500–470 B.C.), a master of the red-figure style in Attic vase painting

Macar One of the *Heliades, he was among the slayers of *Tenages.

Machaon A legendary Greek figure, he was the son of Aesculapius and Epione. As one of Helen's suitors, he fought in the Trojan War, being wounded by Paris but then saved by Nestor. Counted among the heroes who hid in the Trojan Horse, he achieved special significance as one of the most celebrated physicians in Greek mythology. In the Greek camp below Troy, he healed many Greeks, including Philoctetes. He himself was finally killed by Penthesilea or Eurypylus.

Maenads (Greek for "raving ones") Ecstatic women who together with the male Satyrs formed the retinue of the god *Dionysus, they were also called Bacchae or Bacchantes. As members of the Dionysian procession, they allegedly raged through the woods with serpents, daggers, and thyrsos stalks, crying out loudly, dismembering wild animals, and eating raw flesh. The Maenads were a favorite theme of Greek vase painters.

Magna Mater (Latin for "Great Mother") Another name for the Phrygian goddess *Cybele, whose cult was introduced into Rome at the end of the 3rd century B.C.

Maia A Greek mountain nymph, she was the oldest daughter of Atlas and Pleione and one of the Pleiades. Having united with Zeus, she gave birth to Hermes. After the death or transformation of *Callisto, Maia reared *Arcas.

Maira 1. A priest of Aphrodite. 2. The faithful dog of *Icarius. After he had helped *Erigone to find the burial place of her murdered father, he died and was translated to heaven as Sirius (the Dog Star).

Mallophora The epithet under which the goddess Demeter was worshiped at her temple in Megara, because she taught the inhabitants of that city the use of wool.

Mallos A city in Cilicia with a famous oracle founded by Mopsus and Amphilochus.

Mamurius A smith who created the eleven shields (*ancilia*) for Numa Pompilius.—*Salii.

Manes (*Di Manes*) Roman spirits of the dead, they were understood by the Romans as "good gods." Only neglect of the cult of the dead or similar outrages stirred their anger. They could summon living persons to themselves and forbid dead ones entry into the underworld. Thus the inscription "D(is) M(anibus)" is frequently seen on Roman tombstones. The main festival of the Manes was the *Parentalia.

Manto A Greek seer and daughter of *Tiresias, she lived for a long time at Delphi after the death of her father and then married the Cretan Rhacius. She became the mother of *Mopsus (2).

Marathon An ancient site on the east coast of Attica, where the Athenians won a victory over the Persians in 490 B.C. The Athenians who fell were buried in a single grave, which has been preserved. The runner who brought the news of victory to Athens, and is said to have dropped dead there, first emerges in the later tradition. The Greek legend relates that Theseus led the Greeks in full armor and Pan, too, hastened to their aid.

Marathonian bull *Cretan bull.

Marpessa Daughter of Euenus and Alcippe, she was the bride of Idas, who forced Apollo to relinquish her when that god was about to carry her off. Marpessa married Idas and became the mother of Cleopatra. After her husband died, she committed suicide.

Mars A rural Italian god who evolved at Rome into a war god and one of the most important Roman divinities after Jupiter and Quirinus. Although identified with the Greek Ares, his significance far surpassed that of his Greek counterpart. Mars protected the Roman state as it strove for world dominion, awarding it numerous victories in the process. The Romans worshiped him as the father of Romulus and Remus and so as their ancestor. His main festivals were celebrated in the months of March (named after the god) and October. At these festivals the

Mars Roman god of war

*Salii, adorned with their archaic shields and red mantles, performed war dances. In Rome, several temples as well as the so-called Campus Martius, where solemn military gatherings took place, were dedicated to the god. After his victorious battle at Philippi (42 B.C.), Augustus erected a temple to Mars as an offering of thanks for the revenge granted to him by the god against the murderers of Caesar. This temple was consecrated to *Mars Ultor* ("avenger"). Other cult epithets with a warlike accent were *Gravidus* (probably "warrior") and *Invictus* ("invincible").—Nevertheless, Mars was also characterized as a rural god, to whom offerings were made so that he would guarantee a rich harvest and preserve the cattle from sickness.

Marsyas and Apollo

Marsyas A Phrygian satyr and lover of Cybele, he was probably the son of *Olympus. In Greek mythology, he appears as the inventor of the flute and flute playing. According to another version, he discovered the flutes that Athena had thrown away, practiced on them for recreation, and developed such mastery that he dared to challenge Apollo to a musical competition. He further stipulated that the winner should have the right to determine the fate of the loser. Apollo won the contest with his cithara, after which he had Marsyas hung from a tree and flayed alive.

Mater Matuta An ancient Italian goddess whose significance is still disputed today. Regarded as a goddess of dawn, she was also often identified with Ino Leucothea or venerated as a mother goddess. Her festival, the Matralia, took place on June 11.

Matralia *Mater Matuta.

Meander A river god, in Greek mythology, and son of Oceanus and Tethys.—The river of the same name in western Anatolia (known today as the Menderes) arises at Dinar and follows a serpentine course to the Aegean Sea.

Medea In Greek legend, the daughter of King Aeetes of Colchis and an eminent sorceress. With her magical arts she helped the *Argonauts, led by Jason, to obtain the *Golden fleece. Medea married Jason, fled with him to Greece, and bore him two sons. When Jason proved unfaithful to her and turned his attention to Glauke (also called Creusa), a daughter of King Creon of Corinth, Medea exacted a terrible revenge. She sent Glauke a precious robe, which burst into flames when the bride put it on, killing her and her father. In order to wound Jason even more deeply, Medea also murdered their two sons and then escaped to Athens in a chariot drawn by a winged dragon. There she married King Aegeus and gave birth to a son, with whom she returned to her homeland after she had tried to kill Theseus, a son of her husband (at first her husband knew nothing of his paternity, however). At Colchis Medea continued to practice her terrible magic arts.—Since its dramatization by Euripides, the Medea legend has often been treated in literature, including the literature of our own time.

Medica (*Minerva Medica*) An epithet of *Minerva as patroness of Roman doctors.

Meditrina Roman goddess of medicine whose festival, the Meditrinalia, was celebrated on October 11 with drink offerings of juice from the new harvest. The celebration was supposed to bless the worshipers of the goddess with health and well-being.

Meditrinalia *Meditrina.

Medusa In Greek mythology, one of the *Gorgons, who in contrast to her sisters was held to be mortal. When she became pregnant by Poseidon, Perseus cut off her head and presented it to Athena. From then on Athena bore it as the so-called Gorgoneion on her shield. At an early date, an apotropaic significance was ascribed to the Gorgoneion, which accounts for its frequent appearance on temples, tombstones, shields, drinking vessels, etc.

Medusa

Megaira One of the *Erinyes. In a figurative sense, the term also denoted an evil woman or Fury.

Meilichius An epithet of Zeus and Dionysus in the sense of "the mild one" or "the gracious one."

Melampus In legend, one of the most important Greek seers, he was the brother of *Bias (1). As he slept, serpents licked his ears, after which Melampus understood the language of animals. He cured the daughters of *Proetus of their madness and received in exchange a share of their father's rule. Melampus was also connected with the cult of Dionysus; in some versions he is portrayed as its founder and in others as having contained its excesses.

Melanion The husband of the great huntress *Atalanta. According to another version, he was married to *Hippomenes.

Melanippe Daughter of Aeolus and *Hippe, she was the mother by Poseidon of the twins Aeolus and Boiotos. Melanippe's father took her children from her and had them exposed, but a cowherd saved them. Later King *Metapontos and his wife Theano adopted the two children and raised them together with their own two sons. When the four sons got into an argument, Aeolus and Boiotos killed the natural sons of the king; Theano then committed suicide.—Melanippe, who had been blinded by her father, Aeolus, recovered her eyesight with the help of Poseidon and married Metapontos.—According to another tradition, Metapontos and Theano adopted the twins because they were childless. When Aeolus and Boiotos had grown up, they underwent difficult and dangerous conditions searching for their natural mother. Finding her at last, they freed her from the prison in which her father had confined her.

Melanippus 1. Son of Astacus, he was an ally of Eteocles against the *Seven against Thebes. In the battle at Thebes, he mortally wounded *Tydeus. After decapitating Melanippus, Amphiaraus threw his head to the dying Tydeus, who ate the brain of his dead antagonist. Athena, who had been planning to confer immortality on Tydeus, recoiled in horror at this act and renounced her intention. 2. A son of Ares. 3. Lover of *Comaetho (1) and priestess of Artemis at Patrae. Because their families opposed the union of the two young people, they had a secret rendezvous in the temple. Incensed at the desecration of her sanctuary, Artemis inflicted plague and famine on the land. She could only be appeased by the sacrifice of Melanippus and Comaetho. 4. A son of Priam.

Melanthius The highest ranking goatherd of Odysseus. Odysseus killed him in a cruel manner because he had sided with the suitors of *Penelope.—*Melantho.

Melantho Daughter of Dolios, she had seven brothers, including *Melanthius. Servant of *Penelope and lover of Eurymachos, she was hanged for collaborating with the suitors of Penelope. According to another tradition, Dolios and his family were faithful supporters of Odysseus.

Melanthos In Greek legend, a descendant of *Neleus, king of Messenia. After being banished from there, he emigrated to Attica and acceded to the throne as eleventh king of Athens.

Meleager In Greek legend, son of *Oeneus and Althaea, he married Cleopatra, the daughter of *Idas. Meleager was the hero who succeeded in killing the Calydonian boar, which Artemis had sent to devastate the land in revenge for Oeneus's failure to sacrifice to her at the harvest festival (he had forgotten). The most famous heroes of Greece participated in the *Calydonian boar hunt. After Meleager had delivered the death blow to the beast, he got into a fight over the boar skin with his mother's brothers and killed them. Filled with the desire to avenge her brothers' murder, Althaea remembered a prophecy made by the Moirai at the birth of Meleager to the effect that he would live only as long as a log (which was still lying by the hearth) had not been consumed by fire. Taking this log, which until then she had carefully preserved, Althaea threw it into the fire and so accomplished the death of her son.—The legend of Meleager underwent many embellishments and modifications in antiquity.

Melian nymphs (*Meliades*) Guardians of Zeus as a boy, they were often thought to be the oldest of the *Nymphs.

Melicertes God of harbors in Greek mythology, he was the son of Athamas and *Ino, and the brother of *Learchus. In order to save her son from his father, who had gone crazy, Ino tossed him into the sea, where he was transformed into the sea god Palaemon. In memory of this event and in honor of the god, Sisyphus inaugurated the *Isthmian Games.—The legend of Melicertes is presented in the sources with many variations.

Melissa Daughter of the Cretan king Melisseus, she was the sister of Amalthea. The two sisters nurtured the infant Zeus by feeding him goat's milk. Melissa learned how to gather honey and was changed into a bee.—According to other versions, Melissa was a common name for priestesses of different cults and for certain types of nymphs.

Melisseus King of Crete, he was the father of *Amalthea and *Melissa, who cared for Zeus in his infancy.

Melos A Greek island among the Cyclades in the Aegean Sea. Some important ancient works of art were found there, in particular the late Hellenistic Aphrodite of Melos, sculpted in the late 2nd century B.C.

Melpomene The *Muse of tragedy. Artistic representations tend to show her with a tragic mask, a garland, and a club.

Melpomene One of the Muses

Memnon King of the Ethiopians, and son of Tithonus and Eos, he was killed by Achilles at Troy after he himself had killed Nestor's son Antilochus. Memnon was reputed to be the creator of the colossal statues (the "columns of Memnon") of Amenhotep III at Thebes. The legend records that his ashes turned into birds which fought annually around his grave.

Memphis Daughter of the river god of the Nile (Neilos), she married Epaphus, son of Zeus and king of Egypt. Their daughters were Libya and Lysianassa.

Mena Roman goddess of menstruation, she may have been identical with Juno. Young dogs were sacrificed to her.

Menderes *Meander.

Menelaus King of Sparta, in Greek mythology, he was the son of Atreus and Aerope and the brother of Agamemnon; a later version names Pleisthenes and Kleolla as his parents. Menelaus married *Helen, a daughter of Zeus, who bore Menelaus Hermione and probably also Nikostratos. When Helen was abducted by the Trojan Paris, her husband turned to his brother for help. Agamemnon convened Helen's erstwhile suitors as an expeditionary force to make war against Troy. Once Troy had fallen, Menelaus killed Deiphobos, son of Priam, whom Helen had married after the death of Paris. Then he and his wife traveled eventfully back to Greece. According to another tradition, Menelaus did not find his true wife (Helen) until he reached Egypt on his return voyage from Troy. It turned out that she had remained faithful to him all along. After his death, Menelaus was transposed to *Elysium together with Helen.

Menestheus 1. In Greek legend, he ruled Athens during the absence of *Theseus. Commander of the fifty Athenian ships sent to the Trojan War, he was one of the heroes who hid inside the wooden horse. After the war Menestheus went to Melos, where he ascended the throne. 2. Son of the river god *Spercheios and *Polydora (2), he was raised by his mother and her husband, Boros.

Menoeceus 1. Father of the Theban king *Creon (2). 2. A son of King Creon of Thebes. During the siege by the Seven against Thebes, he willingly sacrificed his life because Tiresias had prophesied that the city could only be saved if that precondition were fulfilled. In another tradition he was killed by the Sphinx, who was haunting Thebes.

Menoetius 1. Son of Actor and Aegina, and father of *Patroclus. He is often counted among the Argonauts. 2. Son of Iapetus and *Clymene (1) (or Asia, according to another version). His brothers were Atlas, Epimetheus, and Prometheus. When he contended against the

Mercurius Flying Mercury by G. da Bologna. A certain resemblance to the Greek god Hermes, with whom Mercury was early identified, is unmistakable

Mercurius

gods, Zeus dispatched him to Tartarus by means of a thunderbolt.

Mentor In Greek mythology, a close friend and confidant of Odysseus, whose son (Telemachus) he educated. Mentor became proverbial as a faithful and fatherly counselor.

Mercurius (*Mercury*) Roman god of commerce, he protected merchants and astronomers. He was venerated particularly by the plebeian class, who were chiefly responsible for commercial activity. In Rome, a temple was dedicated to Mercurius in 495 B.C., but he was also worshiped in many Roman provincial cities by people involved in trade. The identification of Mercurius with the Greek god *Hermes occurred at an early date.

Meriones A Cretan who belonged to the tightly knit group of warriors led by *Idomeneus in the Trojan War. He served as the latter's charioteer and as second in command of the Cretan contingent of eight ships. Meriones was also regarded as the best Greek archer after *Teucer (2). Indeed, at the funeral games for Patroclus, he won the archery contest (which had been organized for that occasion). Meriones had in his possession a famous helmet that Autolycus, a son of Hermes, had stolen from Amyntor and given to Odysseus. During the Trojan War he killed many opponents, and he helped Aias locate the body of Patroclus.

Mermeros 1. Son of Jason and *Medea, he was killed either by his mother or by a lioness. 2. Son of *Pheres (2), he was the father of Ilos and an experienced poison maker.

Merope 1. Daughter of Atlas and Pleione, she was one of the Pleiades and unique among her sisters in marrying a mortal, Sisyphus of Corinth. 2. A daughter of Pandareos, she was raised together with her sisters by Athena after Zeus killed their parents. Later the sisters were carried off by the Harpies and forced to serve the Erinyes. 3. Wife of the Heraclid *Cresphontes, she was the mother of Aepytus. The murderer of her husband, Polyphontes, compelled her to marry him. After numerous complications,

Aepytus eventually killed Polyphontes in order to avenge his father and assume power in his native kingdom of Messenia. The story of Merope was treated in dramas by Euripides and Voltaire, among others. 4. Daughter of Erechtheus, she may have been the mother of Daedalus. 5. Daughter of *Oenopion and Helice, she rejected the love of Orion, who then offended her so deeply that her father blinded him. 6. The wife of Polybus (1), she was also called Periboea or Eriboea. When the infant Oedipus was found on Mount Cithaeron, she undertook his care.

Messenia The southwestern region of the Peloponnesus. According to legend, it was named after Messene, wife of Polykaon, alleged to be the first king of Messenia.

Mestor 1. Son of Perseus and Andromeda. 2. An illegitimate son of Priam.

Metanira The mother of *Demophon (2).

Metapontos Possibly a son of Aeolus and brother of *Melanippe, he married Theano, who had two sons and bore him two additional sons. Metapontos believed that all four children were his own and even favored the two elder sons. When he discovered the truth, however, he killed them along with their mother; then he married Melanippe and adopted the twins Aeolus and Boiotos.

Metis The personification of good sense, she was a daughter of Oceanus and Tethys. After she had long resisted marriage with Zeus, she finally became his first wife. Once she was pregnant, Gaia prophesied that she would give birth to a daughter whose cleverness would equal that of Zeus and, subsequently, to a son who would supplant him. Out of envy and fear lest he lose his authority, Zeus swallowed Metis (an occasional motif in Greek mythology). Their daughter, *Athena, was later born from her father's head.

Metope Daughter of the river god Ladon or Peneus, she was the sister of Daphne. She married the river god Asopos, to whom she bore three sons and twenty daughters.

Mezentius An Etruscan king about whom the legendary accounts vary considerably. As the ruler of Caere, he was enlisted as an ally against Aeneas and the Trojans by Turnus, king of the Rutulians, who pledged him half of the grape harvest. Aeneas, who had promised half of the vintage to Jupiter, emerged victorious from the battlefield, whereas Turnus and Mezentius were both mortally wounded.—Following another tradition, the Rutulians called on Mezentius for assistance only after the death of Turnus. The Trojans, led by Ascanius (after Aeneas was spirited away), suffered defeat at the hands of Mezentius, but he offered to observe a truce on the condition that he be granted the entire grape harvest. Aided by Jupiter, to whom the whole vintage had likewise been promised, Ascanius made a surprise attack on the enemy. Although Mezentius was allowed to withdraw, his son Lausus was killed.—Yet another version portrays Mezentius as a tyrannical king who governed his subjects with such cruelty that they finally got rid of him. Mezentius then allied himself with Turnus against Aeneas and was killed either by Aeneas or (in an alternate tradition) by Ascanius.

Midas King of Phrygia from ca. 738 to 690 B.C., he was obliged to pay tribute to the Assyrians from 709 B.C. and was defeated by the Cimmerians ca. 690.—The Midas of legend was a son of Gordias and Cybele. He owned a celebrated rose garden into which the drunken Silenus wandered by mistake. The king received him kindly, entertained him, and sent him back to Dionysus. To thank him for his generosity, Dionysus granted Midas one wish, and Midas wished that everything he touched would turn to gold. He was finally released from his bondage to this deadly wish, which had condemned him to hunger, by bathing in the Pactolus River.—At a musical contest between Apollo and Pan, Midas awarded the victory to Pan. Apollo then caused donkey's ears to grow on Midas, which the latter tried to hide under a kind of leather hood.

Miletus The most important ancient Greek city on the west coast of Asia Minor, it was situated near the mouth of the Meander River. Miletus enjoyed its greatest prosperity from the 8th to the 6th century B.C., and then again in the Hellenistic and Roman periods.

Minerva An ancient Italian divinity, probably of Etruscan origin, she was the tutelary goddess of Rome. More important, though, was her role as patroness of artisans, poets, and teachers, in addition to physicians (as *Minerva Medica*). Probably at the end of the 3rd century B.C., Minerva was identified with the Greek goddess Athena. Her principal temple was located in Rome on the Aventine. Her main festivals, the Quinquatrus or Minervalia, were celebrated on March 19 and June 13, the March festival being attended primarily by artisans and teachers, and the June festival by flute players.

Minerva

Minervalia A collective term for the festivals celebrated in Rome in honor of the goddess *Minerva.—*Quinquatrus.

Minos A prominent figure in Greek mythology, he was the son of Zeus and Europa, the brother of *Sarpedon (1) and *Rhadamanthys, the husband of Pasiphae, and the father of various children, including *Ariadne. Minos was renowned for the justice of his reign as king of Crete, and after his death was installed as a judge in the underworld.—Another tradition puts greater emphasis on his enmity toward the Greeks. To ensure divine legitimation of his rule over Crete, he asked Poseidon to send him a bull from the sea, which he would then sacrifice to the god. Poseidon acceded to his request; in return, however, Minos did not sacrifice the bull but instead incorporated it into his herd. Poseidon punished this breach of faith by causing Pasiphae to conceive an unnatural passion for the animal. Her union with it produced the *Minotaur, which the king locked up in the labyrinth that Daedalus had built for him. The Athenians, defeated by Minos in war, were compelled to send seven youths and seven maidens annually to Crete to serve as fodder for the monster. This atrocity continued until Theseus, with the aid of Ariadne, suc-

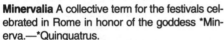

Zeus─┬─Europa

Sarpedon
Rhadamanthys
Minos─┬─Pasiphae

Catreus
Deucalion
Glaucus
Androgeus
Phaedra
Ariadne

Minotaur Theseus slays the Minotaur; after a depiction on a Greek plate

Mnemosyne The mother of the Muses

ceeded in killing the Minotaur and finding his way back to the labyrinth's exit.

Minotaur (Greek for "bull of *Minos") A mythical creature with the body of a man and the head of a bull. It was engendered by the union of Pasiphae, wife of Minos, with a bull from the king's herd. Imprisoned in the labyrinth by Minos, it was finally killed by *Theseus.

Minthe (*Menthe*) A daughter of Cocytus. Because she was desired by Hades, Persephone turned her into the mint plant, many types of which are commonly found in the Mediterranean region.

Misenus 1. Hector's flute player in the Trojan War. After Hector's death, he served Aeneas in the same capacity, even following him from Troy to Hades. When Misenus challenged the gods to a musical competition, he was drowned in the sea by the deeply offended *Triton. Aeneas buried him on what is now called Cape Misenum, which took its name from Misenus. 2. A companion of Odysseus, possibly identical with (1).

Mnemosyne Greek goddess of memory, she became the mother of the *Muses by Zeus.

Mnesimache Daughter of Dexamenos, she was saved by Heracles from a forced marriage with the Centaur Eurytion.

Moira A term for the share that the individual has in the collective fate. It was later personified by the figures of the *Moirai.

Moiragetes This epithet was applied to Apollo and the Delphic Zeus as the leaders of the Moirai.

Moirai Greek goddesses of fate, they symbolized through their actions the working of destiny. Originally there was a multitude of Moirai, but already in the writings of Hesiod they were reduced to three figures: Clotho, daughter of Zeus, who spun the thread of life; Lachesis, who assigned to each individual his or her destiny; and Atropos, who cut the thread of life. The Romans identified the Moirai with the Parcae.

Molion The shield-bearer of Hector, he was killed in the Trojan War by Odysseus.

Molione Wife of the Thessalian king Actor, a son of Phorbas, she gave birth to the *Moliones.

Moliones Cteatus and Eurytus, the sons of Actor (or, in another version, Poseidon) and Molione. They were twin brothers, born from a single egg, whose bodies may have been joined like those of Siamese twins. They fought with their uncle Aegeus against Heracles and were killed by the latter.

Molorchos An old Nemean shepherd, he planted a grove in which the *Nemean games were held. He was killed by the *Nemean lion that Heracles finally strangled to death.

Molossus Son of *Neoptolemus and Andromache. Tormented by jealousy, Hermione, the wife of Neoptolemus, persecuted Andromache and her son so fiercely that the two fled at great hazard to Epirus, where Molossus became a follower of *Helenus.

Moly An herb that protected Odysseus from being enchanted by Circe. It is probably best conceived of as a fabulous, rather than botanically specific, plant.

Momos In Greek mythology, a god of censure and rebuke. Son of Nyx and Erebus, he was banished from Olympus because he mocked and slandered the other gods.

Mopsus 1. A Thessalian who was involved in several important events of Greek legend. He fought with the Lapiths against the Centaurs, went on the *Calydonian boar hunt, and was counted among the Argonauts. When he died of a snake bite, Mopsus received great honors on account of his many heroic deeds. 2. Son of Rhacius (or Apollo, according to another version) and Manto. An eminent prophet from southwestern Asia Minor, he initiated a competition with Calchas, another seer, to determine whose prophetic art was superior. At the competition, Calchas posed the question of how many figs were hanging on a nearby fig tree. Mopsus answered correctly, which meant that Calchas lost the contest. Calchas died after his defeat, thus fulfilling the prophecy he had been given to the effect that, if he should find a seer wiser than himself, his death would be imminent.

Morpheus A Greek god of dreams mentioned only by Ovid, he was the son of *Hypnos. He appeared to sleeping dreamers in the most varied forms.

Morta Another name for *Parca.

Mulberry tree A tree from the *Morus* genus with inconspicuous blossoms in the catkins. The edible, pulpy part is found in the outer sheath surrounding the blossoms. The provenance of the plant is Eastern, and it is associated with the legend of *Pyramus and Thisbe.

Musaeus A distinguished poet and musician, he was probably a legendary figure. The Greeks identified him as a student of Orpheus and ascribed many Orphic writings to him. Musaeus was supposed to have played a role in the founding of the *Eleusinian mysteries.

Musagetes (Greek for "leader of the Muses") One of the epithets of Apollo.

The nine Muses:
Erato (love poetry)
Euterpe (music)
Calliope (epic poetry)
Clio (history)
Melpomene (tragedy)
Polyhymnia (ceremonial song)
Terpsichore (dance)
Thaleia (comedy)
Urania (astronomy)

Muses Feminine deities of the arts and sciences, in Greek mythology they were daughters of Zeus and Mnemosyne or of Uranus and Gaia. Their dwelling places, often situated near springs and brooks, were in Pieria east of Mount Olympus (Pierian Muses), on Mount Helicon in Boeotia (Boeotian Muses), and on Mount Parnassus at Delphi (Delphic Muses). In those locales they would dance and sing, frequently with Apollo *Musagetes as their leader. The Muses were very concerned about their honor and punished any mortal who presumed to equal them in the art of song. Originally they numbered only three, but already in Homer they appear as a group of nine sisters, each of them correlated with a particular artistic function. Most are connected with a symbol, which need not be fixed, however. Poets commonly invoked the Muses at the beginning of their compositions even in Homer's time. This practice was observed later, too, at centers of intellectual life such as schools, philosophical circles, etc.— The Romans identified the Muses with the *Camenae.

Mycenae A fortified settlement in the northeastern Argolid dating from the second millennium

B.C. According to legend, it was founded by Perseus and named after a daughter of Inachus.—Mycenae had a large palace complex with a megaron and served as a royal seat from the 16th to the 12th century B.C. In the 14th century, it was encircled by a wall six meters thick, which also enclosed the rich shaft graves of the 16th-century B.C. rulers; these were discovered in 1876 by H. Schliemann. The main entrance was provided by the Lion Gate. Of the numerous beehive tombs discovered outside the fortified citadel, the "treasury of Atreus" is especially worth mentioning.—In Greek mythology, Mycenae is noted as the seat of the legendary king *Agamemnon.

Mycenae Gold mask—the so-called mask of Agamemnon

Myrmidones An ancient Thessalian people. In Greek mythology, they were comrades-in-arms of Achilles during the Trojan War.

Myrrha The legendary daughter of the Cypriot king Cinyras, although other versions supply her with other fathers. She was also called Smyrna. Either because she committed incest with her father or (following other traditions) because she neglected the worship of Aphrodite, she was punished by being transformed into a myrrh tree; after nine months Adonis emerged from the tree.

Myrtilus Chariot driver of *Oenomaus and son of Hermes, he was both cunning and violent. *Pelops induced him to cause the death of his master (*Hippodameia). When that deed was done, Pelops hurled Myrtilus into the sea so as to rid himself of his confidant. After Myrtilus's death, Hermes placed him in heaven as the constellation Auriga (charioteer). According to another version, Myrtilus atoned for his outrageous act in the underworld.

Mysia An ancient country in northwestern Asia Minor, its principal cities were Troy and Pergamum. From 280 B.C., it was the chief province of the kingdom of Pergamum. In 133 B.C., King Attalus III bequeathed it to the Romans, and in 129 B.C. it became part of the Roman province of Asia.

Naiad One of the nymphs of springs

Naiads In Greek mythology, the designation for water nymphs.

Nana Daughter of the river god Sangarius, she was the mother of Attis.

Narcissus A beautiful youth in Greek mythology, he was the son of the river god Cephisus and Liriope. For scorning the love of the mountain nymph Echo, he was punished by either Nemesis or Aphrodite to the following effect: whenever he bent over a spring to quench his thirst, an overpowering love for his own reflected image seized him. Eventually he was turned into the flower that is named after him.

Nauplius 1. Son of Poseidon and *Amymone, he was a Greek slave trader and founder of the city of Nauplia. 2. A descendant of (1), father of *Palamedes, and helmsman for the Argonauts. On the homeward journey of the Greeks after the Trojan War, he avenged the murder of Palamedes by sending a false signal to the Greek fleet, so that its ships crashed onto the rocks and a large number of the crew died.

Nausicaa In the *Odyssey,* daughter of *Alcinous, the Phaeacian king. Nausicaa came to the aid of the shipwrecked Odysseus, who had been washed up on the shore of her homeland, and escorted him to her father. Nausicaa has often been the subject of literary treatment, e.g., by Sophocles and Goethe.

Naxos The largest island among the Greek Cyclades in the Aegean Sea, it is associated with the legend of Ariadne.

Necklace of Harmonia *Harmonia.

Nectar In Greek mythology, the drink of the gods which, together with *Ambrosia, conferred immortality. Nectar was served by Hebe, daughter of Zeus, and later by Ganymedes.

Neleus King of Pylos, and son of Poseidon and Tyro. Together with his twin brother Pelias, he was exposed and brought up by a mare. In the dispute that developed between the brothers over who should assume power, Neleus acquired Messenia and founded Pylos. He married Chloris, a daughter of Amphion. All of the twelve sons that she bore him, except *Nestor, fell in combat against Heracles. After his death, Neleus was buried in a secret tomb known only to Sisyphus.

Nemea A small valley located southwest of Corinth, containing a Doric temple of Zeus dating from the 4th century B.C., it was the site of the *Nemean games and, reportedly, the place where Heracles killed the *Nemean lion.

Nemean games One of the four Panhellenic athletic competitions, the establishment of which was attributed to the Seven against Thebes. Held every two years at midsummer, they were divided into athletic contests and mounted exercises. From the 3rd century B.C., musical contests were added to the program.

Nemean lion A lion covered with an invulnerable skin, which stalked the valley of *Nemea. Heracles performed his first labor by driving it into a cave and strangling it. Subsequently, he wore the lion skin as a sort of shield and used the lion's head as a helmet.

Nemean lion Heracles strangles the Nemean lion

Nemesis A Greek goddess who originally expressed general opposition to all wrongdoing, she became the personification of compensatory jus-

Nemesis   **Nemesis**

tice. In addition to her role as avenger of human wickedness, she had various other functions. Her most important cult places were located in Rhamnus and Smyrna. Veneration of Nemesis continued for an exceptionally long time, and was still practiced in the Roman imperial period.

Nenia Roman goddess of burial, whose temple stood outside the city gate.—One form of lamentation for the dead had a name like hers; it was performed either by the relatives of the deceased person or by professional mourners. Later the term *Nenia* denoted a literary elegy.

Neoptolemus (actually *Pyrrhus*) Son of Achilles and Deidameia, he was called to Troy during the last phase of the siege because a prophecy had declared that the city could not be taken without him. He was the first of the heroes to enter the wooden horse, and distinguished himself at the conquest of Troy by killing King Priam, Priam's daughter Polyxena, and Priam's grandson Astyanax. After the city had fallen, he received Andromache, Hector's widow, as booty. Neoptolemus married Hermione, who was originally betrothed to him but had meanwhile become the bride of Orestes. He was killed either directly by Orestes, or at the latter's instigation, at Delphi.

Nephele A cloud created by Zeus to resemble Hera, which he passed off on Ixion. The union between Ixion and Nephele produced the Centaurs. Nephele married Athamas and bore him Phrixus and Helle.

Neptune God of running water and later of the sea too, his provenance may have been Etruscan. Neptune coincided with the Greek Poseidon. His festival, the Neptunalia, was celebrated on July 23. Also a god of racecourses, Neptune had a temple near the Circus Flaminius.

Neptune with trident, dolphin, and ship's bow (Hellenistic sculpture)

Nereids In Greek mythology, the fifty daughters of the sea god Nereus and the Oceanid Doris.

Nereids

Delighting sailors with their dancing and sporting, they also helped those in distress at sea.

Nereus In Greek mythology, a sea god and son of Pontus and Gaia, he became the father of the *Nereids by *Doris (1). Endowed with the gifts of metamorphosis and prophecy, he was compelled by Heracles to divulge the way to the Garden of the Hesperides.

Nereus

Nessus One of the *Centaurs. As a result of his attempt to rape Deianira, wife of Heracles, Heracles killed him with his club.—According to another tradition, the weapon of Heracles was a poisoned arrow. As he lay dying, Nessus advised Deianira to preserve his deadly blood as a love charm. When Deianira sent her husband a shirt dipped in the poisoned blood, the so-called shirt of Nessus, it destroyed him.

Nestor A legendary Greek hero and son of Neleus and Chloris, he was king of Pylos. All eleven of his brothers died in combat with Heracles. Nestor took part in several expeditions; even in old age, he entered the Trojan War with a contingent of ninety ships. At Troy he stood out less for his strength as a warrior than for his wise counsels and his eloquence.

Nicomachus Son of Machaon, a famous physician in Greek mythology, he himself also became a doctor. Aristotle traced his descent back to Nicomachus.

Nike (Greek for "victory") In the works of Hesiod, she is goddess of victory and daughter of the Titan Pallas and Styx. She herself was not the author of victory but rather delivered it to the victor. Usually represented with other victory-bearing gods, especially Zeus and Athena, Nike appears in winged form and accompanied with attributes such as a palm branch, garland, etc. Among the Romans, Nike found her counterpart in the goddess *Victoria.

Nike of Samothrace (ca. 180 B.C.)

Nikostrate *Carmenta.

Nimrod The legendary builder of the tower used by the giants when they made their attack on the gods of Mount Olympus.

Nike Image of Nike from a Greek vase painting

Niobe A legendary Greek figure and daughter of Tantalus and Dione, she was the wife of Amphion, ruler of Thebes. Proud of her seven sons and seven daughters (the number of her children

Niobe Artemis and Apollo kill the children of Niobe; vase painting by the Niobe painter

fluctuates in the various traditions), she disparaged the goddess Leto, who had born only two children: Apollo and Artemis. Apollo and Artemis avenged their gravely insulted mother by killing the children of Niobe. Petrified by the grief that she suffered, Niobe was removed to her Lydian homeland as a cliff.—The legend of Niobe received frequent attention from both dramatists (e.g., Aeschylus and Sophocles) and artists.

Nona One of the *Parcae.

Notos (Latin, *Auster*) Son of Astraeus and Eos, he was generally understood as god of the south wind.

Numa Pompilius The legendary second king of Rome (715-672 B.C.), he was reputed to have instilled piety and obedience to law and order in the Romans, built temples, and regulated matters of cult.

Numitor King of Alba Longa, and grandfather of Romulus and Remus. Compelled by his brother Amulius to renounce the throne, he was later restored to office by Romulus and Remus.

Nycteus King of Thebes, he was the husband of *Polyxo (1) and the father of *Antiope.

Nymphs In Greek mythology they were nature divinities, considered to be daughters of Zeus, who normally functioned in groups. They enjoyed great popularity and veneration especially among simple folk. The nymphs inhabited seas (*Oceanids, *Nereids), springs and brooks (*Nai-

ads), and woods and trees (*Dryads). They also appeared in the retinue of higher deities and occasionally took care of divine children, as in the case of Dionysus. Frequently their male partners were Satyrs and Sileni. At times the nymphs were dangerous to humans who approached them too closely. The ancient Greeks regarded a *nympholeptos*, i.e., someone "caught by nymphs," as not only inspired but also insane.

Nysa In Greek mythology, the place where the nymphs raised the child Dionysus, entrusted to them by Hermes.

Nyx (Greek for "night"; Latin, *Nox*) A figure of Greek cosmogony, she was the daughter of Chaos, and the sister and wife of Erebus, to whom she bore Heaven (Aether) and Day (Hemera). Thanatos, Hypnos, Moros, and other daimonic beings were also counted among her children, who may have further included the Hesperides.

Nyx

Oath *Fides.

Obolus A Greek coin worth one-sixth of a drachm. An obolus was placed in the mouth of every deceased person as payment for the ferryman who rowed the dead across the river Styx.

Oceanids In Greek mythology, the daughters of *Oceanus and Tethys. Three thousand in number, they possessed the gift of metamorphosis. The Oceanids lived partly in water and partly on land and had a distinct meaning for human beings.—*Nymphs.

Oceanus In Greek mythology, originally the river flowing around the earth's sphere. Oceanus was thought of in connection with other rivers and seas, although separated from them. Only gradually did the name Oceanus come to refer to the ocean.—Oceanus was personified as a Titan, son of Uranus and Gaia, brother and husband of Tethys, and father of the Oceanids. Because he remained aloof from the battle of the Titans, he was not thrown into Tartarus like his brothers after their defeat, but instead retained dominion over the seas.

Oceanus

Ochimos One of the *Heliades, he married the nymph Hegetoria and became the father of a daughter named Kydippe. He may have been the first human being who offered a sacrifice to Athena.

Ocresia (also *Ocrisia*) A slave from an aristocratic family in the city of Corniculum, where her husband was a member of the royal house. Impregnated, according to legend, by the hearth spirit of the Tarquinians, she gave birth to *Servius Tullius, the sixth king of Rome. The tradition has a series of variations.

Ocypete In Greek mythology, one of the Harpies.

Odysseus (Latin, *Ulixes*) King of Ithaca, son of Laertes and Anticlea, husband of Penelope, and one of the heroes of the Trojan War. He contributed a contingent of twelve ships after he had first tried to avoid joining the expedition (in which he was morally bound to participate as a former suitor of Helen) by feigning madness. To this end, he hitched an ox and a horse to a plow and proceeded to sow salt in the earth. But when someone laid his tiny son Telemachus in

Odysseus Slaughter of the suitors of Penelope by Odysseus

one of the furrows, he immediately desisted from his strange behavior and so was unmasked. Odysseus belonged to the Greek legation that sought in vain to regain Helen peaceably from the Trojans. Similarly, he tended to come to the forefront where diplomatic skills were called for in addition to military ones. Thus he succeeded in extracting the Palladium from Troy and was said to have been decisively involved in the proposal to capture the city by means of the wooden horse. Odysseus's extraordinarily long and adventurous return voyage after the Trojan War is the subject of the *Odyssey. When he finally arrived in Ithaca, his wife, Penelope, could hardly fend off the brazen suitors any longer. She had pledged herself to whichever of them showed himself capable of stringing Odysseus's bow. At the last moment, Odysseus proved himself the only competitor able to do so. He was then recognized by his wife and killed all those who had afflicted her. On the further fate of the hero, the tradition diverges. The best known story is of his being slain by Telegonus, the son Circe had born him: having attained manhood, Telegonus set out in search of his father and, failing to recognize him, killed him with the spine of a sting ray.— Odysseus's many adventures on his homeward journey combine fairy-tale features with heroic elements and motifs characteristic of stories of homecoming. The narrative about Odysseus (or single episodes from it) has provided writers and artists with favorite models since antiquity.

Odyssey The work usually attributed to *Homer in which the adventure-filled homeward journey of Odysseus from Troy to Ithaca is narrated.

Oebalus King of Sparta or, in any case, a member of the Spartan royal family. Son of *Kynortas, he married Gorgophone, his brother's widow.

Oecles Husband of *Hypermestra and father of Amphiaraus, he was probably killed during Heracles' combat with the Trojan king *Laomedon.

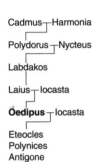

Cadmus—Harmonia

Polydorus—Nycteus

Labdakos

Laius—Iocasta

Oedipus—Iocasta

Eteocles
Polynices
Antigone
Ismene

Oedipus (in antiquity, this name was generally interpreted to mean "swell foot") One of the most important figures in the Theban cycle of legends, he was the son of King *Laius and his queen *Iocasta (in Homer, Epicaste). Laius was warned by the Delphic oracle that his unborn son would kill his own father and marry his mother. Although his wife nevertheless carried the child to term and delivered it, Laius pierced the infant's feet and exposed it on Mount Cithaeron in an effort to avert catastrophe. But the infant was discovered by shepherds and brought to King Polybus and his wife, the childless ruling couple of Corinth, to be raised by them. As a young man, wishing to learn the secret of his origins, Oedipus himself consulted the Delphic oracle, which gave him the same answer that it had given his father. Supposing that the terrible message referred to his foster parents, Oedipus did not go home again so as not to cause them any harm. On his wanderings through Phocis, he encountered Laius, got into an argument with Laius's driver, and killed his natural father. At Thebes he solved the riddle of the *Sphinx; having freed the city from that monster, he was made king and married to the widow of Laius. This marriage produced two sons, Eteocles and Polynices, and two daughters, Antigone and Ismene. After a long period of prosperity, a plague broke out. When the Delphic oracle was consulted, it urged that the murderer of Laius be tracked down. As a result, the fateful truth came to light. Iocasta hung herself. Oedipus blinded himself and was driven into exile by his sons, whom he solemnly cursed. Accompanied by Antigone, he made his way to Attica, where he found refuge in the grove of Colonus until his life's end.—Among the relatively numerous literary adaptations of the Oedi-

Oedipus kills the Sphinx

pus legend, the two Oedipus tragedies of Sophocles are the most significant: in *Oedipus Tyrannus* the life of the hero is portrayed with its horrifying background. *Oedipus Coloneus* depicts Oedipus's last years far from Thebes.

Oeneus King of Calydon, he was the father of several children, including *Meleager, *Tydeus, and *Deianira. Various legends are told about him: according to one, Dionysus bestowed the grapevine on Oeneus. In another, at the insistence of Athena (or Artemis), his land was ravaged by the Calydonian boar because the king had neglected to make a sacrifice to the goddess.

Oeno ("wine maiden") A daughter of *Anius, whom Dionysus ardently adored. Her sisters were Spermo ("seed maiden") and Elais ("olive maiden"). She could bring forth wine from the earth just by touching it.

Oenomaus King of Pisa in Elis, he was probably a son of Ares. His wife, Sterope, bore him *Hippodameia. By forcing each of them to enter a chariot race from which he consistently emerged the victor, Oenomaus succeeded in killing all of his daughter's suitors. Only Pelops was able to outwit the king and so win the hand of Hippodameia for himself.

Oenone Daughter of the river god *Cebren and wife of *Paris, she prophesied that her husband would abduct Helen and so cause the Trojan War. When Paris returned wounded from Sparta, she refused to save him with a remedy that she had in her possession because he had been unfaithful to her with Helen. Finally Oenone committed suicide.

Oenopion King of Chios, he was the son of Dionysus (or Theseus, according to another version) and Ariadne, and the husband of Helice, who bore him a daughter, *Merope (5), in addition to several sons. Dionysus taught him wine growing. Oenopion blinded *Orion in revenge for his rape of Merope.

Oeta A massif in central Greece where legend relates that *Heracles, in torment from the wounds inflicted on him by the shirt of *Nessus, had himself cremated on a funeral pyre.

Ogygie The island on which Odysseus spent seven years with the nymph *Calypso. The precise length of his sojourn there fluctuates in the different traditions.

Ogygus Perhaps a son of Poseidon, he was married to a daughter of Zeus. One strand of the tradition reports that a massive flood broke out at Thebes during his reign over that city. In Attic legend, he appears as the father of the hero Eleusis.

Oiagros A Thracian river god or king of Thrace or both. The tradition usually regarded him as the father of *Orpheus.

Oileus King of Locris, husband of Eriopis, and father of *Aias (1), he was one of the Argonauts and thought to be a lover of Apollo.

Okaleia (*Aglaia*) The wife of Abas, she was the mother of the twin brothers *Acrisius and *Proetus.

Oknos Son of the Tiber, he was the husband of an unrestrained, extravagant woman. The story about Oknos places him among the damned in Hades, where he was forced to twist ropes which a she-ass continually devoured.

Olive tree The tree sacred to Athena.

Olympian games The most important set of *Panhellenic games, they were organized every four years at Olympia in honor of *Zeus. After the initial period when participation in these athletic contests was restricted to prescribed circles, all free Greeks (as long as they were male) were qualified to enter. From 776 B.C. lists of victors were kept, but the games themselves date back before that. Youth competitions were admitted from 632 B.C., and a musical component was also incorporated into the program. The prize was an olive branch. At home the victors enjoyed high honors and various privileges, e.g., tax-exempt status. In the course of Christianization, Theodosius the Great prohibited the games in A.D. 393.

Olympus 1. A mountain range with the highest peak in Greece (2,911 meters), it is located on the boundary between Thessaly and Macedo-

---

Olympus: Mount Olympus was the seat of the great Olympian gods

Greek name	Latin name	Greek name	Latin name
Apollon	Apollo	Hephaestus (Hephaistos)	Volcanus
Aphrodite	Venus	Hera	Juno
Ares	Mars	Hermes	Mercurius
Artemis	Diana	Hestia	Vesta
Athena (Athene)	Minerva	Chronos (Kronos)	Saturnus
Demeter	Ceres	Poseidon	Neptune (Neptunus)
Dionysus (Dionysos)	Bacchus	Rhea (Rheia)	Cybele
Gaia	Terra	Selene	Luna
Hades	Pluto	Uranos	Uranus
Helios	Sol	Zeus	Jupiter

nia near the Thermaic Gulf. The ancient Greeks regarded it as the seat of the chief (Olympian) gods. 2. A famous flute player often regarded as a historical figure. In legend he was either the father of *Marsyas or his student. Pan taught Olympus how to play the syrinx at his home on the Mysian Mount Olympus.

Omphale Queen of Lydia, she was the wife of *Tmolus. After Heracles had killed *Iphitos and committed further crimes, he was obliged to spend one year (in another version, three years) performing menial tasks for Omphale. According to the legend, the queen, who engaged in a love affair with the hero, made him wear women's clothes and do women's work. Another tradition reports that Heracles had become so effeminate that he voluntarily assumed the appearance of a woman.—Heracles in the service of Omphale was a favorite theme of artists.

Olympus Pan instructs Olympus in flute playing

Omphalos A conical block of stone, which after the tripod was the most significant cult object at Delphi, and the subject of various myths and legends. Thus the sanctuary was said to have belonged at one time to a Minoan-Mycenaean goddess, later equated by the Greeks with *Gaia. Legend tells that two eagles (or birds of another type, in another version) were dispatched from either end of the world and met at the Omphalos. Another story identifies the stone as the one that *Kronos swallowed thinking that it was his son Zeus. After he had spit it

Omphalos at Delphi

back out, the stone was brought to the temple of the Delphic oracle.—The Omphalos was often considered to be the seat of prophecy, even though the latter was actually the tripod on which the Python sat down.

Onca A Phoenician goddess identified with Athena, she was introduced into Thebes by Cadmus.

Oneiroi The children of Hypnos or Nyx, they lived near one of the entrances to the underworld.

Opheltes Son of *Lycurgus (2) and king of Nemea, whose nurse and attendant was *Hypsipyle. When Hypsipyle laid him down in the grass so that she could show the Seven against Thebes a spring, the child was killed by a snake. He was buried under the name Archemorus (which means "death-causing"), and his death was read as an evil omen for the Seven. The *Nemean games were established in honor of Opheltes.

Ophion A Titan who may originally have been a god. Perhaps the husband of Eurynome, he ruled over Olympus with her until the two were plunged either into the sea or into Tartarus by Kronos and Rhea.

Opis (also *Upis*) A companion of Artemis, whom Orion sought to dishonor (according to one strand of the tradition), whereupon Artemis killed Orion. Other sources give Opis or Upis as a name or epithet of Artemis.

Ops Roman goddess of the harvest and later of wealth generally. Several festivals were celebrated in her honor, above all the harvest thanksgiving on August 25. Connected with Consus, Ops was thought to be the wife of Saturn and identified with the Greek goddess Rhea. In Rome she was also worshiped as goddess of marriage and family.

Oracle In the religious history of many peoples, an important means of communicating the will of a divinity; it instructed those who consulted it, with reference to their conduct, and informed them about things and events far removed in time and space. The term also designates the place where the divinity was questioned. The oracle functioned through (a) observation or inspection and skilled interpretation of certain signs such as the entrails of sacrificial animals, the flight of birds, the stars, dreams, and the rustling of leaves in sacred groves; or (b) the medium's direct interrogation of the gods whose frequently cryptic answers were construed by interpreters. Famous cult oracular sites in Greek antiquity included Delphi, Dodona, and Olympia. Of much less significance was the consultation of oracles in Italy tied to specific locales.—A related phenomenon was direct, nonlocalized prophesying by charismatic gifted persons, for example, *Cassandra.

Oracle of Delphi *Delphi.

Orchomenus 1. An ancient city in Boeotia, founded in legend by Minyas. 2. An ancient city in Arcadia.

Orcus *Underworld.

Oreithyia 1. One of the *Nereids. 2. A daughter of Erechtheus who was carried off by *Boreas to Thrace. They produced several children.— *Boreades.

Orestes An important legendary Greek figure, he was the son of the Mycenaean king *Agamemnon and *Clytemnestra, as well as the brother of Electra, Iphigenia, and Chrysothemis. When Orestes' father, Agamemnon, was murdered upon his arrival home from Troy by his wife and Aegisthus, Orestes' sister Electra saved him by having him secretly removed to the safekeeping of their uncle Strophius in Phocis. There Orestes grew up with his cousin Pylades. Later he avenged the death of his father by killing his mother and Aegisthus. Afterward he was pursued as a matricide by the *Erinyes until he stood trial in a court of law on the Areopagus. The Erinyes appeared as the plaintiffs, Apollo represented the defendant, and Athena (who cast her vote for Orestes) finally brought about his acquittal. Thus his atonement was solemnized.—According to another tradition, the purification of Orestes occurred when he and his friend Pylades took the cult image of Artemis out

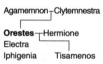

Agamemnon — Clytemnestra

Orestes — Hermione
Electra
Iphigenia   Tisamenos

of Taurus, where Orestes also found his sister Iphigenia again. When they had returned to their homeland, he married Hermione and gave Electra in marriage to Pylades. The legend tells that Orestes died from a snake bite in Arcadia; his son Tisamenos succeeded him as king.—The story of Orestes, with its central motif of blood revenge, which on the one hand is commanded by the gods and on the other severely punished, has been widely treated in literature, perhaps most brilliantly in the entirely preserved trilogy (*Oresteia*) of Aeschylus.

Orestiads Mountain *nymphs who accompanied Artemis on the hunt.

Orion In Greek mythology, a mighty hunter from Boeotia, son of Poseidon and Euryale. Because Orion had attacked *Merope (5) in her sleep, Merope's father, Oenopion, blinded him. With the aid of a youth from the workshop of Hephaestus, whom he carried on his shoulders, Orion walked toward the sunrise seeking to be healed by Helios. When he returned, he attempted to avenge himself on Oenopion but was prevented from doing so by his beloved Eos. Concerning his further fortunes the tradition diverges. Sometimes it is related that Artemis killed him with her arrows either out of jealousy toward Eos or because Orion had been pursuing the goddess or a nymph from her retinue. Another account tells that he boasted of being able to shoot all animals—regarded as the wards of Artemis—and consequently was killed. Orion's pursuit of the virginal Pleiades is also recorded; together with them, he was translated by Zeus to the stars.

Ormenus One of the *Lapiths, he was killed by *Polypoites.

Orpheus A prominent mythical singer and lyre player, he was born to the Thracian river god *Oiagros and the Muse Calliope. Apollo is also occasionally named as his father, with the intent of raising his person and his art to the level of the divine. As a musician, Orpheus had the power to enchant human beings, animals, and plants and to create a state of paradisal calm in which all creatures listened only to him. The soothing effect of his music also came to light

Orpheus with his lyre; painting on a krater from Gela (ca. 450 B.C.)

during the voyage of the Argonauts, when Orpheus (who accompanied the Argonauts) succeeded in calming the storms at sea. The focal event in the myth about Orpheus is his journey to the underworld to recover his beloved wife, Eurydice, who had died from a snake bite. Deeply stirred by Orpheus's music, Hades offered to return his wife to him on condition that he not look back at her as they ascended to the upper world. When Orpheus failed to abide by this condition, he lost Eurydice forever. Varying accounts of his later fate have been handed down. Thracian Maenads are said to have torn him apart after he became a misogynist. Another reason given for his violent death is his refusal to sacrifice not only to Apollo but also to Dionysus. The legend speaks, too, of his head and his instrument floating over the sea, and of his lyre being placed among the stars.—*Orphism.

Orphism A philosophical-religious movement of Greek antiquity named after *Orpheus, which probably arose in Thrace in the 6th century B.C. Spreading over Greece, Crete, southern Italy, and Asia Minor, it was partly concentrated in loose groups. On the basis of a cosmogony and theogony fixed in writing, Orphism functioned as a mystery cult practiced especially by itinerant priests. In connection with purification rites and other ceremonies, it aimed to ensure a blessed afterlife through the observation of a pure, moral-religious "Orphic life" (reduction of rebirths).

Orsedike Daughter of Cinyras, king of Paphos, she emigrated to Egypt after engaging in a love affair.

Orseis A nymph and the wife of *Hellen, she was the mother of *Aeolus, *Dorus, and *Xuthus.

Orsilochos Son of the river god *Alpheus.

Orthros (also *Orthos*) A two-headed dog belonging to the shepherd Eurytion, engendered by Typhon and Echidna. Orthros guarded the cattle of *Geryon, which Heracles stole during his tenth labor; in the process, he killed Eurytion and Orthros.

Osiris An ancient Egyptian god, he was the brother and husband of *Isis. Originally probably a fertility god, he was also god of the moon and the Nile, as well as ruler over the realm of the dead. Greek mythology named Zeus as his father.

Ossa A Greek mountain in Thessaly, 6,490 feet high, which faces Mount Olympus. It was the locale of several legends.

Othryades The only survivor, on the Spartan side, of a battle (ca. 550 B.C.) between 300 Argives and 300 Spartans. Two Argive warriors survived.

Otrere (also *Otrera*) An Amazon queen, she was the mother of Antiope, Hippolyta, and Penthesilea by Ares.

Otus One of the Aloades. Like his brother *Ephialtes, he was a giant who joined battle with the gods.

Ovid (*Publius Ovidius Naso*) A Roman poet, he was born in 43 B.C. at Sulmo and died at Tomis (on the Black Sea) in A.D. 17 or 18. From a distinguished aristocratic family, he received a rhetorical education at Rome and undertook numerous travels, especially in Greece and Asia Minor. In A.D. 8, he was banished by Augustus to the Black Sea for reasons that are not precisely known. A virtuoso in his command of language and verse, witty as well as frivolous in his love poetry, and a master of lively, colorful narrative, Ovid exercised—after Virgil—the strongest influence on medieval Latin and vernacular epic and lyric in addition to Renaissance and Baroque poetry. His early work includes three books of love elegies (*Amores*), the *Heroides* (love letters from the pen of mythical and legendary female figures), a didactic poem about the art of love (*Ars amatoria*), and a companion piece on the cure for love (*Remedia amoris*). In his maturity, Ovid wrote epic works. With his arrangement of myths and legends and his explanation of the Roman religious calendar, Ovid sought to place himself in the service of the Augustan reform movement (*Fasti*, unfinished in six books). The fifteen books of *Metamorphoses* presented legends of transformation from the creation of the world to Caesar's apotheosis. Ovid wrote *Tristia* (poems of lamentation), *Epistulae ex Ponto*, and the libelous *Ibis* during his exile.

Pactolus A small Lydian river taking its rise on Mount Tmolus. According to legend, its sands contained gold after Midas bathed in its waters to free himself from the disastrous gift that turned everything he touched into gold. The wealth of Croesus was said to have derived in large measure from the Pactolus.

Pagasae A harbor in Thessaly where, according to one strand of the tradition, the *Argo was built and put to sea.

Paion (*Paean*) 1. Another name for *Asclepius. 2. Son of Endymion and a Naiad, though other possible mothers are mentioned. When Paion's father organized a race in order to determine who his successor as king of Elis would be, another of his sons, Epeios, won the contest and Paion had to emigrate to Macedonia.

Palaemon Son of Athamas and Ino, he was originally called *Melicertes. After his deification he received the name Palaemon.

Palamedes In Greek legend, son of *Nauplius (2) and Clymene (according to another version, Philyra). Distinguishing himself by his great cleverness and skill, Palamedes invented (among other things) several letters of the alphabet. When the Greek army was being recruited for the campaign against Troy, he unmasked the duplicity of *Odysseus in pretending to be insane so as to avoid participation in the war. After that Odysseus always sought opportunities to do away with his archenemy. Thus it is said that he drowned him while fishing. According to another version, Odysseus forged a letter ostensibly from Priam to Palamedes demonstrating that Palamedes had been bribed to betray the Greek camp. Presenting this document to the assembled army, Odysseus demanded that the tent of the accused be searched. In it the gold that Odysseus had previously hidden there was found; Palamedes was then stoned to death.— A later tradition tells of a well in which Odysseus persuaded Palamedes that a treasure was concealed. When Palamedes climbed down into the well to get the treasure, his adversary killed him by pelting him with stones.

Palatine (Latin, *Palatium*) A group of hills between the Tiber River and the Forum in Rome, named after their point of highest elevation. The oldest Roman settlement, supposedly established by Romulus, was located there. Its extensive sacred structures and upper-class residential quarters gave way to the magnificent buildings of the imperial period.

Pales Roman goddess of shepherds and their herds whose chief festival, the Parilia, was celebrated on April 21. This date was later commemorated as the day of Rome's foundation. Although one strand of the tradition speaks of two Pales, it remains unclear whether the obvious explanation that the two divinities were female and male is correct. Both Pales may have been female. There was certainly a male Pales, but he belonged to the Etruscan Penates.

Palici These Sicilian gods, a pair of twins, are often identified as sons of Zeus and Thaleia, though other parents are also mentioned. They were held to be personifications of natural phenomena (e.g., sulfur deposits) connected with their single cult place, the Lago dei Palici on Sicily. Their sanctuary is frequently mentioned in the tradition as a place of oath-taking and seems to have been especially venerated by slaves.

Palinurus The helmsman on Aeneas's flagship. In the legend he either drowned off the coast of Italy, after he had gone to sleep and fallen into the ocean, or he survived and swam for four days until he reached the Italian coast, where the native inhabitants murdered him. He was forbidden entry into the underworld as long as he remained unburied; Aeneas later provided for his interment. The barbarians who had killed him were punished by a plague. To save themselves from this calamity, they worshiped Palinurus as a hero and named Cape Palinurus after him.

Palladium A cult image of Pallas Athena, depicting her with a shield and raised spear, it was the subject of a rich mythological tradition. The tradition reports that Zeus threw it down from heaven. Possessed by Troy, it was worshiped in the Athena temple there and served to protect the city. Odysseus and Diomedes were supposed to have stolen it in the conviction that without it the Greeks would never be able to conquer the city. According to another version, the Palladium was recovered by Aeneas, who took it with him on his voyage to Italy. Later the Palladium was generally regarded as the protective relic of a city, the loss of which would render that city defenseless.

Pallantia Daughter of Evander and Deidameia, she became the mother of a son (Pallas) by Heracles. According to legend, the Palatine Hill in Rome was named after her.

Pallas In Greek mythology, a frequently used name or epithet applied to the following, among others: 1. Athena, with a meaning that cannot be certainly determined—possible explanations are that she was so called after she had killed a giant by the same name, or on account of the manner in which she swung her spear. 2. A son of Evander and ally of Aeneas, who fell in combat with Turnus. 3. A son of Heracles and *Pallantia. 4. A son of Uranus and Gaia, whose skin Athena stripped off during the battle between the gods and giants, so that it could be used for a shield.

Pan Arcadian god of shepherds and hunters, he was imagined as half-animal and half-human. In Greek myth, he was often identified as the son of Hermes and the nymph Dryope, but the tradition makes numerous other statements about his parentage. Pan resembled the Satyrs and Sileni, whom he frequently joined as a follower of Dionysus or in pursuit of the nymphs. A master flute player, he also knew how to strike "panic fear" into human beings by suddenly appearing. His cult spread all over Greece, though

Pan in the park of the Schloss Nymphenburg

Pan and Panic Fear

he enjoyed special veneration in Attica because, as legend records, before the battle of Marathon he let it be known to the Athenians that he was their friend and would stand by them against the Persians. After the Greek victory, the Athenians dedicated a grotto to Pan on the Acropolis, where they worshiped him. Corresponding to the Greek Pan was the Roman *Faunus.

Panacea (*Panakeia*: Greek for "female all-healer") Goddess of health, she was the daughter of Asclepius and Epione.

Panathenaia The preeminent Athenian festival, it commemorated annually the birthday of the goddess Athena (Small Panathenaia). From ca. 565 B.C., it was observed every four years with special pomp as the Great Panathenaia. The cultic ritual of the festival was richly developed. It began in the evening with singing and dancing on the Acropolis. At dawn the great procession, which is represented on the Parthenon frieze, took place. Apart from its religious character, the festival was equally intended to demonstrate the importance and magnitude of Athens. The Great Panathenaia also served as an occasion for athletic and musical competitions. The chief prizes were the well-known Panathenaic amphoras filled with oil.

Panathenaic amphoras *Panathenaia.

Pandareos King of Cretan Miletus, he was the son of Merops and a nymph. Pandareos stole a golden dog made by Hephaestus, which guarded a cave dedicated to Zeus. Zeus then turned him and his wife into a rock, or else killed the two as they fled to Sicily. Despite the protection extended to them by Hera, Aphrodite, and Athena, the daughters of Pandareos were kidnapped by the Harpies and handed over to the Erinyes as slaves.

Pandion King of Athens, and probably a son of Erichthonius and Praxithea. He married Zeuxippe, the sister of his mother, and became the father of Philomela and *Procne. With *Labdakos he maintained a state of war. One strand of the tradition relates that, after ruling for forty years, he died of grief over the transformation of his daughters into birds.

Pandora (Greek for "the all-endowed") In Greek mythology, she was the first woman, whom Hephaestus created by order of Zeus. Distinguished for her great beauty, she was endowed by the gods with many charming gifts. Brought to earth by Hermes, she arrived with a box containing all the evils of the world in addition to hope. Her task was to punish mankind for the theft of fire by *Prometheus. Although Prometheus warned his brother Epimetheus, the latter married Pandora, who immediately opened the box, unleashing untold disaster on the human race; only hope remained inside the box.—Behind Pandora there may have lurked an ancient earth goddess who bore to Epimetheus the daughter Pyrrha, future wife of *Deucalion (1).

Pandora with the box

Pandrosos One of the daughters of *Cecrops (1), she was the sister of *Aglauros and *Herse.

Panhellenic games The games to which all the Greeks sent representative competitors: the *Isthmian games, the *Olympian games, the *Nemean games, and the *Pythian games.

Panhellenic games
From an Attic vase painting, 5th century B.C. The figures depicted are, from left to right: a runner in heavy armor, a supervisor, boxers, a youth with a surveyor's chain

Panhellenios Epithet of Zeus, the god of all Greeks.

Pankratis Daughter of Aloeus and *Iphimedeia. Together with her mother, she was carried off by Thracian pirates but rescued by her half-brothers, the Aloades.

Panope A *Nereid, she was the eldest of the fifty daughters of Nereus and Doris. When sailors got caught in storms, they called to her for help.

Pantheon A round temple in Rome with interior niches dedicated to all the gods, it was erected

Parcae One of the
singing Parcae; by
Asmus Jacob Carstens
(1754–1798)

under Agrippa in 27 B.C. and domed over by
Hadrian (A.D. 117-138). In 609 Christians con-
verted it into a church.

Panthoos Priest of Apollo at Troy, he served as
counselor to Priam and died in the Trojan War.

Paphia Epithet of Aphrodite, derived from her
temple at Paphos.

Paphos A city on the west coast of Cyprus,
near which (according to legend) *Aphrodite
emerged from the sea.

Parca Roman goddess of birth and one of the
Parcae, she was the companion of Nona and
*Decuma. In cases where mother and child died
in childbirth, Parca was also called Morta.

Parcae Roman goddesses of fate who were
originally birth divinities; they were equated with
the Greek *Moirai. The Parcae usually appeared as a trio with the names *Parca, *Decuma (or Decima), and *Nona.

Parentalia The Roman ceremonies for the
dead performed from February 13 to 21, at
which families remembered their dead and presented offerings at their graves. During the
Parentalia, temples remained closed and weddings were not celebrated.

Parilia The festival of *Pales.

Paris (*Alexander*) In Greek mythology, a son of
*Priam and Hecuba, and brother of Hector.
When Hecuba was pregnant with Paris, she
dreamed that she would give birth to a burning
torch which would set the whole city of Troy on
fire. To avert this catastrophe, the newborn infant was abandoned on Mount Ida; shepherds
raised him there, and he later lived there as a
shepherd himself. There he was also asked to
decide whether Aphrodite, Hera, or Athena was
the most beautiful of the goddesses (the judgment of Paris); the three could not agree because of the golden apple of *Eris. Paris chose
Aphrodite, who had promised him Helen in return. By abducting Helen (the wife of
*Menelaus) to Troy, Paris kindled the flames of
the Trojan War. In the course of it, he killed
Achilles and died himself when his wife

*Oenone refused to save him, with a remedy that she possessed, in revenge for his infidelity.—For the most part, the character of Paris lacks sharply defined features, since the *Iliad* dispenses with details. Nevertheless, in antiquity the judgment of Paris was already a favorite theme of writers and artists. Euripides treated the youth of the hero in his *Alexander*, and Sophocles portrayed the judgment of Paris in his *Crisis*; the two works have survived only in fragments.

Parnassus A limestone mountain range at Delphi, it was regarded in antiquity as the seat of Apollo and the Muses, hence in a figurative sense also as the realm of poetry.

Parthenon The temple of Athena Parthenos on the Acropolis of Athens, it was erected between 447 and 432 B.C. by Ictinus and Callicrates as a Doric peripteral structure. *Pheidias sculpted the chryselephantine cult statue, 39 feet high. The east pedimental sculptures depicted the birth of Athena, and the west pedimental sculptures the controversy between Athena and Poseidon over Attica. The remaining decoration consisted of 92 metopes and the Panathenaic frieze.

Parthenopaeus The son of *Atalanta and Melanion (in other versions, of Meleager or Ares), he courageously went to war with the Seven against Thebes against the will of his mother, who foresaw his death.

Parthenope One of the *Sirens, she was the daughter of *Achelous and a Muse. The legend relates that she, like her sisters, dove into the sea out of grief after Odysseus and his companions had escaped from them. However, Parthenope did not drown but landed at the site of Naples, which therefore took its alternate name from her.

Parthenos Epithet of *Athena.

Partridge *Perdix.

Pasiphae Daughter of Helios and Perseis, she was the sister of Aeetes and Circe. She came from a family endowed with magical powers. Pasiphae's husband, *Minos, prayed to Poseidon for a bull, which he vowed to sacrifice to the god. Breaking his promise, the king incorporated the animal into his herd. Pasiphae fell in love with it and as a result gave birth to the *Minotaur, which was held captive in a labyrinth.

Pasithea 1. One of the Charites (Graces), she was the daughter of Zeus and Eurynome, according to one strand of tradition. She married Hypnos and became the mother of Morpheus. According to another version, she may have been identical with the Grace Aglaia. 2. One of the *Nereids.

Patroclus
The contests held at the celebrated funeral games for Patroclus:
   chariot racing
   boxing
   wrestling
   foot racing
   dueling
   discus throwing
   archery
   javelin throwing
Prizes were awarded to the various victors.

Patroclus Son of *Menoetius (1) and Sthenele, he was the best friend of Achilles. Patroclus went with Achilles to the Trojan War, at which he performed many heroic deeds. When he ventured too far toward the enemy, wearing the armor of Achilles, he encountered Hector and was killed by him. Achilles mourned his friend deeply, and splendid funeral games were held in his honor. The heroic deeds and the death of Patroclus are described in the 16th book of the *Iliad.*

Pax Roman goddess of peace

Pax The Roman goddess corresponding to the Greek *Eirene, she was understood to be the divine personification of peace and was worshiped especially from the Augustan period onward. In 9 B.C. the Ara Pacis Augustae was consecrated on the Campus Martius; its construction had been decreed in 13 B.C. after the victorious return of Augustus from Spain and Gaul. Vespasian erected a temple to the goddess in A.D. 75. The Pax Augusta or Pax Augusti also appeared as a favorite motif on Roman coins.

Peacock The bird sacred to Hera. The hundred eyes of *Argos Panoptes were set in its tail feathers.

Pegasus Representation of the winged horse on a piece of woven material (6th century)

Pegasus A winged horse, which issued from *Medusa when Perseus cut off her head. Bellerophon rode it for his decisive combat with the *Chimaera. Bellerophon's later attempt to fly to Mount Olympus seated on Pegasus brought about his own death and Pegasus's translation to the stars. Of Pegasus it is also told that the stamp of his hoof created two fountains: the Hippocréne fountain in Boeotia and the Pirene fountain in Corinth. At both of these fountains the Muses gathered; Pegasus was their sacred horse.

Peisidice 1. Daughter of *Aeolus and Enarete, she was the wife of Myrmidon, to whom she bore three children. 2. Daughter of *Nestor.

Peisinoe Daughter of *Achelous, and one of the *Sirens.

Peisistratos A son of Nestor, who accompanied *Telemachus to Sparta.

Peitho Greek goddess of persuasion analogous to the Roman *Suada. Often mentioned in connection with Aphrodite, the name Peitho was also transmitted as an epithet of Aphrodite and Artemis.

Pelasgus King of Arcadia, he was born to Zeus and Niobe; according to another version, Gaia was his mother. He married the Oceanid Meliboea, who bore him *Lycaon, his successor on the throne. Considered the founding ancestor of the Pelasgians, Pelasgus cultivated the land and was the first to have a temple to Zeus built in Arcadia.

Peleides (*Peleion*) Epithet of Achilles as son of *Peleus.

Peleus A Greek hero from Thessaly, he took part in the Calydonian boar hunt and the Argonautic expedition. Peleus was a son of Aeacus of Aegina and Endeis, a brother of Telamon, and a half-brother of Phocus. Anxious about their inheritance, Peleus and Telamon killed their half-brother and then had to go into exile. Peleus sought refuge at the court of King Eurytion in Phthia. The king absolved him of fratricide and gave him his daughter Antigone in marriage. She bore Peleus a daughter, Polydora. After he inadvertently killed his father-in-law with a spear during the Calydonian boar hunt, Peleus fled to King Acastus of Iolcus, who purified him for the second time. The wife of Acastus, Astydameia, fell in love with Peleus but found no response

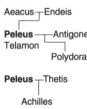

from him. She avenged herself for this rejection by alleging to Peleus's wife that he intended to marry a daughter of Acastus; Antigone reacted by committing suicide. Astydameia also persuaded her husband that Peleus had indecently pursued her. The king took his revenge while on a hunt by stealing the hunting knife of his putative rival and hiding it when Peleus was asleep on Mount Pelion. This left Peleus exposed and unprotected against the Centaurs who lived in the area. Salvation came from *Chiron, who knew how to tame his wild brethren. Peleus returned to Iolcus, conquered the land, and killed the malicious Astydameia.—Another important component of the legend about Peleus is his struggle with the Nereid Thetis, beloved of Zeus. She always managed to evade her suitor by assuming one manifestation after the other. At last, however, they were married at a wedding attended by all the Olympian gods except *Eris. From the union of Peleus and Thetis, Achilles was born. His mother tried to make him immortal by laying him on the fire (or, according to another version, dipping him in the river Styx). Because she was surprised by her husband before finishing the job, Achilles' heel remained vulnerable. Thetis vanished forever into the palace of her father, Nereus.

Peliades Designation for the daughters of *Pelias.

Pelias King of Iolcus, he was the son of Poseidon and Tyro, the brother of Neleus, and the half-brother of *Aeson, whom he forced from power. Pelias commissioned *Jason to obtain the *Golden fleece, hoping that he would die in the attempt and so make no further claims on the throne. Medea wreaked a terrible revenge on Pelias by inducing his daughters, under the pretext that he would thus be rejuvenated, to dismember and cook their father; she then withheld the magic herbs which would have restored his youth. The funeral games arranged for Pelias were famous for their solemnity. One of Pelias's sons, Acastus, ascended the throne, whereas Jason and Medea had to leave the country.

Pelion A richly wooded mountain on the peninsula of Magnesia in Thessaly, with a sanctuary of Zeus at its summit. Legend reports that the wood cut down there was used by the Greeks to build the *Argo*. The wise Centaur Chiron was also thought to have lived in a cave on the mountain.

Pelopia 1. Daughter of Pelias and Anaxabia or Phylomache, she may have been the mother of Cycnus by Ares. 2. Daughter of Thyestes and a Naiad, she was the mother of Aegisthus. In one strand of the tradition she is mentioned as the wife of Atreus.

Peloponnesus (Greek for "island of Pelops") Since the Middle Ages also called *Morea*, this peninsula is joined to central Greece by the Isthmus of Corinth. Culturally a Mycenaean area, it was settled by Dorians during the Dorian migration (ca. 1200–1000 B.C.). Its most important cities were Sparta, Argos, and Corinth.

Pelops 1. In Greek mythology, a son of Tantalus and grandson of Zeus. Tantalus once invited the gods to a meal at which he served them stewed Pelops. The gods perceived his crime, revived Pelops, and provided him with a shoulder of ivory since Persephone had unwittingly eaten that part.—As a young man, Pelops went to Elis to the court of King *Oenomaus and sought the hand of his daughter *Hippodameia, winning her by trickery. After killing his confidant, *Myrtilus, he threw him into the sea. The dying Myrtilus uttered a curse on Pelops and his descendants, which found its most horrible fulfillment in regard to Pelops's sons Atreus and Thyestes. Pelops, who took over the rule of Oenomaus, became the eponym of the Peloponnesus ("island of Pelops"). 2. One of the numerous children of Amphion and *Niobe. 3. Son of Agamemnon and Cassandra.

Peloros One of the *Spartoi, who were born from the dragon's teeth sown by *Cadmus.

Pemphredo Daughter of Phorcys and Ceto, and sister of Dino and Enyo, she was one of the *Graiae.

Penates Roman household gods who protected not only families but also, as state gods, the Roman people in its entirety. Their protective function pertained to the storerooms and the interior of the house. They were worshiped in the vicinity of the hearth where, like the Lares, they received a daily meal and were included in the events of the household.—According to legend, Aeneas brought the state Penates with him from Troy to Italy. Veneration of the Penates occurred first in Lavinium and later in Rome, where it came under the authority of the Pontifex Maximus.

Peneleos An Argonaut and son of Hippalcimus. As one of Helen's (former) suitors, he contributed fifty ships from Boeotia to the Trojan War effort. He was killed by *Eurypylus (2), an ally of the Trojans.

Penelope Daughter of Icarius of Sparta and Periboea, she was the wife of *Odysseus, to whom she probably bore a second son after his return from the Trojan War; Telemachus was their first

Penelope The wife of Odysseus at her loom; Greek vase painting (ca. 440 B.C.)

son. One strand of the tradition also designates her as the mother of Pan by Hermes. She remained faithful to Odysseus throughout his twenty-year absence by constantly devising ways to ward off her importunate suitors. Thus she maintained that she must weave the shroud for her father-in-law before she could think about remarrying, but then during the night she would unravel what she had woven that day. Penelope became the paradigm of a faithful wife.

Peneus Thessalian river god and son of Oceanus and Tethys. Before the erection of a temple to Peneus, his image was set up on the bridges that crossed the Peneus River.

Penthesilea An Amazon queen, and daughter of Ares and *Otrere. After the death of Hector, she came to the aid of the Trojans and was killed by Achilles, who fell in love with his dying adversary.

Pentheus King of Thebes, and son of Echion and *Agave (1). His violent death at the hands of his mother was closely linked with the cult of Dionysus, which he would not sanction (because of its orgiastic aspects) despite the opposition of the god's worshipers. His conduct and fate demonstrate the difficulty of adapting Dionysiac religion to Greece.

Penthilus Illegitimate son of Orestes and Erigone. His successors in the royal dynasty founded by him at Mytilene were called the Penthilides.

Peparethos Son of Dionysus and *Ariadne.

Perdix (*Talos*) An Attic inventor, he was the nephew and pupil of *Daedalus, whose wealth of ideas he threatened to surpass. According to legend, he invented the saw and perhaps also the compass and potter's wheel. When Daedalus killed Perdix out of envy, Athena changed the dead man into a partridge.

Pergamos A legendary son of Neoptolemus and Andromache. One strand of the tradition reports that he emigrated to Mysia, conquered the city of Teuthrania, changed its name to Pergamum, and became its king.

Pergamum A city in Mysia (northwest Asia Minor), today called Bergama. It was the site of many sanctuaries, among them the Pergamum altar, purportedly dedicated to Zeus. Legend tells that Pergamum was named after *Pergamos.

Periander Tyrant of Corinth from 627 to 585 B.C., under whose rule Corinth experienced a renascence. A patron of poetry and the great sanctuaries, Periander was numbered among the Seven Wise Men of Greece.

Periboea (*Eriboea*) 1. The second wife of Telamon and the mother of *Aias the Great, she set out with Theseus for Crete to be sacrificed to the Minotaur. Minos fell in love with her, but she rejected him and returned home to Greece. 2. Wife of the Corinthian king Polybus and foster mother of *Oedipus. 3. Wife of *Oeneus.

Periclymenus 1. An Argonaut and son of *Neleus and Chloris. Gifted with the ability to change his form, he was nevertheless killed by Heracles after turning himself into an eagle. 2. Son of Poseidon and Chloris (a daughter of Tiresias), he was the chief defender of the Thebans in the battle of the Seven against Thebes. He killed *Parthenopaeus, among others.

Perieres Son of *Aeolus (1) and Enarete. His wife *Gorgophone, a daughter of Perseus, bore him several children.

Perigune Daughter of *Sinis Pityocamptes ("spruce bender") and, by Theseus, the mother of a son, Melanippus. She introduced the cult of asparagus.

Perimedes A companion of Odysseus on his journey into the underworld.

Perimele A daughter of Aeolus, she had many brothers and sisters. Pursued by Achelous, she bore him two sons named Hippodamas and Orestes, according to one strand of the tradition. For this Aeolus threw her into the sea, where Poseidon transformed her into an island.

Periphas King of Thessaly, son of Lapithes, and brother of *Phorbas. He married Astyageia and became the father of many sons, including Antion.

Periphetes 1. A son of *Kopreus, he was killed in the Trojan War by Hector or Teucer. 2. Son of Hephaestus or Poseidon (in a rarer version, of Daedalus), he was a lame bandit with a bronze or iron club, accordingly named Corynetes ("club man"). Periphetes spread fear and panic because he attacked travelers with his club. Theseus finally killed him.

Pero Daughter of *Neleus and Chloris, she had many suitors and eventually married *Bias (1), to whom she bore several children. Pero was praised for her beauty.

Perseis (*Perse*) An Oceanid, she married Helios and bore him Aeetes, Circe, Pasiphae, and Perses.

Persephone A goddess of the underworld in Greek mythology, she was the daughter of Zeus and *Demeter and the wife of *Hades. Persephone persuaded her husband to let her live in the upper world for part of the year as goddess of growth (in relation to the cycle of vegetation). She received the name *Kore in certain contexts. Veneration of Persephone occurred primarily through the *Eleusinian mysteries. *Proserpina was her Roman counterpart.

Persephone

Persephone The goddess as queen of Hades

Perses 1. The oldest son of Perseus and Andromeda, and the legendary ancestor of the kings of Persia. 2. A Titan, son of *Crius, and father of Hecate. 3. Son of Helios and Perseis, and brother of Aeetes, Circe, and Pasiphae. He seized the throne of Aeetes, king of Colchis, but was deposed by the children of Aeetes.

Perseus An important hero of Greek legend, he was the son of Zeus and Danae. Because an oracle had indicated that Acrisius, the father of Danae, would die at the hands of a grandson,

Acrisius—Eurydice
Zeus—Danae
Perseus—Andromeda

Perses Alcaeus Sthenelus Heleios Mestor Electryon—Anaxo Gorgophone

Zeus—Alcmene
Heracles

Perseus with the head of Medusa; by Benvenuto Cellini (1500-1571)

Perseus with the head of Medusa

he locked his daughter up in an underground chamber or an ivory tower. But Zeus approached her anyway, in the form of a shower or cloud of gold. As a result, Danae gave birth to Perseus, and when her father learned of this, he had mother and child put out to sea in a chest. Instead of drowning, however, they drifted ashore at the island of Seriphus and were hospitably received by *Polydectes, king of the island. Having fallen in love with Danae, Polydectes tried to get rid of the youthful Perseus by ordering him to capture the head of the Gorgon Medusa. Equipped with a magic purse, a magic hood, and winged shoes (objects that he had obtained with the help of Hermes and Athena), Perseus started on his way. He came upon the mortal Gorgon Medusa—whose petrifying gaze was supposed to kill him—lying fast asleep together with her two immortal sisters. By using his shield as a mirror, he averted the petrifying effect of her gaze and cut off her head. Depositing it in his pouch, he escaped from the two sisters by putting on his magic hood. On his homeward journey he rescued *Andromeda, who had been exposed to a sea monster, and made her his wife. Perseus turned Polydectes to stone by means of the Gorgon's head, which he then gave to Athena, and crowned the fisherman Diktys (brother of Polydectes) king of the island. The oracular saying that he would kill his grandfather was fulfilled when he unintentionally struck Acrisius with a discus during a game. Perseus assumed the kingship of Tiryns in exchange for that of Argos, and founded Mideia and Mycenae. He was the ancestor of Heracles and the Heraclids.—The unusually detailed stories about Perseus have certain traditional variations, but the core of the legend is not affected by them.

Petasus In ancient Greece a broad-brimmed hat, worn by Macedonians in the time of Alexander the Great for traveling as well as combat. The winged petasus was a characteristic feature of Hermes, who is often represented wearing this headgear.

Phaeacians A people mentioned in the *Odyssey* who inhabited the island of Scheria. They were famous for their ships, each of which (according to legend) could reach its goal even without a helmsman and in the thickest fog. The Phaeacian king, *Alcinous, extended help to Jason and Medea and received Odysseus hospitably after he had suffered shipwreck. At the court of Alcinous, Odysseus told of his lengthy adventures on his homeward journey from Troy. To speed him along, Alcinous let Odysseus take one of the Phaeacian ships with him. However, an angry Poseidon turned it into stone.—In ancient legend the country of Phaeacia was famous for its wealth and reputed to be a land of milk and honey.

Phaedra Daughter of the Cretan king Minos and his wife Pasiphae, she was the sister of Ariadne and the wife of Theseus. Phaedra fell in love with her stepson Hippolytus, who refused her seductive advances. Fearing discovery by her husband, Phaedra accused Hippolytus to Theseus of having pursued her, whereupon Theseus, who believed her, prayed to Poseidon to destroy his son. As Hippolytus rode along the shore in his chariot, a bull rose up from the sea and the frightened horses dragged Hippolytus to his death. Phaedra committed suicide.—Hippolytus was worshiped in Troezen, in addition to Athens and other places later on. He played a sacrificial role in the "Potiphar" narrative (just outlined), variations of which occur frequently in Greek legend. His fate was treated by Sophocles and twice by Euripides, though only the later version of Euripides has been preserved.

Phaethon In Greek mythology, a son of *Helios, who permitted him to drive the sun chariot for one day. Approaching the earth too closely, Phaethon would have set the world on fire but was killed by Zeus with a thunderbolt. He plunged into the Eridanus River. His lamenting sisters, the Heliades, were turned into poplar trees.

Phaethusa One of the *Heliades. Daughter of Helios (perhaps also of Apollo), she was the sister of *Lampetia, and the half-sister of Phaethon. After Phaethon's death, Phaethusa mourned so deeply for him that she turned into a poplar tree; her tears became amber.

Phaidimos One of the numerous children of Amphion and *Niobe.

Phaistos 1. Son of Zeus and Europa, he was the father of *Rhadamanthys, according to Cretan tradition. 2. King of Sicyon and son of Heracles, he left his homeland after an oracle advised him to emigrate to Crete.

Phaisyle One of the *Hyades and daughter of Atlas and Pleione.

Phaleros An Argonaut and the eponym of the harbor of Phaleron.

Phantasos Son of Somnus and god of dreams, he appeared in people's dreams. Phantasos possessed the power of turning himself into earth, rock, water, trees, and other natural objects.

Phaon In Greek legend, a very old, ugly boatman from Mytilene (on Lesbos). Aphrodite gave him a small container of ointment, from which he gained great beauty. According to a later tradition, the lyric poet Sappho fell in love with him but killed herself when he rejected her.

Pharos An island near Alexandria on which a lighthouse 590 feet high was constructed by Sostratos under Ptolemy II. Completed in 280 B.C., the lighthouse was counted among the Seven Wonders of the World.

Phasis (the present-day Rion or Rioni) A river of Colchis arising in the Caucasus mountains and flowing into the Black Sea. Legend tells of the Argonauts sailing along this river.

Phegeus 1. King of Phegea in Arcadia and son of Inachus. As a priest of Apollo, he purified Alcmaeon, one of the Epigoni against Thebes, for the murder of his mother, but later killed him on account of another crime. One strand of the tradition also speaks of Phegeus himself being killed, probably together with his wife. 2. A companion of Aeneas on his journey from Troy to Italy, who was killed by Turnus.

Pheidias (*Phidias*) A Greek sculptor from Athens, born ca. 490 B.C. He was a friend and adviser of Perikles, who appointed him artistic director of the revision of the Athenian Acropolis. Together with Polyclitus, Pheidias embodied the zenith of Greek plastic art. His most famous works (which can be roughly reconstructed from copies and descriptions) were the gold and ivory images of Athena Parthenos for the Parthenon in Athens and of Zeus for the temple of Zeus at Olympia. The ascription to him of other works is highly speculative.

Pheme (*Fama*) The Roman personification of quickly spreading rumor. In mythology, she was the daughter of the earth. Elevated to divine status by the time of Hesiod, she appeared in Virgil's epic as a horrifying creature with many jabbering mouths. Ovid represented her as a herald of truth and falsehood.

Phemius A singer and faithful servant of Odysseus, who was compelled by the suitors of Penelope to serve them. After his homecoming, Odysseus spared Phemius.

Pheres 1. A son of Jason and Medea. One strand of the tradition reports that Medea killed him as a child or that he was stoned to death by the Cretans. 2. The father of *Mermeros (2), the renowned maker of poison.

Pherusa One of the *Nereids.

Phidias *Pheidias.

Philammon Son of Apollo and *Chione (1), he was the twin brother of Autolycus, whose father however was Hermes. He married the nymph Argiope. An outstanding musician and poet, Philammon died in battle while defending the temple of Apollo at Delphi against *Phlegyas.

Philemon and Baucis An old Phrygian married couple whom Ovid describes in his *Metamorphoses* as living together harmoniously in a humble cottage. Once Zeus and Hermes, disguised as travelers, stopped at their hut and were treated with great kindness. To show their appreciation, the divine wayfarers turned the couple's cottage into a temple, in which Philemon and Baucis then served as priest and priestess. Having asked to be allowed to die together, Philemon was transformed in old age into an oak tree and Baucis into a linden tree.— The motif of the gods visiting human beings in disguised form and testing them with respect to hospitality is relatively frequent in Greek legend. Combined with it is the theme of the gods rewarding or punishing a friendly or unfriendly reception. In this story, for example, a flood was sent to punish all those who had not received them.

Philippides (*Phidippides*) A famous Athenian runner. According to legend, he covered the 150 miles between Athens and Sparta in two days in order to get help from the Spartans against the Persians, who had landed at Marathon.

Philoctetes A hero from Thessaly, he was the son of *Poeas and Demonassa. Philoctetes is said to have been the only friend of Heracles who was willing to kindle the funeral pyre on which Heracles lay outstretched when that hero urgently implored him. For this deed he was given Heracles' famous bow with the poisoned arrows and became a famous archer himself.— In the Trojan War Philoctetes, as one of Helen's suitors, contributed a contingent of seven ships. During a temporary stopover en route to Troy, a snake bit him, inflicting a wound which did not heal and emitted a noxious odor. Because of the wound, the Greeks left Philoctetes on the island of Lemnos, where he passed many solitary years. His rescue followed only after it was prophesied to the Achaians, whose nine-year siege of Troy had proved futile, that they would not capture the city without the bow and arrows of Heracles. Having been brought to Troy, Philoctetes killed Paris and found a cure for his suffering. After the fall of the city, he returned uninjured to his homeland. One strand of the tradition reports that he also went to Italy and founded several cities there.—All three of the great Greek tragedians (Aeschylus, Sophocles, and Euripides) wrote a tragedy about Philoctetes, but only the one by Sophocles has survived.

Philoetius The cowherd of Odysseus, Philoetius remained faithful to his master during the latter's long absence and fought with him (after his return) against the suitors of Penelope.

Philomela The sister of *Procne. After *Tereus had raped her, he tore out her tongue, condemning her to silence.

Philomelus Son of Jason and Demeter, and brother of Plutos, he was reputed to be the inventor of the chariot.

Philonoe A daughter of *Iobates, she married *Bellerophon, to whom she bore several children.

Philonome The second wife of Cycnus, king of Coloni. She tried to seduce her stepson Tenes, but was rebuffed by him. Believing his wife at first, Cycnus put his son and his daughter Hemithea in a chest and cast them out to sea. The two floated ashore onto the island of Leukophrys, where the inhabitants made Tenes their king and named their island after him. Later when Cycnus discovered his wife's treachery, he set sail to seek reconciliation with his children. Tenes remained adamant, however; he cut through the rigging of his father's ship and drove it away from his territory.—According to another version, Cycnus soon realized that his wife was lying and buried her alive.

Philyra Daughter of Oceanus and Tethys, she may have been the wife of Nauplius, to whom she bore several children. By Kronos she became the mother of the Centaur *Chiron, whose hybrid form was accounted for in legend with two possible explanations: either Kronos had turned himself into a stallion in order to conceal himself from his lawful wife, Rhea, or Philonome had assumed the form of a mare in order to escape the god. When she gave birth to Chiron, she was appalled at the infant's appearance and prayed to Zeus to change her into a linden tree.

Phineus 1. King of Salmydessos in Thrace and son of Agenor (according to another version, Phoenix). Phineus was a prophet about whom legend gives varying accounts. His first wife was

*Cleopatra (1). After her death he married Idaia, who persecuted her two stepchildren with implacable hatred, inducing her husband to blind them or have them blinded. When the Argonauts passed through Salmydessos and saw what had happened, they deprived the king of his own sight to punish him for his shameful deed.—According to another version, Helios blinded Phineus either because when faced with the choice between death and blindness he had preferred blindness, or because he had betrayed the secrets of the gods. Finally, the Harpies punished him further by taking away his nourishment and defiling whatever remained so that Phineus came close to starvation. Out of compassion or in exchange for Phineus's promise to show them the way, the Argonauts ordered the *Boreades to banish the Harpies once and for all. 2. An uncle of Andromeda.

Phlegethon (*Pyriphlegethon*) One of the rivers of the underworld, it was pictured as a stream of fire into which robbers, murderers, and others were thrown.

Phlegyas A Lapith and ancestor of the Thessalian Phlegyae, he was a son of Ares and Chryse (or Dotis, in another version). His children were *Coronis (1) and possibly Ixion. When Apollo carried off Phlegyas's daughter, he burned down the god's temple at Delphi. The legend reports that Apollo then killed him, dispatched him to Hades, and suspended a huge stone over his head. Other traditions speak of him also as a ferryman in the underworld.

Phlogios One of the four horses of Ares.

Phobetor God of dreams and a legendary son of Somnus. In dreams he could assume the aspect of animals, for example, birds or snakes.

Phobos 1. God of panic fear, he was born to Ares and Aphrodite. He and his brothers accompanied their father into battle.—*Deimos and Phobos. 2. One of the four horses of Ares.

Phocis In antiquity a coastal region in central Greece situated north of the Corinthian Gulf, it included Mount Parnassus and the prominent cities of Delphi, Amphikleia, and Crisa.

Phocus Son of Aeacus of Aegina and *Psamathe (1), he emigrated to Phocis and colonized the area near Delphi. Eventually he was killed by his half-brothers Peleus and Telamon.

Phoebe 1. Epithet of Artemis as goddess of the moon. 2. Daughter of the Titan Uranus and Gaia, she was the wife of Coeus and by him the mother of Leto and Asteria; Apollo and Artemis were her grandchildren. Before the advent of Apollo, she was often considered the mistress of Delphi. 3. Daughter of Leucippus (a descendant of Perseus) and Philodike.

Phoenix 1. King of Phoenicia and son of Agenor, he was the husband of Perimele and by her the father of Astypaleia and Europa. In addition, he probably had a series of sons from extramarital unions. When *Europa was forcibly abducted, Phoenix sent his brothers and children out to retrieve her. 2. King of the Dolopians, he was the son of Amyntor and Hippodameia (or Kleobule, according to another version) and a participant in the Calydonian boar hunt. One form of the tradition relates that Phoenix was incited by his mother to seduce the concubine of his father, whom the latter loved very deeply. On discovering the intrigue, Amyntor condemned his son to perpetual childlessness. Phoenix then fled to Peleus, whose son Achilles he tutored, receiving in return sovereignty over the Dolopians. According to another version, Amyntor blinded Phoenix on account of his shameful act, but he was healed by *Chiron. 3. The Greek name of the bird venerated by the Egyptians as sacred, which they regarded as a manifestation of Re or Osiris. Because it rose again newly constituted after being consumed by fire, this bird symbolized eternal life for the Greeks.

Phoibos Another name for Apollo as god of sun and light.

Pholus A Centaur famed for his friendly nature, who once entertained Heracles hospitably. When Heracles asked for wine that belonged to all the Centaurs in common, Pholus finally acquiesced, with the result that the other Centaurs appeared and a fierce struggle ensued in which Heracles retained the upper hand. Pholus met his death while scrutinizing an arrow tipped with the Hydra's poison that had just fallen on his foot.

Phorbas 1. Son of Lapithes (a descendant of Apollo) or of Triopas, and king of Thessaly. Emigrating to Elis, he assisted the king there, Alektor, in his combat with Pelops. In return he received part of the dominion over Elis, which he bequeathed to his son Augeas. Of Phorbas it is also told that he colonized Rhodes and freed it from a plague of serpents. 2. A leader of the Phrygians in the battle against the Greeks during the Trojan War. He possessed large herds and was beloved of Hermes.

Phorcys 1. An ancient sea god and son of Pontus (according to another version, Oceanus) and Gaia. Among his several siblings were Thaumas and Nereus. Marrying Ceto, Phorcys became through her the father of the *Graces and the *Gorgons. Occasionally the Hesperides are also identified as his daughters. 2. A Trojan killed in the Trojan War by *Aias the Great. 3. An ally of Turnus in his combat with Aeneas.

Phoroneus The legendary first king of Argos, his several children included a daughter, Niobe, who was thought to be the first mortal woman and Zeus's first love. Of Phoroneus it is related that he was the first human being in the Argolid to erect an altar to Hera. Moreover, one strand of the tradition asserts that it was Phoroneus rather than *Prometheus who first brought fire to mortals.

Phosphorus The morning star. Phosphorus was the Greek name for the planet Venus when seen before sunrise.

Phrixus Son of Athamas and Nephele in Greek mythology, he was the brother of *Helle. Wishing to get rid of Phrixus and his sister on account of her own children, his stepmother Ino used a drought as the pretext for falsifying an utterance of the Delphic oracle to the effect that Phrixus and Helle would have to be sacrificed. Nephele came to the aid of her children with a golden ram, intended to carry them back to Colchis. En route, Helle fell to her death but Phrixus reached their destination. Received by King *Aeetes, he was married to the king's daughter Chalciope. The golden ram's fleece was hung up in the grove of Ares.—*Argonauts.

Phrontis One of the sons of *Phrixus and *Chalciope.

Phrygia An ancient province in the interior of western Asia Minor inhabited by Indo-European Phrygians, who probably immigrated from Thrace ca. 1200 B.C. Their empire, founded ca. 800 B.C. with its capital at Gordion, was destroyed by the Cimmerians at the beginning of the 7th century B.C. Their worship was devoted chiefly to the goddess *Cybele.

Phthia 1. A daughter of Amphion and *Niobe, who was killed by Artemis. 2. The capital of Achaea in Thessaly, also called Phthiotis. In legend it is frequently referred to as the birthplace of Achilles and the adopted home of Peleus.

Phthios A son of Poseidon and the eponym of *Phthia (2).

Phylacus The father of *Iphiclus, who promised freedom to the prophet *Melampus, as well as his own or his son's cattle, if the seer would reveal why Iphiclus was childless. The different versions of the legend vary in detail.

Phylios A king of Thrace who may have been the father of *Phyllis.

Phyllis In Greek legend, a Thracian princess whose father may have been Phylios (another version names Lycurgus). She fell in love with *Demophon (1), who either promised to marry her or actually did, but then departed for Athens. Since he did not return for a long time, Phyllis believed that he had abandoned her. She therefore killed herself and was transformed into a leafless almond tree. The tree put forth leaves when Demophon returned to Thrace and embraced it.—This story belongs to the genre of plant metamorphosis narratives, which was especially popular in the Hellenistic age.

Phyxios God of fugitives; his name was an epithet of Zeus.

Picus An ancient Roman nature divinity, he was often identified as the son of Saturn and Venilia. One strand of the tradition, preserved by Virgil, names him as the father of *Faunus and the grandfather of Latinus. The legend relates that Circe fell in love with Picus, but turned him into a woodpecker when he rebuffed her. Other traditions also connect the name Picus with "woodpecker," hence the story that he provided Romulus and Remus with nourishment. Among the Romans the woodpecker always played a certain role, for example, in augury.

Pieria A district in northern Greece (Macedonia), it was the legendary birthplace of the Muses or *Pierides.

Pierides 1. Epithet of the *Muses. 2. The nine daughters of *Pieros, who challenged the Muses to a singing competition. Defeated by their rivals, they were changed into magpies or jackdaws.

Pieros King of Pella in Macedonia, he was the father of the *Pierides and possibly the father of Hyacinthus by the Muse Clio .

Pietas Worshiped by the Romans as the divine personification of "reverence," Pietas was understood as the virtue of performing one's duty toward the gods and the fatherland but also, in the private realm, toward one's parents and children. In 181 B.C. a temple was dedicated to Pietas in Rome, and she had another sanctuary (not datable) in the vicinity of the Circus Flaminius. Pietas was also a favorite subject on coins, especially as *Pietas Augusta* during the imperial period. Occasionally individual Romans received the epithet *pius* as a mark of high honor. Their prototype, *pius Aeneas*, was considered the purest embodiment of Roman Pietas.

Pietas Roman goddess

Pillars of Heracles The ancient term for the cliffs on either side of the straits of Gibraltar. According to legend, they were erected by Heracles when he crossed the channel between Spain and Africa as a way of demonstrating his presence.

Pilumnus An ancient Roman peasant god, he was the legendary inventor of the pestle.

Pindar (*Pindaros*) A Greek poet from the vicinity of Thebes, he lived from ca. 522 or 518 until 445 B.C. From an aristocratic background, he was educated as a poet, musician, and choral leader in democratic Athens. Nevertheless, he kept his ties with the declining aristocracy, for whom his victory odes constituted a memorial. Restricting himself to choral lyric, Pindar brought this genre to perfection. Of his poems, the paeans and dithyrambs (hymns for festivals of Apollo and Dionysus) are preserved only in fragments, but the Epinician odes (victory songs distributed in four books according to the place of the competition) are nearly complete. These poems were written in the Doricizing, artificial dialect of choral lyric, each using new metrical forms (and melodies) and arranged in a pattern of strophe, antistrophe, and epode. The middle part treats a mythical event, thus moving the victor toward proximity with the gods and heroes. Pindar's language is often original, dark, and solemn.

Pirene Daughter of the river god Achelous, she was a nymph of the fountain by the same name, which was sacred to the Muses. The fountain sprang up under the hoofprint of *Pegasus.

Pirithous King of the Lapiths, he was the son of Ixion (or Zeus, in another version) and Dia, and the husband of Hippodameia, daughter of Adrastus. At his wedding, a battle arose between the Lapiths and the *Centaurs from which Pirithous emerged victorious.—Pirithous was the best friend of *Theseus, with whom he performed many daring exploits. For example, they tried to abduct Persephone and had to atone for their crime in Hades.

Pisa An area on the lower Alpheus River, which flows past Olympia. According to legend, it was conquered by immigrants from Elis, who accompanied Nestor to the Trojan War. From ca. 570 B.C., Pisa belonged to Elis.

Pisander A leader of the Myrmidons who accompanied Patroclus when the latter entered the battlefield wearing the armor of Achilles.

Pitane A Laconian nymph who became the mother of Evadne (1) by Poseidon.

Pittacus An arbiter between the nobility and the common people in Mytilene on Lesbos, he lived from 648 to 570 B.C. After the promulgation of superior legislation, he retired. Pittacus was counted among the Seven Wise Men of Greece.

Pittheus King of Troezen, he was a son of Pelops. One part of the legend names him as the father of Aethra and so the maternal grandfather of Theseus.

Pitys A nymph who was loved by both Boreas and Pan. As she fled from Boreas (or Pan, according to another version), she fell on a rock and was turned into a stone pine.

Plataea An ancient Boeotian city located south of Thebes. There in 479 B.C. the Greeks, led by Pausanias, won a victory over the Persians, led by Mardonius. According to legend, the place-name could be traced back to a daughter of *Asopos and Metope.

Pleiades
The seven daughters
of Atlas and Pleione:
Alcyone
Asterope
Electra
Celaeno
Maia
Merope
Taygete

Pleiades In Greek mythology, the seven daughters of Atlas and the Oceanid *Pleione. The following star legend is connected with them: the famous hunter *Orion fell in love with the mother of the Pleiades, Pleione, and pursued her and her daughters for a long time. Finally Zeus put an end to the pursuit by translating Orion and the fugitives to heaven as constellations.

Pleione Daughter of Oceanus and Tethys, she was the wife of Atlas, to whom she bore numerous children, including the *Pleiades.

Pleisthenes A legendary Greek figure whose origin is a matter of great controversy. Frequently identified as king of Argos and Mycenae, he may have been the son of Atreus, but Pelops and Hippodameia are also mentioned as parents, which would make him a brother of Atreus and Thyestes. Homer refers to him frequently as the father of Agamemnon and

Menelaus. A further alternative is that Pleisthenes was the bastard son of Thyestes and Aerope, and thus the brother of Tantalus. A final possibility is that several persons with the same name are involved; this would account for the different theories.

Pluton (Latin, *Pluto*) An epithet of the Greek god *Hades, meaning "the wealthy one." Taken over by the Romans as a divinity, he was called Pluto or Dis Pater by them.

Plutos Greek god of wealth, he was the son of Iasion and the grain goddess Demeter, according to Hesiod. Viewed at first as a god who bestowed rich harvests, he evolved gradually into a god of all things signifying wealth. As lord of treasures from the earth, he came to be more and more closely associated with *Pluton, god of the underworld.—Aristophanes' familiar comedy *Plutus* portrays the blind god distributing his gifts unjustly among mortals until he is healed in a sanctuary of Asclepius.

Pluvius Roman god of rain. His name is also an epithet of Jupiter.

Podalirius Son of *Asclepius and Epione, he was a physician like his brother *Machaon, who is frequently mentioned together with him. Podalirius took part in the Trojan War and healed many heroes there, including Philoctetes. His cult was concentrated chiefly in Thessaly, southwest Asia Minor, and southern Italy. Possibly Carian in origin, he was reputed to be the founder of Syrnos.

Podarces The younger son of *Iphiclus. After the death of his brother *Protesilaus, he assumed command of the contingent of ships that Protesilaus had contributed for the Trojan War.

Podarge One of the *Harpies, and daughter of Thaumas and Electra, she was thought to be the mother of the windswift, immortal horses *Balios and Xanthus.

Poeas An Argonaut and son of Thaumakos, he was the husband of Demonassa and father of *Philoctetes. The tradition sometimes names Philoctetes and sometimes Poeas as the person who kindled the funeral pyre on which *Heracles lay atop Mount Oeta; the robe of Nessus had eaten into his skin and was torturing him horribly. In return for this act of friendship, Poeas received the bow and arrows of Heracles.

Poena Roman goddess of punishment, she corresponded to *Nemesis in Greek mythology.

Poliporthes (also *Ptoliporthes*) The son of Odysseus and Penelope who, according to legend, was conceived when Odysseus returned home after an absence of twenty years. His brother was Telemachus.

Polites 1. A son of Priam and Hecuba, of whom legend tells that he was the last of Priam's fifty sons to fall in the Trojan War (one son survived). 2. A boatman of Odysseus who was changed into a pig but regained his human form from Circe.

Pollux The Latin name for Polydeuces.— *Dioscuri.

Polybotes A giant and son of Gaia. In the battle with the gods, who triumphed over the giants, Poseidon vanquished Polybotes by means of a piece of land that had broken off from the island of Cos; subsequently the small island of Nisyrus arose from it.

Polybus 1. A king of Corinth who together with his wife Periboea or Merope raised the foundling Oedipus. 2. A suitor of Penelope. 3. One of the numerous sons of Antenor and Theano.

Polyclitus The
Doryphorus of Polyclitus
(ca. 430 B.C.)

Polyclitus A Greek sculptor from Argos, who lived from 460 to 420 B.C. He and Pheidias were the leading masters of Greek classical art. He devoted himself entirely to the masculine figure, which he brought to canonical status by achieving a balanced relationship between the standing leg and the free leg. Among his outstanding works are the *Doryphorus*, the *Diadumenus*, and the cult statue of Hera at Argos.

Polycrates Tyrant of Samos from 538 to 522 B.C., he controlled the Aegean Sea, had splendid buildings constructed, and patronized poets and scholars. Polycrates was taken prisoner by the Persians and crucified.—Schiller's ballad "The Ring of Polycrates" drew on an account by Herodotus.

Polydamas 1. Son of the Trojan *Antenor and Theano, he was the husband of *Lykaste, a daughter of Priam. Like his father, he was accused of betraying the Trojan cause in the war with the Achaians. 2. Son of the Trojan *Panthoos and Phrontis, he was a close friend of Hector, the two having been born (according to legend) on the same night. Gifted with the ability to foretell the future and to read the flight of birds, he fought bravely in the Trojan War. He was killed either by Achilles or by one of the two *Aiases.

Polydamna Wife of the Egyptian king Thoon, who kept watch over the mouth of the Nile, she taught Helen the use of healing herbs.

Polydectes King of Seriphus, he received Danae at his court; she had been repudiated by her father and had borne a son (Perseus) to Zeus. Polydectes fell in love with Danae, but she did not requite his love. In order to remove Danae's son, who functioned as his mother's guardian, from the scene, Polydectes ordered him to fetch the head of the Gorgon Medusa. The young man succeeded in performing this task with the help of the gods. Upon returning to the court, he showed Polydectes his booty, the sight of which turned the king to stone.

Polydeuces The Greek name for one of the two *Dioscuri.

Polydora 1. Daughter of *Meleager and Cleopatra. According to one strand of the tradition, she married *Protesilaus. 2. Daughter of Peleus and Antigone (or Polymela), half-sister of Achilles, and wife of Boros. Through the river god *Spercheios, she became the mother of Menestheus.

Polydore One of the fifty daughters of *Danaus, she married Dryops and murdered him on their wedding night.

Polydorus 1. King of Thebes, son of *Cadmus and Harmonia, husband of Nycteus, and father of *Labdakos. According to the legend, he died when his son was still a child. 2. The youngest son of Priam and Laothoe (in another version, Hecuba). Since he was too young to take part in the Trojan War, Polydorus was sent to the Thracian king Polymestor with an abundance of treasures for safekeeping. But Polymestor killed him and seized the treasures for himself.—In another version Polydorus was killed by Achilles.

Polyeidus A prophet from Corinth, he recalled to life *Glaucus (3), a son of Minos from Crete, who had fallen into a honey jar and drowned.— Polyeidus advised *Bellerophon on how to capture *Pegasus.

Polyhymnia The *Muse of ceremonial song, to whom other functions were also ascribed. For example, she was considered the Muse of geometry and choreography and even sometimes of agriculture.

Polyhymnia One of the Muses

Polymela Daughter of the Thessalian king Actor, she was the first wife of Peleus, according to one strand of the tradition, and the mother of a daughter likewise named Polymela. She is said to have hanged herself because she believed that her husband Peleus had left her for another woman.

Polymestor King of Thrace, he was the husband of Ilione and the father of *Deipylos. After he had killed *Polydorus (2) in order to take possession of the latter's fortune, the victim's mother (Hecuba) wreaked her revenge, according to one strand of the tradition, by blinding Polymestor and killing his son.

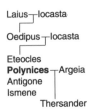

Laius┬Iocasta

Oedipus┬Iocasta

Eteocles
Polynices┬Argeia
Antigone
Ismene
      Thersander

Polynices In Greek mythology, he was the son of *Oedipus and *Iocasta, the brother of *Eteocles, *Ismene, and *Antigone, and the son-in-law of *Adrastus (1). After their father had gone into exile, the brothers agreed to alternate the rulership of Thebes between them every year. But Eteocles, who was chosen to hold the first term, refused to honor the agreement; the result was the expedition of the *Seven against Thebes.

Polypemon (also *Damastes*) Another name for *Procrustes.

Polypheides Member of a famous family of seers, he was the son of Mantios, brother of *Cleitus, and father of Theoklymenos, who could likewise tell the future.

Polyphemus A famous *Cyclopes, he was born to Poseidon and the nymph Thoosa. When Odysseus came upon the cave of Polyphemus as he journeyed homeward with his companions, the giant ate several of the companions. However, Odysseus then succeeded in making Polyphemus drunk and gouging out his one eye. By tying themselves to the bodies of Polyphemus's sheep, the involuntary guests of the Cyclopes were able to escape.—In Hellenistic literature Polyphemus's love for the beautiful Nereid *Galatea is frequently treated along with the story of Acis (the son of a nymph) and Galatea, in which the jealous Polyphemus crushed Acis to death. Galatea then turned her lover Acis into a river god, and his blood into a fountain that gushed forth from the rock with which Polyphemus had killed him.

Polyphemus The blinding of the one-eyed Cyclops; from an early Greek vase painting (6th century B.C.)

Polyphontes 1. Son of Autophonos, he was a Theban who helped Eteocles to defend Thebes against the Seven. Aepytus killed him. 2. The murderer of *Cresphontes of Messenia and his two elder sons, Polyphontes seized the throne and forced the king's widow, Merope, to marry him. She bore him three children. Aepytus, the youngest son of Cresphontes, who had escaped death at the hands of Polyphontes, killed him when he reached manhood.

Polypoites 1. Son of Odysseus and Kallidike, who succeeded her mother on the throne of the Thesprotians. 2. Son of *Pirithous and Hippodameia; as a suitor of Helen, he took part in the Trojan War. Said to have been among the heroes who hid inside the wooden horse, he distinguished himself at the funeral games for Patroclus.

Polyxena A figure not mentioned in Homer who is named in other traditions as the youngest daughter of Priam and Hecuba. One version reports of her that she accompanied her father when he went to the Greek camp to ransom the dead body of his son Hector. Later, after the fall of Troy, the shade of Achilles is supposed to have demanded the sacrifice of Polyxena in order to secure favorable winds for the Greek fleet, and so Neoptolemus cremated Polyxena on his father's grave. Euripides locates the event not at Troy but in Thrace, where the Achaian ships lay becalmed. Here Odysseus played a particularly reprehensible role by insisting on the sacrifice of Polyxena, whereas Agamemnon interceded to try to save her.

Polyxo 1. Wife of Nycteus, king of Thebes, and probably the mother of *Antiope. 2. Priestess of Apollo on Lemnos and nurse of *Hypsipyle. In the legendary account of her, she urged the women of Lemnos to kill their husbands and later counseled the queen of Lemnos to receive the Argonauts for the sake of repopulating the island.

Pomona Roman goddess of gardens

Pomona Roman goddess of gardens and fruit trees, she was venerated in a grove situated on the outskirts of Rome. No festival dedicated to her is known. She was widely regarded as the wife of Vertumnus but also as the beloved of Picus. Over time her cult lost much of its meaning.

Pontos (Latin, *Pontus*) 1. An ancient coastal region in northeast Asia Minor bordering on the Black Sea. In 280 B.C. it withdrew from the Seleucid kingdom as the Pontic kingdom, and in 63 B.C. it became the province of Pontus under Roman hegemony. 2. Both son and husband of Gaia, he was the father of numerous children, including Thaumas, Nereus, Phorcys, and Ceto. Pontos was thought to personify the broad sea.

Portunus Roman god of harbors whose main festival, the Portunalia, was celebrated on August 17. From the fact that he was represented with a key and that this key played a major cultic role, it can be inferred that he simultaneously functioned as god of doors. He was known to the Greeks under the name of *Melicertes (*Palaemon*).

Poseidon Greek god of the sea, he was the son of Kronos and Rhea and one of the twelve Olympian gods. Usually represented with a trident, which he used to churn up the sea or to split chunks of rock, he was also imagined as equine in form. His wife, Amphitrite, bore him several children. In addition, he possessed a great number of illegitimate offspring, including monsters and giants, from his numerous love affairs. A famous legend tells of how he and Apollo built the walls of Troy for an agreed-upon payment; when they were cheated of their wages, Poseidon dispatched a monster from the sea to which Hesione, the king's daughter, was supposed to be sacrificed. This was one reason for Poseidon's fierce opposition to the Trojans in the Trojan War and his support for the Greeks.—It is uncertain whether Poseidon was always the foremost sea god. In any case his cult extended over all of Greece from an early date, and socially prominent families especially liked to call him their ancestral father.—Poseidon's Roman analog was *Neptune.

Poseidon with his trident

Poseidon with dolphin

Potamiades A designation in ancient literature for the river nymphs.

Potina Roman goddess of medicines for children.

Praxiteles A Greek sculptor active in Athens from ca. 370 to 320 B.C. Celebrated for his marble statues, he also sculpted statues in bronze. His figures are characterized by a fine-lined harmony, a naturalistic handling of anatomy and drapery, and a convincing rendering of inner states. His chief work is the *Aphrodite of Cnidos* (it survives in Roman copies), the first known life-sized Greek representation of the nude female body. The original of his *Hermes with the infant Dionysus* is preserved in Olympia (with the back part unfinished).

Priam Legendary king of Troy, son of Laomedon, and husband of Hecuba, he had fifty sons and a number of daughters, his most noted children being Hector, Paris, Helenus, Deiphobos, Cassandra, and Polyxena. Some of his progeny

Priam Depiction of Priam on an amphora; work of the Attic vase painter Euthymides (turn of the 6th or 5th century)

derived from his numerous concubines. It was during Priam's reign that the Trojan War took place, in which he lost almost all of his sons. The death of Hector particularly grieved him, and he went at night into the Greek camp to ransom the corpse from Achilles. When the enemy conquered the city of Troy after a siege lasting for years, the aged Priam sought refuge at the altar of Zeus, where he was nevertheless slain by Neoptolemus. The tradition reports that he remained unburied and without the funeral honors due to him as king.

Priapus Probably the name of a fertility god from Asia Minor whose original center of worship was Lampsacus on the Hellespont. He was reputed to be the son of Dionysus and Aphrodite, though occasionally Hermes is given as his father. According to legend, Priapus once approached the sleeping nymph *Lotis, but the braying of a donkey woke her in time. In his anger Priapus killed the donkey, which was placed among the stars.—As a fertility god, Priapus was actually represented in the form of a wooden figure painted red with a large phallus; such figures also served as scarecrows in gardens. During the time of Alexander the Great, Priapus's cult spread over large portions of Greece and beyond. Worshiped in addition as a god of love, Priapus functioned as guardian of sailors and fishermen.

Procas King of Alba Longa, whose legendary reign occurred twelve generations after Aeneas.

Procles Son of the Heraclid Aristodemus and brother of Eurysthenes, he was raised by his uncle Theras after his father died. Later he founded a kingdom in Lacedaemon.

Procne Daughter of Pandion and Zeuxippe, she was the wife of *Tereus, Thracian king and son of Ares. He fell in love with Procne's sister *Philomela, seduced her, and then cut out her tongue so that she would not divulge anything to his legitimate wife. Nevertheless, Philomela succeeded in representing what had happened on a piece of material and had the latter secretly conveyed to her sister. Procne avenged the wrong done to her by killing Itylus, the son she had born to Tereus, and serving him to her husband at a meal. Tereus overtook Procne and her sister in flight, and all three were turned into birds: Procne into a nightingale, Tereus into a hoopoe, and Philomela into a swallow.—The legend about Procne has other versions too.

Procris In Attic legend she was the daughter of Erechtheus and the wife of *Cephalus, who killed her probably by mistake.

Procrustean bed *Procrustes.

Procrustes (actually *Damastes) A legendary Greek figure, he was a huge monster and highwayman who stretched or truncated the limbs of travelers until they fit into either his short or his long bed. Because he stretched the limbs of short people, he received the name Procrustes ("the stretcher"). Procrustes was overcome by *Theseus, who put an end to his evil doings.—"Procrustean bed" has the figurative meaning of a rigid schema demanding laborious adaptation by the individual.

Proetus Son of Abas, a king of Argos, he was the twin brother of *Acrisius, with whom (legend tells) he was already at enmity in their mother's womb. Driven out of Argos, he became king of Tiryns. When his wife *Anteia (also named Stheneboea) conceived a passion for *Bellerophon only to be rejected by him, she intrigued for so long against him that her husband banished Bellerophon from the court.—The daughters of Proetus were punished with madness because they despised the cult of Dionysus. According to another tradition, Hera, having been insulted, inflicted sickness on them. However, with the possible exception of one daughter (Iphinoe), they were healed by the prophet *Melampus in exchange for the surrender of part of the kingdom of Tiryns.

Promachos 1. Son of King *Aeson of Thessaly and his wife Alkimede, he was the brother of Jason and the half-brother of Pelias. 2. Son of Parthenopaeus by Clymene and one of the Epigoni, he was killed at Thebes.

Iapetus—Clymene
|
Epimetheus
Atlas
Menoetius
Prometheus
|
Deucalion—Pyrrha

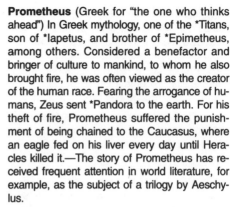

Prometheus (Greek for "the one who thinks ahead") In Greek mythology, one of the *Titans, son of *Iapetus, and brother of *Epimetheus, among others. Considered a benefactor and bringer of culture to mankind, to whom he also brought fire, he was often viewed as the creator of the human race. Fearing the arrogance of humans, Zeus sent *Pandora to the earth. For his theft of fire, Prometheus suffered the punishment of being chained to the Caucasus, where an eagle fed on his liver every day until Heracles killed it.—The story of Prometheus has received frequent attention in world literature, for example, as the subject of a trilogy by Aeschylus.

Prometheus An eagle devours the liver, i.e., vital energy of Prometheus; painting on a bowl from Caere

Pronoia Possibly the mother of *Deucalion by Prometheus.

Proserpina The Latin name for the Greek goddess *Persephone, whom the Romans incorporated into their cultic life.

Proserpina

Prometheus as sculptor

Protesilaus Thessalian king and son of *Iphiclus and Diomedeia, he married *Laodameia (1) (or Polydora, according to another version). As one of Helen's suitors, he entered the Trojan War with a contingent of forty ships. At Troy he was the first to disembark and the first Greek to meet his death.

Proteus An old man of the sea, he was a son of Oceanus and Tethys and the father of Eidothea. He lived on Pharos and kept watch over the seals of Poseidon. Like many sea gods, he possessed the gifts of transformation and prophecy. One strand of the tradition also identified Proteus as king of Egypt.

Proto One of the *Nereids.

Protogeneia 1. Daughter of *Deucalion and Pyrrha. 2. Daughter of Erechtheus and Praxithea, whose father was probably *Cephissus.

Psamathe 1. A *Nereid who did not return the love felt for her by Aeacus. Yet since she could not elude him, she became the mother of *Phocus by him. Later she married Proteus. 2. Daughter of Krotopos of Argos, she became the mother of *Linus (1) by Apollo.

Psyche An unusually beautiful king's daughter who aroused the jealousy of Venus. Venus persuaded her son Amor to fill Psyche with love for the ugliest man of all. Instead, however, Amor himself fell in love with Psyche. He put her in a splendid palace where he visited her every night, though he insisted that she neither ask him to tell her his name nor demand to see him. But goaded by her two sisters, who stirred up doubt and curiosity in her, Psyche lit a lamp one night and recognized Amor, whose beauty compared with her own, to be her lover. Amor woke up, expressed his anger at her for disobeying him, and left her. In despair Psyche set out in search of her beloved. On her way she came to a temple of Venus. Venus treated her like a slave, forcing her to perform onerous tasks, which Psyche was only able to manage with the help afforded her by the compassion of others. Finally Zeus took pity on her, immortalized her, and (with the consent of Venus) reunited her with Amor.—The tale of Amor and Psyche, handed down in the *Metamorphoses* of Apuleius, exerted a lasting influence on subsequent literature and art. It has also received many allegorical interpretations.

Psyche in mourning

Psychopompus Epithet of Hermes as guide of souls into the underworld.

Ptah The chief god of Memphis in Egypt, he was usually represented anthropomorphically and was worshiped from the time of the fifth dynasty as a creator god. The Greeks frequently connected him with Hephaestus.

Pterelaus King at Taphos and son of Taphius, he was either the son or (according to another version) the grandson of Poseidon. In the legend Pterelaus, father of six sons and a daughter named *Comaetho (2), had a golden hair, which made him immortal. Because her father would not tolerate her love for his enemy Amphitryon, Comaetho pulled this hair out. As a result, the Taphians were conquered and Pterelaus died. Amphitryon also killed Comaetho.

Pygmalion 1. Brother of *Dido, who fled from him and founded Carthage. 2. King of Cyprus and a misogynist, he nonetheless fell in love with the ivory image of a woman that he himself had created. Aphrodite acceded to his request that she vivify his creation. The two then married and had a child named Paphos.

Pylades Son of *Strophius, who was king of Phocis and an uncle of *Orestes. Orestes grew up at the court of Strophius. As his cousin's best friend, Pylades later married Orestes' sister *Electra.

Pylon One of the *Lapiths, he was killed by Polypoites.

Pylos A Greek port city in Messenia situated on the Gulf of Navarino on the Ionian Sea. According to legend, the area was ceded to Neleus after Pelias drove him out of Iolcus. Pylos was also thought to have been the home of the Homeric king Nestor.—In 1939, the remains of a Mycenaean palace (possibly Nestor's), including a two-story, richly furnished megaron along with a late Mycenaean citadel, were uncovered near a group of beehive and chamber tombs from the Mycenaean period.

Pyramus and Thisbe A Babylonian story tells of this young couple whose parents did not wish them to marry. The lovers could only speak with each other through a chink in the common wall of their adjoining houses. One day they agreed to meet secretly at the tomb of Ninus outside the entrance to the city. Arriving there first, Thisbe was forced to flee by a lion, which snatched her veil and tore it up. When Pyramus appeared and saw the veil, he believed that his beloved had been killed; in his grief he committed suicide. Thisbe returned, found her dead lover, and likewise ended her life.

Pyrene A woman who gave birth to a snake after she had been raped by Heracles.

Pyrgo Having served Priam as his children's nurse, she migrated with Aeneas from Troy to Italy.

Pyriphlegethon Another name for the underworld river *Phlegethon.

Pyrrha 1. Daughter of *Epimetheus and Pandora. She married her cousin *Deucalion (1), the son of Prometheus, and bore him several children. Legend presented her as the first mortal woman and, together with her husband, as a survivor of the great flood. 2. Daughter of Creon. 3. The name given to Achilles when he lived disguised as a girl at the court of Lycomedes, king of Scyros.

Pyrrhus Another name for *Neoptolemus.

Pythia The prophetess who served as the female medium for the oracle of Apollo at Delphi. Although an older woman, she dressed like a young maiden. During the time of the oracle's greatest success, her office was held by more than one person. Although the details of oracular consultation are disputed, probably the responses were transposed by priests into verses that were often enigmatic. Hence the use of the term *Pythian* to mean "puzzling" in the sense of "hard to interpret."

Pythian games The Panhellenic games staged at Delphi at the foot of Mount Parnassus that were founded, according to legend, by Apollo after he had killed the Python. Despite the athletic events, these games were predominantly musical in character. Originally they took place every eight years, but from 582 B.C. they were held every four years. At first hardly less important than the Olympian games, they suffered a decline from the end of the second century B.C. In the fourth century B.C., the names of the victors (*Pythionikai*) in the contests were published.

Python In Greek mythology, a mighty dragon or serpent that lived in the vicinity of Delphi and was killed by Apollo. The *Pythian games are supposed to have been named after the monster.

Quadriga In antiquity a chariot for racing, combat, or triumphal procession equipped with four horses yoked in a single row. The term was also used for the chariot in which Helios made his legendary daily journey across the heavens.

Quadriga Zeus in a quadriga fells the Titans

Quinquatrus Name given to the Roman festival in honor of *Minerva.

Quirinal (Latin, *collis Quirinalis*) One of the seven hills of Rome, located northeast of the Capitol. On it were the temple of Quirinus, the baths of Diocletine and Constantine, and the Palazzo del Quirinale, erected between 1574 and 1740 as the summer residence of the pope.

Quirinus 1. The name under which Romulus shared in divine honors after he had been translated to the realm of the gods. 2. A Roman war god who may also have been an agrarian god. He was worshiped together with Jupiter and Mars until this older triad was replaced by the divine trinity of Jupiter, Juno, and Minerva. Quirinus functioned as god of the nonaristocratic Roman citizenry and gave his name to the Quirinal, the hill on which his cult had been especially practiced from of old. Here in 292 B.C. a temple was dedicated to him which Augustus rebuilt when it was destroyed by fire. Quirinus was identified with Romulus at some point after the latter had been made divine as Quirinus (1).

Rainbow *Iris.

Raven A white bird sacred to Apollo. The god made its feathers black because it brought him bad news.

Remus The twin brother of *Romulus, with whom (according to legend) he was exposed as an infant. Romulus killed Remus when the latter ridiculed the newly founded Rome by leaping over its low city wall.

Rhacius The husband of *Manto and perhaps the father of *Mopsus (2).

Rhadamanthys A son of Zeus and Europa, he was the brother of Minos and, in many versions, also of Sarpedon. Before the reign of Minos he ruled Crete. Greek mythology praised his sense of justice and designated him a judge in the underworld along with Minos and Aeacus.

Rhampsinitus An Egyptian pharaoh, possibly Ramses III. Herodotus tells stories of thievery concerning his treasury.

Rhea (*Rheia*) Daughter of Uranus and Gaia and sister of the Titans, she married her brother Kronos. The mother of numerous gods, including

Rhea The goddess on her throne

Rhea The goddess hands Kronos a stone instead of the infant Zeus

Zeus, she was worshiped as a mother and earth goddess under the most diverse names: Bona Dea, Magna Mater, Cybele, et al.

Rhea Silvia A Roman vestal virgin also called *Ilia. Through Mars she became the mother of Romulus and Remus, although isolated sources name other fathers of the twins. Her uncle or father, Amulius, had her thrown into the Tiber to punish her for her pregnancy, but the river god made her his wife.

Rhesus King of Thrace and son of Eioneus (in another version, of Strymon), he was an ally of the Trojans. Among his possessions were two white horses and a golden chariot. Because of an oracle to the effect that Troy would remain invincible if Rhesus's horses could drink from the Scamander River, Diomedes and Odysseus captured them and killed Rhesus.

Rhodes The chief island of the Greek Dodecanese, located on the southeast rim of the Aegean Sea about 12 miles off the coast of Asia Minor. Sacred to Helios, it was named after *Rhodos (according to legend). Already thickly settled by Greeks in the Mycenaean period, it came under Dorian control ca. 1000 B.C. Its three most prominent city-states were Lindus, Ialysus, and Camirus. In antiquity the island was particularly famous for its *Colossus of Rhodes, counted among the Seven Wonders of the World.

Rhodope 1. A nymph and the wife of Haimos, she was transformed by the gods into a mountain after she and her husband assumed the names Hera and Zeus for themselves. 2. A mountain chain in the Balkan Peninsula between Macedonia and Thrace, with an altitude of 9,596 feet at its highest point.

Rhodos (also *Rhode*) Usually mentioned as the daughter of Poseidon and Amphitrite, she was either the lover or the wife of *Helios, whose official wife was *Perseis. Otherwise the eponym of the island of *Rhodes.

Rhoikos 1. A young man who spared the life of a dryad only to be blinded by her in response to an insult from him. 2. A centaur who was killed by Theseus at the wedding of *Pirithous and Hippodameia. 3. A giant killed by Dionysus in the war between the gods and the giants.

Ripheus 1. A Centaur whose height was so great that he towered above the trees. He was killed by Theseus at the wedding of *Pirithous and Hippodameia. 2. A Trojan companion of Aeneas whom the Greeks killed.

Robigo Roman goddess of grain or of the rust that could attack the grain.

Robigus Roman god of grain or of grain rust, whose festival was celebrated on April 25. He was often invoked together with *Flora.

Rome (*Roma*) The capital of the Roman Empire. Its origin and early history are bound up with a series of legends. Probably even from the fifth century B.C. the Greek historians connected the founding of Rome with the fall of Troy (an event dated much earlier), tracing the former back either to Aeneas, who fled from Troy to Italy, or to one of his descendants. The other version of Rome's founding revolves around *Romulus and Remus and the successors of Romulus, with certain functions concerning the consolidation of the state being attributed to each one.

Romula Designation for the fig tree under which a shepherd allegedly found Romulus and Remus.

Romulus Legendary founder and first king of Rome, he was the twin brother of *Remus.— *Romulus and Remus.

Romulus and Remus The pair of twins who are closely connected with the legend of Rome's founding. Their mother was Rhea Silvia (or Ilia), a daughter of King Numitor of Alba Longa, who was driven from the throne by his brother Amulius. Amulius appointed his niece as a vestal virgin, thereby forcing her to remain chaste so that his sovereignty would not be threatened by any male offspring she might produce (i.e., from Numitor's line). When Rhea Silvia nevertheless bore the twins Romulus and Remus to Mars, Amulius tried to get rid of the

Rome Personification of Roma as goddess of the city; after a miniature from the lectionary of Heinrich II

The Seven Hills of Rome
- Aventine
- Caelius
- Capitoline
- Esquiline
- Palatine
- Quirinal
- Viminalis

Rome
The seven mythical kings of Rome:
- Romulus
- Numa Pompilius
- Tullus Hostilius
- Ancus Marcius
- Tarquinius Priscus
- Servius Tullius
- Tarquinius Superbus

Romulus and Remus The Capitoline she-wolf who, according to legend, rescued the twins from the Tiber and suckled them

children by ordering that they be drowned in the Tiber. They were saved and nursed by a she-wolf, however, and then brought up by the herdsman, *Faustulus, and by *Acca Larentia. Learning about their real parentage once they had grown up and become herdsmen themselves, the two dislodged the usurper Amulius from the throne of Alba Longa and reinstated their grandfather Numitor as king. Then they resolved to found a new city on the spot where they had been saved. Unable to agree on a numen for the place, they consulted the gods by reading the flight of birds. The heaven-dwellers decided in favor of Romulus by sending him twelve birds and his brother only six. Therefore, the new city was called Rome. The offended Remus provoked Romulus so thoroughly that Romulus killed him and thus became sole king of Rome. As such, he attempted to populate the city by granting the right of asylum to many aliens and inviting the neighboring cities to a great festival for which he had numerous Sabine women captured in order to remedy the dearth of women in Rome. Eventually a reconciliation was achieved with the Sabines, whose king, Titus Tatius, governed Rome together with Romulus for several years. Subsequently Romulus again ruled alone until he was transported to heaven during a terrible thunderstorm that erupted during a military parade. The Romans then accorded Romulus divine honors under the name Quirinus. He came to be regarded as the author of Rome's oldest political and military institutions.

Rosalia A Roman festival celebrated in May or June, at which the tombs of the dead were adorned with roses in their honor. Probably oriental in origin, the festival is attested only for the imperial period, not in the age of the Roman Republic.

Rumina An Italian goddess, the meaning of whose name is not entirely clear. In antiquity it was probably derived from *rumis* ("mother's breast"), making Rumina a goddess of nursing, or suckling. Her sanctuary was located on the spot where legend related that Romulus and

Remus had been nursed by the she-wolf. Worshipers offered milk to the goddess, but not animals and presumably not wine either. Today the name Rumina is also occasionally derived from *ruma*, the Etruscan name for Rome. In that case, Rumina would be understood as a tutelary goddess of the city.

Rutulians (*Rutuli*) An Italian people whose most important king was Turnus. In the legend about Aeneas and his arrival in Italy, Turnus played a prominent role, including competition with Aeneas for the hand of *Lavinia. There is no account of the Rutulians in the historical period.

Sabazius A Thracian-Phrygian god equated by the Greeks with Dionysus.

Sabines (*Sabini*) In antiquity, a people of central Italy who played an important role in the mythical history of Rome (*Romulus and Remus). Generally the Sabines are counted among the most ancient inhabitants of the Roman hills (along with the Latins). Although defeated in the Sabine War of 304 to 290 B.C., they were granted Roman citizenship in 268 B.C.

Saces A friend of Turnus who urged him not to engage in combat with Aeneas.

Sagittarius The great constellation of the archer and the ninth sign of the zodiac. In the ancient imagination, Sagittarius was usually associated with *Krotos, a son of Pan.

Salacia Roman goddess of spring and wife of Neptune, she was known to the Greeks under the name of Amphitrite.

Salamis 1. A Greek island in the Saronic Gulf, west of Athens. Contested by Athens and Megara in antiquity, it was conquered by Athens in the 6th century B.C. In 480 B.C. the Greeks won their naval victory over the Persians at Salamis. 2. Daughter of Asopos and Metope, she was abducted by Poseidon to an Aegean island of the same name.

Salii Brotherhoods of priests consisting in each case of twelve members subject to a director. Attested for Rome (as well as some of the central Italian cities), they were divided into the Salii of the Palatine and the Salii of the Quirinal. In the spring and fall, mostly at the beginning and end of a military expedition, wearing war costumes, they performed dances in honor of the war god Mars (and other gods, too), for which they carried ancient shields. The legend about these mysterious shields, called *ancilia*, relates that a single such shield once fell from heaven at the instance of the gods as a pledge of sovereignty and public prosperity. Anxious lest the shield get lost, Numa Pompilius had eleven more of them copied from the original by a certain Mamurius. As recompense, Mamurius asked that he be mentioned in the song sung by the Salii while they danced.

Salmacis A spring in Caria near Halicarnassus, it was the scene of one of the stories of metamorphosis told by Ovid. The nymph of the spring (who went by the same name) fell passionately in love with *Hermaphroditus, a divine hermaphrodite born to Hermes and Aphrodite. When Hermaphrodites did not respond to her, Salmacis implored the gods to join her body with his forever. After the two had been joined at the spring, everyone who bathed in it was turned into a hermaphrodite. In antiquity, the legend was interpreted as an etiological explanation of hermaphroditism.

Salmoneus Son of *Aeolus and Enarete, he is mentioned in the *Iliad* as king of Elis. Reputed to be the founder and ruler of Salmonia (which was named after him), Salmoneus is characterized especially in later legend as a hubristic person who sought to equal the gods, Zeus foremost among them. Thus it is told that he rode in a chariot whose wheels produced a noise like thunder, and that he tried to imitate lightning with burning torches. Roused to anger, Zeus finally killed him, dispatched him to the underworld, and destroyed his city.—Salmoneus belongs to the roster of god-despisers, who are frequently encountered in Greek legend.

Salus In Roman religion, salvation in the sense of public well-being, she was personified and worshiped as a goddess until the imperial period as Salus populi Romani and thereafter as Salus Augusta. Her cult centers were concentrated in Rome and central Italy. When the god Aesculapius found acceptance in Rome, Salus was additionally worshiped as goddess of personal health and widely identified with the Greek *Hygieia.

Sangarius A Phrygian river god and son of Oceanus and Tethys, he was the father of several children, including *Nana. In the process of eating a piece of fruit from an exceptionally beautiful almond tree that grew beside a river, Nana felt herself becoming pregnant; in another version she plucked an almond blossom and adorned her bosom with it. The child she bore, named Attis, was exposed and nursed by a goat. It went on to fulfill a very unusual destiny.

Sarapis *Serapis.

Sarpedon The name of two important legendary heroes regarding whom the tradition gives differing reports, so that neither parentage nor deeds can be assigned to one or the other with absolute certainty. 1. Son of Zeus and Europa, he grew up in Crete and emigrated to Asia Minor when his brother acceded to the Cretan throne. 2. Son of Zeus and Laodameia, he led the Lycians in the Trojan War as an ally of Priam. Although killed by Patroclus according to the will of Zeus, he was returned to his homeland by Hypnos and Thanatos and buried there with all due honors.

Saturn

Saturn (*Saturnus*) Probably an ancient Etruscan god taken over by the Romans as a god of peasant life. Nevertheless, the derivation of his name from the Latin *serere* ("to sow") is untenable. Identified as the husband of *Ops, he was equated with *Kronos from about the 3rd century B.C. Saturn also appears in the tradition as king of Latium. The idea of a Golden Age in which mankind experienced a happy, carefree existence is associated with him. His festival was the *Saturnalia, and his temple, which

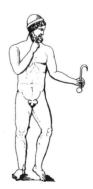

Saturn

housed the state treasury, stood at the foot of the Capitol.

Saturnalia The festival celebrated in ancient Rome, usually from December 17 to 19, in honor of *Saturn. During this festival, the observance of class differences was suspended and a gay, carnivallike atmosphere prevailed.

Satyrs Wood spirits and vegetation daimons with animal ears, tails, horns, and hoofs, they resembled the *Sileni and were often equated with them. Wild and fond of wine, they belonged to the retinue of Dionysus. Hesiod presented them as brothers of the nymphs. In Greek drama, the satyr play received its name from them. This merry, light-hearted sequel to the tragic performances treated comic and grotesque themes as well as occasional coarse and obscene ones.

Satyrs A Satyr enjoying a drink

Scales *Libra.

Scamander A river arising on Mount Ida in the Troad and its god of the same name; the latter was called Xanthus in the language of the gods. A son of Oceanus and Tethys, he had several children, among them probably *Teucer, king of Troy. The name Xanthus alluded to the god's ability to give his hair a golden color. Scamander helped the Trojans in the war against the Greeks by letting his river overflow its banks and flood the surrounding land.

Schoeneus Perhaps the father of *Atalanta.

Sciron 1. Son of Pelops or Poseidon, he was a brigand who compelled passing travelers to wash his feet, whereupon he would throw them into the sea. Sciron was killed by Theseus, who threw him into the sea. 2. The northwest wind, son of Astraeus and Eos.

Scorpius (*Scorpio*) The eighth sign of the zodiac, it represents the scorpion that Artemis commanded to kill Orion.

Scylla 1. A terrible sea monster in Greek mythology, she was the daughter of Cratais and probably Phorcys, although the tradition mentions other parents as well. Her legendary dwelling place was a cave facing *Charybdis; to-

Scylla

gether they formed a narrow channel in the straits of Messina that posed the gravest danger to sailors. For example, it devoured several companions of Odysseus as he passed through with his ship. The noise it let out in the process resembled the barking of a dog. At a relatively early date, the expression "between Scylla and Charybdis" became proverbial for a situation menaced on both sides, i.e., one without a solution. 2. Daughter of King Nisus of Megara. Her love for Minos of Crete, who was besieging Megara, caused her to cut off her father's crimson locks, which had conferred immortality on him. This enabled Minos to occupy Megara and kill the king. Scorning Scylla's love, Minos proceeded to tie her to the stern of his ship and drag her through the sea. In another version, Scylla was turned into the sea bird Ciris.—The story of Nisus and Scylla exemplifies the ancient belief that the hair on a person's head had special powers.

Sea nymphs In Greek mythology, a collective term for the *Oceanids and the *Nereids.— *Nymphs.

Securitas The personification of security, venerated as divine by the Romans. With the advent of the Pax Augusta, an epoch of peace began for the Romans. When they saw this peace imperiled in later times, they appealed to Securitas for help. In so doing, a distinction was made between the Securitas of the emperor and the Securitas of the Roman people. Both were represented on Roman coins.

Selene Greek goddess of the moon, she was the daughter of Hyperion and the Titan Theia, although other parents are also named. The sister of Eos and Helios, she may have been the last wife of Helios, too. The legend tells of her traveling across the heavens in a chariot drawn by oxen or horses. By Zeus she became the mother of Pandia; in addition she had fifty daughters by *Endymion, whom she visited at night in order to unite with him.—The name Selene derives from the Greek *selas*, meaning "brightness," "light." There was no developed cult of the moon among the Greeks. Suggestions of such a cult are found only in the Peloponnesus after the classical period. In folk beliefs, on the other hand, Selene played a considerable role with respect to becoming and passing away, growth and fertility, etc.—Often equated with Artemis, Selene was identified by the Romans with *Diana.

Selloi An old family line of Dodona, whose priest Perseus consulted on his way to encounter Medusa.

Semele A Theban princess, she was the daughter of *Cadmus and Harmonia. When Zeus conceived a passion for Semele, Hera—his lawful and jealous wife—assumed the appearance of Semele's childhood nurse and counseled her to ask Zeus to manifest himself to her in his full divinity. As a result of following this advice, Semele was killed by one of Zeus's lightning flashes. But the Olympian father was able to save his yet unborn son, Dionysus. Later the dead Semele was released from the underworld either by Zeus or by her son, and ranged among the immortals on Mount Olympus.—Probably the original Semele was a Thracian earth goddess.

Serapis (also *Sarapis*) The name is formed from the combination of *Osiris and Apis, a bull sacred to the Egyptians that was connected by cult with Memphis, the city of the dead. Serapis was raised to the level of a god by Ptolemy I in order to unify the Egyptian and Greek inhabitants of his kingdom under one cult. Until well into the Roman imperial period, Serapis remained the Egyptian divinity with the most widespread cult after *Isis. In the Greek sphere as well, he had numerous temples and sanctuaries, where Isis was often worshiped with him. In 166 B.C. the veneration of Serapis was adopted in Athens as a state cult.

Servius Tullius The legendary sixth king of Rome (578-534 B.C.), whose origins may have been Etruscan.—During his long reign, he enlarged Rome, built new temples, and furthered the development of religious life. He was said to have created the Servian Constitution (dividing the citizenry into centuries according to ownership). The tradition relates that he was killed by his son-in-law Lucius, who then usurped the throne.

Sestos An ancient Greek city located on the European side of the Dardanelles at their narrowest point, opposite Abydos. Xerxes arrived at Sestos after crossing over from Asia to Europe in 480 B.C., and in 334 B.C. Alexander the Great embarked from Sestos en route to Asia.—In legend Sestos is known above all for its association with *Hero and Leander.—During the Trojan War the inhabitants of Sestos were allies of the Trojans.

Seven against Thebes The most important strand in the cycle of Theban legends, and the theme of numerous literary works. It began with the conflict between the two sons of Oedipus, *Eteocles and *Polynices. Cursed by their father, they agreed to share their sovereignty over Thebes by alternating the office annually. Coming to power first, Eteocles drove his brother out. Polynices fled to the court of King *Adrastus (1) in Argos and married his daughter Argeia. As it became clear that Eteocles would not adhere to the yearly rotation contract, Adrastus made preparations to launch the expedition of the Seven against Thebes, in which the other participants were Tydeus, Capaneus, Eteocles, Hippomedon, Parthenopaeus, *Amphiaraus, and Polynices. The catastrophic conclusion to

Seven Sages
Bias of Priene
Chilon of Sparta
Cleobulus of Lindus
Periander of
    Corinth
Pittacus of Mytilene
Solon of Athens
Thales of Miletus
The group of individu-
als designated as the
Seven Wise Men
varied at first; those
listed here were
chosen in the 4th
century B.C. from a
pool of about twenty
persons.

**Seven Wonders of
the World**
The Egyptian
    pyramids
The hanging
    gardens of
    Semiramis
The cult statue of
    Zeus by Pheidias
    at Olympia
The Artemision at
    Ephesus
The tomb of
    Mausolus at
    Halicarnassus
The Colossus of
    Rhodes
The lighthouse on
    Pharos
In some sources the
Walls of Babylon and
the so-called Zeus
altar at Pergamum
were also counted
among the Seven
Wonders, a
departure from the
list given above.

the undertaking was already anticipated at
Nemea, where the commanders-in-chief caused
the death of *Opheltes. Except for Adrastus, all
of the seven perished at Thebes. The prophet
Amphiaraus would have been able to save himself if the earth had not swallowed him up as he
fled with horse and chariot. Since both Polynices
and Eteocles had fallen, their uncle Creon (2)
acceded to the throne. His express prohibition of
burial for Polynices was defied by Antigone.—
Ten years later the *Epigoni succeeded in conquering Thebes and destroying it.

Seven Hills of Rome *Rome.

Seven Wise Men (*Seven Sages*) Seven Greek
philosophers and statesmen of the 7th and 6th
centuries B.C., to whom pithy sayings concerning mostly political and ethical matters were ascribed.

Seven Wonders of the World The name given
in antiquity to the seven most impressive artistic
masterpieces of that era.

Shield of Mars The sacred shield (*ancile*)
guarded by the *Salii.

Sibylline books A collection of prophecies in
nine (later ten) books ascribed to the Sibyl of
Cumae by the Romans. They were stored in an
underground room of the Jupiter-Capitolinus
temple and consulted in emergencies by the
Senate through a college of priests. After being
destroyed by fire in 83 B.C., they were replaced
and transferred to the temple of Apollo on the
Palatine by order of the emperor Augustus.
Their further fortunes are shrouded in uncer-
tainty. In A.D. 405, destruction of the Sibylline
books may have been commanded by the
Christian general Stilicho.—The following legend is told in connection with the original collection. Disguised as an old woman, the Cumaean
Sibyl offered the nine Sibylline books for sale to
the last king of Rome, Tarquinius Superbus. Tarquinius found the price too high, so she burned
three of the books and offered the remaining six
to him at the same price. Again he refused to
buy, so the Sibyl destroyed three more of the
books. Finally Tarquinius purchased the three

that were left, even though they cost as much as the original nine would have cost.

Sibyls In antiquity, the term (probably of Anatolian origin) for female prophets who foretold the future in a state of ecstasy and whose prophecies usually announced impending disaster. Although mortal, they were extremely old. Thus, the Sibyls of Cumae attained a legendary age of 1,000 years. Originally only one Sibyl was known, the supposed daughter of Zeus and Lamia; Dardanus, king of Troy, was also mentioned as her father. Later a generic name evolved out of the personal name, giving rise to a series of Sibyls. The most important Sibyls were the Erythraean Sibyls in Greece and the Cumaean Sibyls in Italy, the latter characterized by Ovid in his *Metamorphoses* as the voice of Apollo and invested with everlasting glory by Virgil. The *Sibylline books were also attributed to her.

Sicily The largest island in the Mediterranean, it was separated from Italy by the straits of Messina. The legendary role of Mount Aetna on Sicily led to the assumption that the famous divine smith *Hephaestus had one of his workshops there.

Sicyon An ancient Greek port city located west of Corinth, which achieved its greatest eminence in the 7th and 6th centuries B.C., especially under the tyrant Cleisthenes. In 303 B.C., it was removed to an inland site. Sicyon was famed for its arts and crafts as well as its schools of painting, sculpture, and bronze casting (Lysippus). Archaeological remains of the new city laid out in 303 B.C. have been preserved.—Apis, who began the succession of Sicyon's mythical kings, was followed by nine generations of kings bearing the same name.

Side The first wife of Orion, she was dispatched to the underworld by Hera (in other versions by Orion or Zeus) because she had presumptuously boasted that she was more beautiful than Hera.

Sidero The second wife of *Salmoneus and the stepmother of *Tyro. One strand of the tradition reports that she was killed by Neleus and Pelias because she had tried to persuade Salmoneus to kill Tyro.

Sileni Half-human, two-legged equine creatures, they resembled the *Satyrs and were often identified with them. Members of the retinue of Dionysus, they were sometimes understood as older Satyrs. One of them, Silenus, was thought to be the teacher of Dionysus and leader of the chorus of Satyrs.

Sileni Silenus with a wineskin

Silvanus Roman god of woods and fields, he was worshiped especially by peasants and regarded as the personal god of freedmen and slaves. Despite his lack of a sanctuary or an official cult, many offerings were presented to him annually in the woods in order to dispose the god favorably toward his worshipers. He was frequently associated with *Mars in the latter's capacity as an old Italian rural god. Linked also to Faunus, occasionally he likewise took on a prophetic character. Thus from Rome's early history, the legend is told of how at night, during a fierce, still-undecided battle between Romans and Etruscans, with a loud voice Silvanus pronounced the Romans victorious on the basis that they had lost one less man than the Etruscans had.

Silvia *Rhea Silvia, mother of Romulus and Remus.

Silvius The last son of Aeneas and Lavinia, born to the couple when they were relatively old. According to one strand of the tradition, the boy was not born until after the death of his father; anxious about the safety of the child in her womb, Lavinia fled into the woods and gave birth to Silvius there (hence his name). In other versions, Silvius was said to be the son of Ascanius. He was widely regarded as the predecessor of the kings of Alba Longa.

Sinis Son of *Polypemon (also called Damastes or Procrustes), he was a giant to whom the epithet Pityocamptes ("pine bender") was applied because he waylaid travelers and tied them to pine branches that he had bent down. Then he let the branch fly up again, sending the victim to his death. *Theseus used the same method to kill Sinis.

Sinon A relative and assistant of Odysseus who served as a spy for the Greeks in the Trojan War. At the moment when the Greeks appeared to be sailing away from Troy, he let himself be captured by the Trojans and persuaded them to drag the wooden horse into their city as a votive offering to Athena. That night he used a beacon to signal the Greeks to return. Virgil narrated the episode in detail. It was also treated in some Greek and Roman tragedies that have been lost.

Sinope Daughter of Asopos, she was pursued by Apollo, Zeus, and others but resisted them all because she preferred to remain a virgin. Nevertheless, one strand of the tradition reports that she bore a son, *Syros, to Apollo.

Sirens (Greek, *Seirenes*) In Greek mythology, they were fabulous creatures, usually imagined as having the bodies of birds and the heads of women (occasionally also endowed with such features as beards). Generally held to be the daughters of Phorcys and Ceto or of Achelous and a Muse, they distinguished themselves by their exceptional vocal artistry. Legend tells of how they lived on an island (perhaps in the Tyrrhenian Sea) where they ensnared sailors by enchanting them with their sweet song, causing the latter to forget their homeward journey. Then the sailors' ships ran up against the island reefs, where the Sirens fell upon the men and sucked out their blood or devoured them. The only sailors to escape them were the Argonauts, thanks to Orpheus, and Odysseus with his companions, because Circe had warned Odysseus to stop his companions' ears with wax and to

Sirens Odysseus and the Sirens; the scene shows Odysseus, who had stopped his comrades' ears with wax, tied to the ship's mast so as not to be drawn into the spell cast by the sweet song of the Sirens; stamnos by the Siren painter (ca. 475 B.C.)

269

Sirens One of the Sirens

have himself bound fast to the mast of his ship.—The number of Sirens varies according to the source. In Homer, two sisters are mentioned, whereas later accounts commonly speak of three, sometimes with a fourth in the background. Originally the Greeks pictured the Sirens as beautiful maidens like the Muses. As composite creatures, their appearance was first influenced by oriental art. Characteristics of the Harpies and Ceres were also sometimes attributed to them. Because they were understood in folk belief as spirits of the dead, they intruded into Christian art, often serving on early Christian tombs as symbols of resurrection. On the other hand, they embodied the sensuality and allurements of this world, too.

Sirius The Dog Star: the brightest star in the heavens, it represented the faithful hound of Orion.

Aeolus—Enarete
     |
Sisyphus—Merope
     |
Glaucus—Eurymede
     |
Bellerophon

Sisyphus In Greek legend, son of the Thessalian king *Aeolus and Enarete. The builder and first king of Corinth, he married *Merope (1), becoming the father of *Glaucus (4) and the grandfather of Bellerophon. A master of trickery and malice, he entered the tradition as one of the foremost offenders against the gods. In addition to his many other crimes, Sisyphus succeeded in bringing Thanatos under his control, so that it was not possible for anyone on earth to die until Ares liberated Thanatos. In connection with his own death, Sisyphus forbade his wife to bury him and entreated Hades to permit him to return to the earth in order to call his wife to account for her grievous omission. Actually he wanted to arrange things so that he would not have to stay in the underworld. However, when he finally died at a ripe old age, a severe retribution for his wicked life awaited him in Hades: for all eternity he was assigned to roll an enormous boulder up a mountain, but each time just before reaching the summit the boulder would roll back down to the starting point because of its great weight. Thus a task involving futile effort came to be described as "Sisyphean."—The story of Sisyphus was treated in ancient literature, especially in dramas

Sisyphus with the boulder as a penitent in the underworld; after a Greek vase painting

by the three great Attic tragedians Aeschylus, Sophocles, and Euripides.

Smintheus Epithet of Apollo as "mouse god," i.e., protector of the fruits of the earth against pests and vermin.

Smyrna Another name for *Myrrha.

Sol Roman sun god, corresponding to the Greek *Helios. His main temple stood on the Quirinal in Rome. During the imperial period, his significance increased as the Romans adopted various oriental sun gods, attaching such epithets as *invictus*, *aeternus*, and *divinus* to them. Under the emperor Antoninus Pius, Sol was worshiped together with Zeus at Heliopolis (Baalbek), where huge temples were erected to them. Elagabalus (really Heliogabal) bore the name of the sun god and made him the highest god of the Roman state. Aurelian, too, accorded Sol special veneration. He assumed the title *Sol invictus* for himself and was represented on coins with Helios's crown of solar rays.

Solon An Athenian statesman of noble birth, who lived from ca. 640 to 560 B.C. He implemented comprehensive reforms and created the political system of meritocracy, or timocracy. Also a composer of elegies in the service of his public policy, Solon was counted among the *Seven Wise Men of Greece.

Solymi A powerful line of Lycian warriors, successfully resisted by Bellerophon.

Somnus The Roman god of sleep, analogous to the Greek god Hypnos, he was the father of numerous sons, including *Phobetor.

Sophocles A Greek poet and playwright born at Colonus (in Attica) in 496 B.C., he died in 406 B.C. at Athens. In 443 he served as treasurer of the naval league, and in 441 (together with Pericles) as *strategos*. Moreover, as a citizen he exercised various other functions. Younger than Aeschylus and older than Euripides, Sophocles produced a kind of drama that likewise fell naturally between his predecessor and successor. By introducing a third actor and raising the number of choral members from twelve to fifteen, he

Sophocles: of his more than 120 works, seven have been preserved:
Ajax
Antigone
Trachiniae
Oedipus Tyrannus
Electra
Philoctetes
Oedipus Coloneus
Among his satyric plays, the *Ichneutae* is especially known.

Sophocles

could shape the dramatic performance with greater freedom and suspense. The role of the chorus in his plays diminished as dialogue gained prominence. The action was grounded in the human characters, even if in the end they had to submit to the gods and the fate imposed by the gods. Of the 123 dramas written by Sophocles, seven tragedies have survived.

Soteira Epithet of the goddesses Athena, Artemis, and Persephone.

Soter 1. An epithet of Zeus in his capacity as savior. 2. Name applied by the Greeks to those gods who rescued people from danger. 3. A Roman god of deliverance from danger.

Soteria The thankful offering of someone who has been rescued from danger. The term also denotes public festivals of thanksgiving that were celebrated in remembrance of particular events, especially military and political victories.

South wind The Greek *Notos, known to the Romans as *Auster.

Sparta A Greek city in the Peloponnesus, south of which are located the ruins of ancient Sparta. Also called Lacedaemon in antiquity, Sparta was the most important Greek city-state after Athens. The Lacedaemonians were reputed to be exceptionally disciplined warriors.

Spartoi (Greek for "the sown ones") The ancestral heroes of the Thebans, whose origins are linked to the legend about *Cadmus. Cadmus destroyed a dragon which had killed some of his companions, extracted its teeth, and sowed the teeth in the earth. All but five of the warriors who consequently sprang up from the soil killed each other off. The survivors helped Cadmus build the citadel of Thebes.

Speio One of the *Nereids.

Spercheios A river in southern Thessaly whose god, a son of Oceanus and Tethys, bore the same name.

Spermo A daughter of *Anius who ardently revered Dionysus. Simply by touching the earth, she could bring forth grain from it.

Spes The Roman personification of hope, she was worshiped as a goddess and had cult places at several sites in the Roman Empire. Most important was her temple at Rome, pledged to her during the First Punic War in the hope of a military victory. Spes was further invoked by all persons concerned with achieving success in the most varied enterprises.

Spes Goddess of hope

Sphinx Fabulous creature with a lion's body and a human head. Although variously interpreted, it was at first generally understood as an emblem of sovereign power. Among the ancient Egyptians, it served as a guardian in front of temples; the oldest known representation is the one at Gizeh with the likeness of the pharaoh Chephren. In Syria, the male head favored by the Egyptians was transformed into a female head. From Syria the Sphinx, depicted with wings extended, spread to Crete. In Greece in the 6th century B.C. it often functioned as a crowning element on grave steles or as a votive offering (e.g., the famous Sphinx of the Naxians at Delphi dated to 560 B.C.). In the 5th and 4th centuries B.C., it often functioned decoratively. In Roman art, the Sphinx frequently appeared on the side panels of sarcophagi.—In Greek mythology, the Sphinx was the daughter of Typhon (or Orthos, according to another version) and *Echidna. By order of Hera (who thus sought to avenge the crime of *Laius against Chrysippus), she sat before one of the gates of Thebes, or by the marketplace, and killed every passerby who could not solve the riddle she posed: "What goes first on four, then on two, and finally on three legs?" (The answer was "man.") When Oedipus found the solution, the monster plunged into an abyss, with the result that Thebes was liberated from her death grip.

Sphinx from a Greek amphora

Sphinx of the Naxians (Delphi)

Staphylus 1. A goatherd of *Oeneus, he discovered wild vines and gave their fruit to his master. Dionysus, who (according to another version) had given the king a grapevine, taught Oeneus how to press wine from the fruit. 2. The son of Dionysus (or Theseus) and Ariadne, he was an Argonaut and king of one of the Aegean islands. When his daughter Rhoeo became pregnant by

Apollo, he had her thrown into the sea in a chest. Rhoeo gave birth to *Anius on Delos.

Stentor In Homer's *Iliad*, he was a Greek herald at Troy who had the vocal power of fifty men. It is said that he died after he had competed with Hermes in a contest of vocal strength and lost. The expression "stentorian voice" is still used today.

Sterculus King of Latium, he was a son of Faunus and possibly the father of *Picus. Often equated with Saturn, he is recorded in legend as an inventor of agricultural equipment and the first person to use manure.

Sterope 1. Wife of *Oenomaus. 2. A daughter of *Acastus.

Steropes One of the Cyclopes, son of Uranus and Gaia, and brother of Brontes and Arges.

Stheneboea Wife of King *Proetus of Tiryns. She slandered *Bellerophon, as in the Potiphar story, and later suffered his revenge.

Sthenele Daughter of *Acastus and sister of Laodameia and Sterope, she married *Menoetius (1) and became the mother of *Patroclus.

Sthenelus The name of several Greek heroes, including: 1. Son of Actor and comrade of Heracles in his combat with the Amazons. After he was killed, his ghost appeared to the Argonauts. 2. Son of *Capaneus and Evadne who, as a suitor of Helen, took part in the Trojan War and drove the chariot of his friend Diomedes. Counted among the warriors who hid inside the wooden horse, he was also one of the Epigoni. 3. Son of Perseus and Andromeda, he was king of Mycenae and married to Antibia (in another version, Nikippe), who bore him several children.

Sthenno A *Gorgon and daughter of Phorcys and Ceto.

Striges In the popular Roman conception, the Striges were vampirelike birds, possibly offspring of the *Harpies. Shrieking over infants in their cradles, they fell on them and sucked out

their blood. To gain protection from these fiends, apotropaic measures were resorted to such as substitute sacrifice or the blessing of thresholds. Force could not be used against them, since it would only increase the danger radiating from them.

Strophius 1. King of Phocis and son of Krisos, he married Anaxabia, a sister of Agamemnon, who bore him *Pylades. Having raised his nephew Orestes, Strophius distanced himself from his son when, along with Orestes, he murdered *Aegisthus and Orestes' mother, *Clytemnestra. 2. Son of Pylades and *Electra, he had a son who was also called Pylades.

Strymo A daughter of the river god *Scamander. Beloved of *Laomedon, she was his wife as well, according to one strand of the tradition.

Strymon A river in Thrace with a river god of the same name.

Stymphalides Large man-eating, predatory birds, which shot their dangerous feathers at people like arrows. Inhabiting the swamps of Stymphalus, they posed a constant threat until *Heracles (as one of his labors) startled them with a clapper donated by Athena and then killed them with his arrows.

Styx 1. In Greek mythology, one of the rivers of the underworld, across which Charon ferried the souls of the dead. The Greeks were accustomed to swear by it. 2. An Oceanid and the eldest daughter of Oceanus and Tethys. In legend she was the first to rush to Zeus's aid when the Titans attacked him. Styx ruled over the river Styx in the underworld.

Suada Roman goddess of persuasion, analogous to the Greek *Peitho.

Suculae Roman name for the *Hyades.

Summanus Epithet of Jupiter, of obscure origin. It may be that in the course of time Summanus evolved into an independent god whose province was defined as encompassing nocturnal thunder and lightning, while thunderstorms were attributed to Jupiter.—In another version the epithet seems to apply to Hades, with reference to his power over the nocturnal heavens.

Sunflower *Klytia.

Sychaeus (also called *Acerbas*) The husband of *Dido, he was killed by Dido's brother *Pygmalion (1). Although Sychaeus received no burial at first, his widow subsequently erected a monument to him at Carthage. She remained faithful to him, turning away all suitors, until Aeneas arrived in her kingdom.

Syleus A Lydian giant who forced passing travelers to perform hard labor in his vineyard, he was killed by Heracles.

Symplegades In Greek mythology, two cliffs located where the Bosporus empties into the Black Sea. As soon as a ship passed between them, they clashed together. Only when the *Argo had barely survived the passage unscathed, were the Symplegades finally brought to a standstill.

Syrinx An Arcadian Hamadryad beloved of Pan. As the god pursued her, she cried to the river nymphs for help, and they turned her into a bundle of reeds. From the reeds Pan made a flute, called the Syrinx flute or the pan-pipe.

Syros Son of Apollo, perhaps by *Sinope, and the eponym of Syria.

Taenarum The southernmost promontory of the Peloponnesus, which today is called Cape Matapan. On the east side of the cape was a sanctuary of Poseidon with a cave, regarded in antiquity as one of the entrances to the underworld.

Tages A figure connected with the ancient Etruscan mysteries, he surfaces in the writings of Roman authors. Probably a child of divine parentage who came into the world in a furrow not far from Tarquinii, Tages possessed the gift of prophecy, which he taught to the Etruscans.

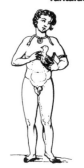

Tages

Talaus An Argonaut and son of Bias and Pero, he was the father of several children, including *Adrastus (1). His wife (and their mother) may have been Lysimache.

Talos 1. A giant forged by *Hephaestus at the request of Minos, who served as guard over the island of Crete. He threw boulders at strangers who wished to land on the island; if they survived that, he would jump into a fire, bring it to white heat, and kill them by embracing them while laughing his sardonic laugh. Only Medea succeeded in putting an end to his gruesome conduct. She knew that he had only one artery running through his entire body; when he threatened the Argonauts on their homeward journey, she slit open his vein at the ankle bone, with the result that he bled to death.—In another version, the giant met his death when *Poeas hit the vulnerable spot on his foot with a bow shot. 2. Also called Perdix, he was a nephew of *Daedalus. His uncle murdered him out of jealousy, because Talos excelled him as an inventor.

Talthybius Agamemnon's chief herald in the Trojan War. After the death of his lord, he became the herald of Orestes. His family held the office of herald as a hereditary possession at Sparta. There and elsewhere Talthybius was venerated as a hero after his death.

Tanagra Probably a daughter of Aeolus and Enarete, she had seven brothers and six sisters (in another version, four).

Tanaquil The Etruscan wife of Tarquinius Priscus, the fifth legendary king of Rome.

Tantalus A legendary Greek figure and the ancestor of an accursed lineage, to which Iphigenia also belonged, he was a son of Zeus (or Tmolus, according to another version) and the father of Pelops and Niobe. From the mountains of Sipylos in Asia Minor, he ruled over a mighty empire and was noted for his proverbial wealth. Since he was the son of a god, the gods favored and trusted him, often inviting him to dine at their table. But instead of showing his gratitude, he stole some *Ambrosia, a food reserved for the gods, and gave it to mortals to eat; moreover, he divulged divine secrets to humans. The culmination of his outrages occurred when he invited the Olympians to dine with him and proceeded to serve them his son. He was punished for this crime by being banished to the underworld, where he suffered from constant hunger and thirst, because the water in which he stood vanished as soon as he wanted to drink from it and the boughs laden with delicious fruit that surrounded him shrank back whenever he reached for one. A strand of the tradition also relates that a huge stone, suspended over his head, continually menaced him. Tantalus became the most famous penitent in the underworld. The Tantalids had already achieved a high degree of notoriety among the Greeks through the many atrocities that they committed.

Taphius King of Taphos and son of Poseidon and Hippothoe, he was the father of *Pterelaus, who succeeded him on the throne.

Tarchon King of Etruria, and an ally of Aeneas in Italy.

Tarpeia A young Roman woman, she was the daughter of Spurius Tarpeius and identified by one strand of the tradition as a vestal virgin. During the Sabine siege of Rome, undertaken to avenge the rape of the Sabine women, Tarpeia betrayed the Capitol to the enemy. Her motives are variously reported: either she was attracted by the Sabines' finery, which she hoped to receive as a reward, or she was in love with Titus Tatius, the Sabine commander. Contrary to her expectations, the Sabines hurled their shields at her until she was crushed by them. Or else she fell off a rock, which was subsequently named the Tarpeian Rock after her.

Tarquinius Priscus The fifth legendary king of Rome, who allegedly ruled from 616 to 578 B.C. Son of the Corinthian Demaratus, he reputedly brought Etruscan cult forms to Rome and annexed many ancient Latin cities. He may also have built the temple of Jupiter on the Capitol in addition to the Cloaca Maxima (as drainage for the Forum), although these structures are sometimes attributed to his successor. Enlarging the number of patrician families and the Senate, Tarquinius Priscus also added to the equestrian centuries and the tribunes. He is said to have been murdered by two sons of his predecessor, Ancus Martius.

Tarquinius Sextus Son of *Tarquinius Superbus, the last mythical king of Rome. According to one strand of the tradition, he brought on the demise of the Roman monarchy by his violation of Lucretia and was assassinated by the inhabitants of Gabii.

Tarquinius Superbus In legend the seventh and last of the mythical kings of Rome, whose rule allegedly ran from 534 to 510 B.C. Represented as the typical tyrant, he was said to have overthrown his father-in-law, Servius Tullius. Other crimes were also imputed to him, such as the arbitrary administration of justice and taxation, and betrayal of the Latin League. The tradition reports that the violation of Lucretia, wife of King Tarquinius Collatinus, by either Tarquinius Superbus or his son Sextus (which resulted in Lucretia's suicide), led to the overthrow of Tarquinius Superbus by Brutus and so to the end of the Roman monarchy.

Tartarus In Greek mythology, a son of Gaia, but also the name of the region below Hades, which formed the deepest layer of the underworld. The enemies of the gods, e.g., the Titans, were banished to Tartarus. Yet it also served as a generalized abode for penitents and demons in contrast to Elysium, home of the blessed after their death.

Tatia Daughter of *Titus Tatius, who shared his sovereignty over Rome for a time with Romulus. Tatia married *Numa Pompilius.

Taurus The constellation of the Bull and the second sign of the zodiac.

Taygete One of the *Pleiades. Daughter of Atlas and Pleione, she became the mother of *Lacedaemon by Zeus.

Tegea Head of a woman (possibly the work of Scopas)

Tecmessa Daughter of *Teuthras (1), she became the Trojan concubine of *Aias the Great and the mother of a son, Eurysaces.

Tegea An ancient city in southeast Arcadia, subject to Spartan hegemony from the middle of the 6th century until the beginning of the 4th century B.C. From 248 to 222 B.C. it was a member of the Achaian League.—At Tegea are the remains of the temple of Athena Alea (4th century B.C.) with pedimental sculpture by the famous Greek sculptor Scopas. An earlier temple, erected in the 7th century B.C., which had wooden columns, burned down in 394 B.C.

Telamon A legendary Greek hero. In the tradition preserved by Hesiod, he was a son of Aeacus of Aegina and Endeis, brother of *Peleus, and half-brother of *Phocus. Fearing that their stepbrother might do away with them for the sake of their inheritance, he and Peleus killed Phocus and then fled from Aegina; Telamon went to Salamis. Since the king of Salamis had no son, Telamon succeeded him on the throne. He married Periboea or Eriboea (in another version, Glauke) and became the father of *Aias (2). Telamon accompanied Heracles on his expedition against Troy, receiving the daughter of King Laomedon, Hesione, as his reward. Their son Teucer took part with Aias in the Trojan War. Telamon himself participated in the Argonautic expedition and the Calydonian boar hunt.

Telamos A Cyclops who prophesied that Odysseus would rob *Polyphemus of his eye.

Telchines Daimonic or dwarflike creatures described quite variously in Greek mythology and associated particularly with the island of Rhodes. Imagined as expert smiths and helpers of Hephaestus, they were credited with many useful inventions. Another version portrayed them as men of the sea who were masters of all kinds of magical arts, but also characterized by such negative features as envy, malice, and the evil eye. Perhaps they came to the Greeks as gods of the pre-Greek population, and then sank to the level of lower, daimonic beings.

Teledamos Son of Agamemnon and Cassandra. He and his twin brother, Pelops, were murdered in childhood by Aegisthus.

Telegonus Son of *Odysseus and *Circe. While searching for his father, whom he had never seen, Telegonus killed him with a spear tipped with a sting-ray spine, having failed to recognize him. Eventually he married Penelope, the legitimate wife of Odysseus, and fathered Italus, eponym of Italy.—The motif of father and son confronting each other in ignorance of each other's identity is a very old one in world literature. Its occurrence in the case of Telegonus has been handed down to us in the *Telegonia* of the epic poet Eugammon (of Cyrene) and in a tragedy of Sophocles preserved only in fragments.

Telemachus Son of *Odysseus and *Penelope, he is the protagonist of the first four books of the *Odyssey*, entitled after him the *Telemachia*. Still a boy when his father left for the Trojan War, Telemachus later supported his mother against the importunate suitors. After the war ended and Odysseus still did not return home, he set out in search of his father or at least for news of him. Once Odysseus finally arrived on Ithaca, Telemachus assisted him in killing the suitors, and after his death Telemachus succeeded him on the throne.—The traditional reports concerning his marriage vary. According to later legend, he married *Circe, who bore him a son, Latinus (in another version Latinus was a son of Odysseus). But Nausicaa and Polykaste are also mentioned as wives of Telemachus.

Teleon Possibly the father of the Argonaut *Butes, who may alternatively have been a son of Poseidon.

Telephassa The wife of Agenor, king of Sidon and Tyre. She bore him several children, including their daughter *Europa, who was abducted by Zeus. The tradition reports that Telephassa accompanied her sons in the search for their lost sister.

Telephus King of Mysia, and son of Heracles and the priestess *Auge (1), he was exposed as an infant and suffered an eventful destiny. According to legend, he played a role in connection with the Trojan War stemming from the proclamation of an oracle that without his help Troy could not be defeated. Telephus guided the Greeks to Troy but did not himself engage in the fighting.

Telesphorus God of convalescence. He was a companion of *Asclepius, the god of healing.

Telete One of the *Pierides (2).

Teleutas Another name for *Teuthras.

Tellus Roman earth goddess analogous to the Greek Gaia but also associated with Demeter and Ceres. Her main festival was celebrated on April 15.

Temenus 1. Son of Aristomachus, descendant of Hyllus, and one of the *Heraclids. After his successful conquest of the Peloponnesus, he acquired the throne of Argos. However, he was murdered by his sons because he had bequeathed his sovereignty not to them but rather to his son-in-law *Deiphontes, the husband of his daughter Hyrnetho. 2. Son of a man named Pelasgus. At Stymphalus in Arcadia, he constructed three sanctuaries to Hera, in which the goddess was worshiped (respectively) as a child, a woman, and a widow.

Tempestas Roman goddess of winds and stormy weather.

Tenages One of the *Heliades, he is reported to have been the first mortal to make a sacrifice to Athena. According to legend, he was murdered by his brothers.

Tenedos A small Aegean island that was sacred to Apollo in antiquity. The Greek forces concealed themselves on the far side of Tenedos, away from Troy, after they had left the wooden horse outside the walls of the city.

Tenes The legend about this figure relates to the island of Tenedos, Tenes being the eponym of it. He was the son of King *Cycnus (1) and Procleia. His stepmother, Philonome, tried to seduce him, but he rejected her advances. She then slandered him to her husband, maintaining that Tenes had made advances to her. Cycnus reacted by having his son thrown into the sea in a chest, which drifted ashore onto Leukophrys. Tenes became king of the island, and the island then took its name from him. He rejected the attempts at reconciliation made by his father, who had at last realized his wife's injustice.—Later Tenes was killed by Achilles when he tried to prevent the latter from landing on the island.

Tereus King of Thrace and son of Ares, he was the husband of *Procne, a daughter of Pandion. Tereus fell passionately in love with Procne's sister *Philomela and raped her. Then he cut out her tongue so that she could not betray him. Nevertheless, Philomela succeeded in portraying the wrong that had been done to her on a piece of fabric and sending the fabric to her sister. Procne avenged herself on her husband by killing their son Itys (also Itylus) and serving him to his father for dinner. When Tereus perceived the outrage his wife had perpetrated, he pursued both sisters in their flight from him. The legend relates that all three were finally transformed into birds.

Terminalia The festival celebrated on February 23, the last day of the old Roman year, in honor of the god *Terminus.

Terminus Roman god of boundaries (or boundary stones). The *Terminalia was celebrated in his honor on February 23. At that festival neighbors from adjoining properties adorned their boundary stones with flowers and sprinkled them with blood. According to legend, the cult of Terminus was very old. The god's main sanctuary at Rome was located within the temple of Jupiter on the Capitol. When the Jupiter temple was built, Terminus is supposed to have refused to yield any space to the new god; thus he belonged to the former generation of gods.

Terpsichore The *Muse of the dance, she is often represented in a dancing position with the lyre and plectrum.

Terra Mater A later name for the Roman earth deity *Tellus.

Terpsichore One of the Muses

Tethys A female Titan and (according to Hesiod) daughter of Uranus and Gaia. She married her brother Oceanus and through him became the mother of countless children, which included the rivers and springs above and beneath the earth. Foremost among them were the Oceanids.

Teucer 1. Probably the son of *Scamander, who immigrated to Troy and was made its first king. He had a daughter, *Bateia (2), whom he married to Dardanus. 2. Son of Telamon and Hesione, he set off for the Trojan War with his half-brother Aias. He likely joined the heroes who hid inside the wooden horse. Considered the best archer on the battlefield at Troy, he displayed his talent particularly well at the funeral games for Achilles. Teucer's efforts to secure a dignified burial for his brother are reported in the *Ajax* of Sophocles. Nonetheless, his father banished him from his native land when he returned home because of the bad treatment Aias had received at the hands of the Greeks, which Teucer had not been able to prevent. Teucer then journeyed to Cyprus, where he founded the city of Salamis, named after his hometown.

Teuthras 1. King of Phrygia and also called Teleutas, he was the father of *Tecmessa, who became the concubine of Aias. 2. Husband of *Auge (1).

Thaleia (*Thalia*) 1. One of the three daughters of Zeus and *Eurynome, she was counted among the Graces and widely regarded as the mother of the *Palici. 2. Daughter of Zeus and *Mnemosyne. As the Muse of comedy, she was often represented with a mask and crown of ivy or a crook.

Thaleia One of the Muses

Thales A Greek natural philosopher from Miletus, he was born ca. 625 B.C. and died ca. 547 B.C. In Aristotle's view, Thales was the founder of Ionian natural philosophy. He identified water as the basic substance of all things, investigated magnetism, and predicted the solar eclipse of 585 B.C. Moreover, he brought Egyptian knowledge of geometry to Greece. From the 5th century B.C., Thales figured as one of the *Seven Wise Men.

Thallo A daughter of Zeus and Themis, she personified the season of spring and was a sister of *Karpo.

Thamyris A Thracian described as a musician in the *Iliad*, and possibly the lover of *Hyacinthus. Having asserted his superiority to the Muses as a singer, he lost a musical contest with them. On account of his pride, they blinded him, robbed him of his voice, and destroyed his lyre.

Thanatos In Greek mythology, he personified death. A son of *Nyx, Thanatos was usually represented as a winged youth like his brother *Hypnos but, in contrast to the latter, with an extinguished or overturned torch in his hand. Though much noticed in poetry and art, Thanatos played only a minor role in the official cult except at Sparta. Otherwise he was an object of folk belief. A famous legend tells of how the cunning *Sisyphus overpowered Thanatos so that nobody on earth could die anymore until Ares liberated death.

Thargelia An Ionian festival celebrated especially in Athens before the harvest (April to May). Dedicated to Apollo, it involved numerous rites of purification, the expulsion of a scapegoat, and the offering of sacrifices as well as competitions in choral singing.

Thasos A Greek island in the northern Aegean, it was colonized by Ionians in antiquity. Legend reports that it was named after a son of Agenor and Telephassa.

Thaumakos The father of *Poeas.

Thaumas A sea god, and son of Oceanus (or Pontus, according to another version) and Gaia. He married Electra, a daughter of Oceanus and Tethys, and gained importance as the father of *Iris, the *Harpies, and the wind squalls.

Theano Priestess and prophetess of Athena at Troy, she was the daughter of the Thracian king *Kisseus (3) and wife of *Antenor, to whom she bore numerous children. She or her husband (in another version) gave the Palladium to the Greeks. After the fall of Troy, she went to Italy and founded Padua. Another branch of the tradition speaks of her emigration to Illyria.

Thebe Daughter of the river god Asopos and Metope, she was abducted by Zeus, according to one strand of the tradition. However, it may actually have been one of her sisters who was abducted.

Thebes 1. In antiquity the capital of Boeotia, it was a bastion of aristocratic values until 395 B.C., mostly in contrast to Athens. Allied in the Persian Wars with Persia and in the Peloponnesian War with Sparta, Thebes achieved hegemony in Greece with its victory over Sparta at Leuktra in 371 B.C. (Spartan domination of Thebes was thrown off by Pelopidas in 379 B.C.) Theban hegemony came to an end with the death of the Theban general Epaminondas in 362 B.C., and the city lost its independence when defeated at Chaeronea in 338 B.C. Destroyed by Alexander the Great in 335 B.C., Thebes was rebuilt in 315 B.C. From 146 B.C. it came under Roman rule.—The Theban cycle of legends played a central role within the Greek world of legends. According to tradition, the seven-gated city was founded by *Cadmus, husband of *Harmonia. The *Spartoi erected the citadel, and *Amphion and Zethus built the walls. The power struggle waged between *Eteocles and Polynices, the sons of *Oedipus, occasioned the expedition of the *Seven against Thebes, which ended in a double failure. Only their sons, the *Epigoni, succeeded in capturing the city, which they leveled to the ground.— Thebes also claimed to be the birthplace of a whole series of important Greek figures, among them Heracles and *Tiresias. 2. An ancient city in upper Egypt, founded at the end of the 3rd century B.C.

Theia A female *Titan who married her brother *Hyperion and became the mother of Eos, Helios, and Selene.

Theias King of Assyria, and possibly the father of *Myrrha (Smyrna), though she was formerly regarded as the daughter of Cinyras.

Theiodamas King of the Dryopes and father of *Hylas.

Themis A female Titan and, according to Hesiod, the second wife of Zeus, she was the mother of the *Horae and the *Moirai in addition, possibly, to Prometheus. Considered to be the personification of order and right, of justice and lawfulness, Themis was frequently invoked by persons taking oaths. She also functioned as a goddess of oracles, and was said to have occupied the seat of the Delphic oracle until Apollo took it over. Sometimes she was identified with Gaia, goddess of the earth.

Themisto Daughter of Hypseus, king of the *Lapiths, she was the wife of Athamas, king of Thebes, who had formerly been married to *Ino. According to a version that contradicts the legend of Athamas and Ino, Ino returned to her husband with her children, Learchus and Melicertes, after surmounting an attack of madness. Athamas had remarried, believing his first wife to be dead, and in the meantime his second wife, Themisto, had had two children of her own. Plagued with jealousy, Themisto ordered her own children to wear white and those of Ino to wear black as part of a plot to get rid of her stepchildren. The children's caretaker knowingly reversed Themisto's instructions, with the result that Themisto inadvertently killed her own children while Ino's children survived. In despair over what she had done, Themisto committed suicide.

Theoklymenos A son of *Polypheides, he belonged to a famous family of seers. He foretold, among other events, the return of Odysseus from the Trojan War and the death of Penelope's suitors.

Theophane A beautiful young girl who was abducted by Poseidon and bore him a ram with a golden fleece. Capable of flying and speaking, the ram played a decisive role in the legend of the Argonauts.

Thera The southernmost island among the Cyclades, and a volcanic area. Behind it the mythical Atlantis was sometimes imagined.

Therimachos A son of Heracles and Heracles' wife Megara. The brother of *Creontiades, he was killed by his father.

Thermodon A river in Cappadocia. One strand of the tradition reports that the Amazons made their home on its banks.

Thersander Son of Polynices and Argeia, and one of the *Epigoni. He gained the participation of Alcmaeon and Amphilochus in the campaign by presenting the cloak of Harmonia to their mother Eriphyle. After the capture of Thebes, Thersander became king of the city.—He also set out for the Trojan War with a contingent of forty ships but met his death at the hands of Telephus during the disembarkation at Mysia. According to another version (Virgil), Thersander survived and hid inside the wooden horse.

Thersites Presented in the *Iliad* as the ugliest man who fought at Troy. From a lower-class background, he was scorned by the Homeric aristocracy. Later accounts provided him with a more illustrious genealogy though, making him a son of Agrius, one of the brothers of the Calydonian king *Oeneus. At the assembly of the army, he spoke against the opinion of Agamemnon and was soundly thrashed by Odysseus. When he mocked Achilles' love for Penthesilea, who died in the fighting, Achilles struck him dead in a fit of rage.

Theseus One of the most important heroes of Greek mythology, he was the son of Aegeus, a king of Athens (another version gave Poseidon as his father) and Aethra, a princess of Troezen. Theseus was brought up by his mother's father, *Pittheus, because Aegeus had ignored the warning of the Delphic oracle against the pleasures of wine and love. Before Aegeus returned to Athens, he hid a sword and a pair of sandals under a huge stone and instructed Aethra to send him their son as soon as he was able to roll away the stone. When the time came, The-

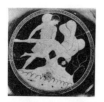

Theseus in combat with Sciron; Greek vase painting (ca. 480 B.C.)

seus set out for Athens by the overland route. On the way he performed various deeds reminiscent of the labors of *Heracles. He killed the club-bearer *Periphetes (2), the pine-bender *Sinis, and the Crommyonian sow; pushed *Sciron (1) into the sea, overcame *Kerkyon in a duel, and put an end to the cruel activity of *Procrustes. On his arrival in Athens, the sorceress Medea, his father's companion, attempted to do away with him. First she persuaded the king to assign their guest the task of destroying the *Cretan bull, and then she tried to poison him. Aegeus finally recognized his son by the sword that he carried and awarded him his rightful inheritance. Theseus did not hesitate to contend with the *Minotaur, to whom the Athenians were compelled to offer annual human sacrifices. He sailed to Crete and, aided by *Ariadne, a daughter of King Minos, succeeded in subduing the monster in the labyrinth. On their return voyage, he and his companions forgot the agreement they had made with Aegeus that they would hoist white rather than black sails if the expedition were successful. Instead the ship was inadvertently fitted with black sails, and when the king awaiting their arrival on the Acropolis saw the sails he threw himself into the sea, assuming in his despair that his son had died.—Theseus acceded to the throne of Athens and became a national hero of Attica. He was credited with uniting several Attic communities and regarded as a wise ruler who enjoyed great esteem in the rest of Greece, too. Theseus's further adventures included the victory over the Amazons, whose queen (Hippolyta, or Antiope) he married. Together with his friend *Pirithous, he took part in the Calydonian boar hunt and the abduction of Helen from Sparta. Their attempt to remove Persephone from Hades led to their own detention there, but Heracles finally freed them.—After the death of Hippolyta, Theseus sent his son *Hippolytus to the court of Pittheus, who granted Hippolytus his inheritance. Theseus himself married *Phaedra, a sister of Ariadne. She fell passionately in love with her stepson, who rejected her. She then slandered him to her husband, and he had his son dragged to death; Phaedra committed suicide. Later Theseus had to face an insurrection at Athens plotted by a successor of the first kings during his absence. He retired to the court of King *Lycomedes of Scyros, who received him hospitably at first but then treacherously hurled him down from a rock into the sea.—After the Persian Wars, during which legend records that Theseus appeared to the Greeks at the battle of Marathon and encouraged them, the bones of Theseus were transferred to Athens. There he was venerated in the context of a state cult as one of the fathers of Atherlian democracy.

Thespius King of the Boeotian city of Thespiae, he was the son of Erechtheus, according to one strand of the tradition. Thespius extended hospitality to Heracles when the latter sought asylum. Wishing to acquire descendants for himself from such an illustrious hero, he had Heracles sleep with all fifty of his daughters. In one version Heracles spent one night with each daughter, in a second with all of them in seven nights, and in a third with all of them in one night. Most of the sons produced from these unions were said to have colonized Sardinia later.—Thespius also purified Heracles after he had murdered his wife Megara and their children in a fit of madness.

Thessalos King of Thessaly, and son of Heracles and Chalciope. His two sons, Antiphos and Pheidippos, took part in the Trojan War with a fleet of thirty ships.

Thessaly A region in northern Greece between Olympus, Pindus, and the Aegean Sea, it functioned historically as a transit corridor. Occupied by immigrants from northwest Greece until the end of the 7th century B.C., Thessaly was politically unified in the first half of the 4th century B.C. for a time. In 354 B.C. it came under Macedonian rule. A region to which a series of myths was attached, it also derived significance from the presence of Mount Olympus.

Thestius 1. King of Aetolia, and son of Ares or Agenor, he was the father of several children, including *Leda. According to one legendary account, the sons of Thestius were killed by *Meleager when they attempted to steal the hide of the Calydonian boar from Atalanta. 2. The father of *Calydon (1).

Thetis Daughter of Nereus and Doris, she was the sister of the *Nereids. Both Zeus and Poseidon pursued her, but withdrew when they learned of a prophecy to the effect that Thetis would bear a son whose strength would exceed his father's. After this only a mortal could be considered as a possible husband for the sea goddess. The best candidate proved to be Peleus, who won Thetis after a wrestling match during which she turned herself into the most varied animals. All of the Olympian gods were invited to the couple's wedding except for *Eris, who avenged this insult by indirectly causing the Trojan War. Thetis bore her husband seven children. In another version she bore only one son, Achilles, whom she sought to immortalize by holding him in the fire or in a pot of boiling water. When Peleus discovered her doing this, she vanished into the underground palace of her father, Nereus. But she continued to extend a protecting hand to her son by trying to warn him of various dangers.—Another equally old version of the Thetis legend relates that the Nereid refused Zeus's advances out of gratitude to his wife, Hera, who had raised her. An intimacy with Hephaestus is also mentioned; Thetis concealed him in the sea for years, and in return Hephaestus helped her on many occasions, e.g., by forging armor for Achilles.

Thisbe The beloved of Pyramus, after whose suicide she likewise killed herself.—*Pyramus and Thisbe.

Thoas 1. King of Lemnos, son of Dionysus (or of Theseus and Ariadne), and father of Hypsipyle, he was the only man to survive the slaughter by the Lemnian women of their husbands. 2. King of the Taurians, he was the son of Jason and Hypsipyle. He wanted to sacrifice Orestes and Pylades to Artemis, but they were saved by Iphigenia. 3. A king of Aetolia who, as one of Helen's suitors, entered the Trojan War with a fleet of forty ships. He was among the heroes who hid inside the wooden horse.

Thoon ("the swift") 1. In Greek mythology, a giant and son of Gaia who was killed in the Gigantomachy at Phlegra by the Moirai. 2. An Egyptian king and the husband of *Polydamna.

Thoosa A nymph and daughter of Phorcys who was probably the mother of the Cyclops *Polyphemus by Poseidon.

Thootes The herald of *Menestheus.

Thrace According to the ancient Greeks, a geographical area encompassing the eastern Balkan peninsula as far as the Danube in addition to the Thracian islands (Thasos, Samothrace, etc.). The Roman province of Thracia (A.D. 46) comprised only the part between the Aegean Sea and the Balkan mountain range.—Originally inhabited by Indo-European Thracians, Thrace was colonized by Greeks from the 8th century B.C. Philip II brought it under Macedonian control, in 281 B.C. it gained independence, and in A.D. 46 it was conquered by Rome.—Thrace was reputed to be the homeland of some legendary figures, the most prominent among them being the mythical singer *Orpheus.

Thrasymedes Son of Nestor, he was a shepherd who accompanied his father in the Trojan War.

Thyestes Son of *Pelops and *Hippodameia, brother of *Atreus, and father of *Aegisthus. Atreus and Thyestes murdered their stepbrother Chrysippus, which brought down on them the solemn curse of Pelops and expulsion from their native land. Hatred then developed between the two brothers, giving rise to more and more novel deeds of vengeance on either side and exerting a tragic influence on their descendants.

Thyiades The companions of Dionysus, also called *Maenads or Bacchantes.

Thyrsos A long staff ending in a pine cone, around which vine leaves and bands were usually wound. It served as a sign of Dionysus and his retinue. Artistic representations always show the god with this symbol.

Tiber The main river of central Italy, arising in the Etruscan Apennines; flowing through Umbria, Campagna, and Rome; and emptying into the Tyrrhenian Sea at Ostia, where a delta gradually accumulated. Originally called the Albula River, it played a particular role in the legends about Rome and was venerated by the Romans as divine.

Tiberinus The sacred name of the *Tiber, which the Romans venerated as divine. Legend reports that Tiberinus was an Italian king who drowned in the Albula, after which the river was renamed in honor of him.

Tilphussa A prophetess and daughter of the river god Ladon, who lived as a nymph near the spring of the same name in Arcadia or Boeotia, where there was an oracle of Apollo. The prophet *Tiresias drank from this ice-cold spring, fell ill, and died soon thereafter.

Tiphys The helmsman of the *Argo, distinguished for his dexterity. He died on the voyage to Colchis and was replaced by Ancaeus or Erginos.

Tiresias The most important prophet in the Theban cycle of legends, he was the son of Eueres and the nymph *Chariklo. The accounts of his fate differ widely. Thus in the course of an argument between Zeus and Hera about men's and women's enjoyment of lovemaking, Tiresias is said to have declared that the pleasure experienced by women was nine times that of men. For this, the scandalized goddess blinded him while Zeus endowed him with the gift of prophecy, the art of observing the flight of birds, and a long life. According to another version, he was struck by Pallas Athena with blindness because he had seen her naked in her bath.—The story of Tiresias's double sex change is also well-known: once as he was climbing up Mount Cyllene, he was suddenly attacked by a pair of copulating serpents. After he had killed the female serpent, he turned into a woman. About seven years later the event recurred, except that this time Tiresias killed the male serpent and changed back into a man.—The tradition narrates several exemplary occasions on which Tiresias demonstrated his prophetic gift: he foretold the fate of Oedipus and the destiny of the *Seven against Thebes. Ten years later, during the siege of Thebes by the *Epigoni, he advised the Thebans to leave their city. Fleeing with them, Tiresias drank from the ice-cold spring of Tilphussa, fell ill, and died soon afterward.

Tiryns A prehistoric fortress city in the Peloponnesus founded by Helladic people in the 3rd millennium B.C., conquered by early Greeks ca. 2000 B.C., and established as the seat of a Mycenaean sovereign from the 15th century B.C. In the 13th century B.C., immense fortification walls were constructed. The city was destroyed in the 12th century B.C. by the Doric migration. Next to Mycenae it was the chief center of Mycenaean culture. According to legend, Heracles spent his early years there.

Tisamenos A son of Orestes who succeeded his father in office and probably fell in battle against the Heraclids. According to another version, he was driven out of Argos and Sparta and met his death when he sought to expel the Ionians from Achaea.

Tisiphone 1. Daughter of Alcmaeon (one of the Epigoni) and his wife Manto, she was the sister of Amphilochus. In an attack of madness, Alcmaeon left his children behind with Creon of Corinth. Jealous of Tisiphone's beauty, the wife of Creon sold her into slavery, with none of the involved parties realizing at first that the buyer was Tisiphone's father. When Alcmaeon later returned to Corinth to reclaim his children, he recognized his daughter and also got his son back. 2. One of the *Erinyes, a daughter of Gaia, and the sister of *Alecto and *Megaira. Her name was interpreted as meaning "avenger of murder."

Titans The children of Uranus and Gaia, they belonged to the generation of gods who ruled before the Olympians. Usually six sons and six daughters are mentioned; in Hesiod's *Theogony* they appear as couples. Under the leadership of *Kronos, the youngest Titan, the Titans hurled

Titans

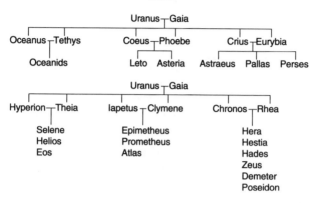

Uranus — Gaia

Oceanus — Tethys	Coeus — Phoebe	Crius — Eurybia
Oceanids	Leto Asteria	Astraeus Pallas Perses

Uranus — Gaia

Hyperion — Theia	Iapetus — Clymene	Chronos — Rhea
Selene	Epimetheus	Hera
Helios	Prometheus	Hestia
Eos	Atlas	Hades
		Zeus
		Demeter
		Poseidon

their father, Uranus, into Tartarus. Kronos swallowed his children except for Zeus, who escaped thanks to a trick. When Zeus reached adulthood, the struggle for world domination that he finally won began. Uranus and all who sided with him, especially the Titans, were thrown into Tartarus but (according to some sources) later pardoned.—What meaning the Titans and their battle had for the history of religion is disputed. The phenomenon presented here (which can also be observed in other cultures) likely consists of one generation of gods cutting off an earlier generation. This does not entail a view of the Titans as the gods of the pre-Greek population who were then repressed, though not wholly eliminated from consciousness, after the Hellenes migrated into Greece.

Tithonus Son of the Trojan king Laomedon, brother of Priam, and husband of *Eos (dawn). The latter bore him Memnon, who played an important role in the Trojan War. With fervent entreaties Eos persuaded Zeus to bestow eternal life on her husband, but neglected to include eternal youth in her request. As a result, Tithonus contracted more and more, to the point where he finally gave the impression of a driedup insect. According to one strand of the tradition, in old age he became a grasshopper.

Titus Tatius King of the Sabines, he ruled Rome jointly with Romulus for a while after the rape of the Sabine women (*Romulus and Remus). The legend reports that he was killed in Laurentum because he broke the law.

Tityus A giant and son of Gaia, or of Zeus and Elare, a daughter of Orchomenus. His birth occurred under the earth, because Zeus wanted to protect his mother from Hera's jealousy; thus he was called "offspring of the earth." When he tried to insult Leto, he was killed by her children, Apollo and Artemis, and thrown into Hades, where he became one of the great penitents. Chained to the ground, he was tormented by two vultures picking at his liver, which constantly grew back again.

Tlepolemus 1. King of Rhodes, he was a son of Heracles and Astyoche (in another version of Astydameia) and the father of a son, Deipylos. Originally Tlepolemus lived in Argos, where he (probably inadvertently) killed his kinsman *Licymnius. On account of this act, he fled to Rhodes and founded several important cities there. As a suitor of Helen, he entered the Trojan War with a contingent of nine ships and met his death in battle. 2. A son of the Trojan Damastor, he was killed in the Trojan War by Patroclus.

Tmolus King of Lydia, he was the husband of *Omphale, who engaged in a love affair with Heracles. The legend presented Tmolus as the arbiter in a musical contest between Apollo and Pan. He was said to have been killed by Artemis because he had abducted one of her companions.

Toxeus 1. Son of *Oeneus, he was killed by his father because he leapt over the moat that protected the city of Calydon. 2. An uncle of Meleager who participated in the *Calydonian boar hunt.

Trident A three-pronged javelin and the symbol of Poseidon, or Neptune, as god of the sea.

Trioditis An epithet of *Hecate.

Trident A symbol of Neptune as god of the sea

Triopas In Greek legend, a frequently occurring name, associated most notably with: 1. A king of Thessaly, the husband of Hiskilla, and the father of the *Erysichthon who was punished with insatiable, ravenous hunger because he had felled a tree in the sacred grove of Demeter. 2. One of the *Heliades and a king of Rhodes, who went into exile because he was implicated in the murder of his brother *Tenages.

Triptolemus An Eleusinian prince and son of Celeus and Metanira; his parents may also have been Oceanus and Gaia or other persons altogether. He was favored by Demeter, who gave him wheat, bidding him to spread agriculture and her veneration over the whole earth. The arts of reaping and threshing, and from the Hellenistic period onward also of ploughing, were connected with him. Occasionally he was also identified as one of the judges of the underworld. After his death Triptolemus was divinized; among his sanctuaries were those at Athens and Eleusis.

Triptolemus with sickle and ears of wheat in a serpent chariot

Triton A sea god with a human upper body and a fishlike lower body. Son of Poseidon and Amphitrite, he was vanquished in combat by Heracles. Triton may have been an ancient god of fishermen and sailors. In Boeotian legend, where he played a major role, he is portrayed as a nature daimon imbued with savage qualities who attacked the women of Tanagra and was killed either by those women themselves or by Dionysus, to whom they cried out for help. In the Argonautic legend, he appeared to the Argonauts on Lake Tritonis in Libya and gave

Triton with a human upper body and a fishlike lower body

*Euphemus a clod of earth, which guaranteed his future sovereignty. Equally familiar is the story of Triton's musical contest with *Misenus (1), from which he emerged victorious; he then cast his defeated opponent into the sea.—Later Triton was widely spoken of in the plural. Thus, with the Nereids, the Tritons came to form the counterpart to the Satyrs and nymphs living on the mainland.

Trivia An epithet of Diana and Hecate as goddesses of intersections, or crossroads, i.e., guardians of forks in the road.

Troad A region in Asia Minor east of the Dardanelles, where Troy was situated.

Troezen An ancient city in the southeast Argolid with a well-known Aesculapius sanctuary and sanatoria. It was the home of several important Greek heroes, including Theseus and his son Hippolytus.

Troilus The youngest son of Priam and Hecuba, whose father is occasionally also given as Apollo. An oracle stated that Troy could not be taken until Troilus reached the age of twenty. He was slain by Achilles in the Trojan War before he attained that age.—The love affairs of Troilus with Chryseis, Briseis, or Cressida derive from a chivalric romance of the 12th century A.D., the *Roman de Troie* of Benoit de Sainte-More, which was influenced by a Greco-Latin prototype. Other versions of the story, e.g., those of Shakespeare and Chaucer, go back to this medieval work.

Trojan War The ten-year war of the Hellenes against *Troy, which represents one of the most important cycles of legends in antiquity. Although the conquest of Troy VIIa may constitute the historical core of the cycle, this is only a conjecture and cannot be proved.—According to the legend, the event that triggered the armed confrontation was the abduction of *Helen by the Trojan prince *Paris. The most eminent heroes of the time made their appearance on both sides of the conflict during the siege of the city. Each of the Olympian gods also chose one side or the other to favor. The

Iliad (*Homer) begins in the tenth year of the war but depicts only about fifty days of the action. The leitmotif of the epic is the wrath of Achilles over Agamemnon's appropriation of Briseis (a king's daughter), who had been awarded to Achilles, and the complications arising from it in the Greek camp. Nothing is told of the city's capture, which was finally accomplished through a stratagem devised by Odysseus. *Epeios constructed a large wooden horse in which thirty of the most valiant Greek heroes concealed themselves. The rest of the Greeks burned their encampment and pretended to sail away. Despite the warnings issued by the priest *Laokoon, the Trojans—believing that the siege was over and their success assured—dragged the horse into the city. The Hellenes inside the horse emerged from their hiding place and opened the city gates, so that the Greeks (who had returned from *Tenedos) had free access. A horrible bloodbath ensued, during which even Priam and those of his sons who still survived were killed. The women gathered around their queen, *Hecuba, but were carried off to captivity and slavery. *Aeneas succeeded in escaping, bearing his father, Anchises, on his shoulders and taking with him the images of the city's gods for his flight to Italy.—The Trojan War received several dramatic treatments in antiquity, the most familiar being Euripides' *Trojan Women* and *Hecuba*, and Seneca's *Trojan Women*.

Trophonius Son of *Erginos or Apollo (in another version). An architect, he built the temple of Apollo at Delphi, according to legend. Together with his brother *Agamedes, he also erected the treasury of the Boeotian king Hyrieus, mounting one of the stones in such a way that the brothers would be able to remove it without being noticed and so steal part of the king's treasure. When Agamedes finally walked into a trap set by Hyrieus, Trophonius struck off his brother's head and caused it to disappear so that no suspicion would fall on him. He himself fled but, in answer to the prayer of Hyrieus, was swallowed up by the earth.—The legend has a series of variations which refer to related circumstances and indicate that the treasury in question actually belonged to Augeas of Elis.

Tros 1. Eponym of the Trojans, he was a son of Erichthonius and Astyoche, and the husband of Callirhoe. 2. A Trojan and son of Alastor, he was slain by Achilles in the Trojan War.

Troy A prehistoric fortress city of unknown name on the northwest coast of Asia Minor. Equated with Homer's Ilium in the historical period and later called Ilium, it was explained as the Troy of Greek legend. Heinrich Schliemann, who based his search for Troy on the ancient sources, especially the site specified in Homer's *Iliad*, discovered the ancient city in the tell at Hissarlik in modern Turkey, and excavated it from 1870 to 1894 (as of 1882, together with Wilhelm Dörpfeld). Nine occupational layers were uncovered and later subdivided into forty-six phases. Most of the settlements, which varied considerably in extent and significance, had been destroyed by fire, though earthquakes and enemy conquests also appeared as agents of destruction. Thus Troy VIIa fell victim to enemy attackers ca. 1240–1200 B.C., but whether the core of the Trojan legend is to be sought here remains uncertain. The dating of strata also fluctuates.—According to the myth, *Dardanus, son of Zeus, was the forefather of the Trojan royal line. The city took its name from his grandson Tros. One of his descendants was the prolific *Priam, during whose reign the Trojan War is supposed to have taken place.

Tullia Two daughters of the mythical Roman king Servius Tullius, about whom closely interwoven stories are told. One of the daughters, probably the younger, was married to Aruns Tarquinius, and the other to Tarquinius Superbus. The wife of Aruns induced her brother-in-law, Superbus, to kill her husband and her sister and then to marry her. After this double murder, she had her father, Servius Tullius, dethroned and killed by Superbus. She herself rode in a chariot over the corpse of her father.

The site of this crime was thereafter called *vicus sceleratus*.

Tullus Hostilius The third legendary king of Rome, his reign is dated from ca. 672 to 640 B.C. Son of Numa Pompilius and father of Ancus Martius, he was a warlike ruler who destroyed Alba Longa and successfully fought against the Sabines. The legend reports that Jupiter struck him with lightning.

Turnus King of the Rutulians and son of Daunus and Venilia, he was a fearless warrior who competed for the hand of *Lavinia. The legend focuses on his struggle with Aeneas after the latter had arrived in Italy, having fled from Troy. Whether Turnus was an ally of Latinus or took the field against Latinus and Aeneas together is unclear. The tradition relates that he fell in a duel with Aeneas and was dispatched to the underworld.

Tyche Among the Greeks this term referred to providence in the sense of good or bad fortune that the individual is powerless to influence. During the Hellenistic period, the idea prevailed that each person had his particular Tyche as well as his personal daimon. Moreover, a number of cities each had its own Tyche, which was worshiped by the inhabitants. In personified form, Tyche appears in Hesiod as one of the Oceanids and in Pindar as a daughter of Zeus. She was widely represented with a rudder, a cornucopia, or the infant Pluto on her arm. As a sign of the insecurity of good fortune, she often stood on a sphere or wheel.—*Fortuna was the Roman analog of the Greek Tyche

Tydeus Son of King *Oeneus of Calydon and Periboea, he had to flee from his father's court after killing his uncle (in another version, his brother). He went to the court of King Adrastus at Argos, where Polynices of Thebes had also sought asylum. The king gave each of them one of his daughters in marriage. To Tydeus he gave Deipyle, who bore her husband a son, Diomedes. Tydeus participated in the expedition of the *Seven against Thebes, killing Ismene, the beloved of *Periclymenus (2), at the behest of Athena. When he himself was mortally wounded, the goddess wanted to make him immortal but decided otherwise when the dying Tydeus devoured the brain of his adversary Melanippus out of hatred.

Tyndareos King of Sparta, son of Oebalus and Bateia (or, in another version, of Perieres and Gorgophone), and husband of Leda. Tyndareos became the father of Clytemnestra and of one or, according to many traditions, both of the *Dioscuri. Leda's daughter Helen, however, was generally regarded as a daughter of Zeus. Banished from Sparta by *Hippocoon (1), Tyndareos later received his throne back from Heracles.

Tyndarides The patronymic of the *Dioscuri as children of Tyndareos.

Typhon (*Typhoeus*) Son of Tartarus and Gaia (or Hera, in another version). Classified among the giants, he was a colossal monster with serpent feet and one hundred serpent heads, all of which possessed a horrifying voice. With Echidna he fathered numerous monsters such as Cerberus, the Chimaera, and the Crommyonian sow. Typhon's struggle with Zeus for world dominion ended with his banishment to Tartarus. According to another version, Zeus hurled Mount Aetna or another mountain at him; entombed in the mountain, he occasionally moved underneath it, his movements being manifested as volcanic eruptions. There is also a tradition which tells of the terrified gods fleeing from Typhon to Egypt, where they were turned into animal figures symbolizing the Egyptian gods.

Tyro Daughter of *Salmoneus and Alkidike. After Poseidon approached her in the form of the river god Enipeus, whom she loved, she gave birth to the twins *Pelias and *Neleus. Because she feared Sidero, the second wife of her father, who had done her great injustice, she abandoned her infants. The children were nourished by animals and then raised by a shepherd. Later the twins found their mother again and avenged themselves on Sidero by killing her. Tyro married her uncle Cretheus of Iolcus, to whom she bore the sons Aeson, Pheres, and Amythaon.—The motif of twins deriving from a god and a mortal, who are abandoned as infants but later assume their rightful position, occurs with relative frequency in Greek mythology.

Udaios One of the *Spartoi who survived the combat between the warriors generated from the sown teeth of a dragon.—*Cadmus.

Ulixes The Latin name for *Odysseus.

Underworld In Greek mythology, the subterranean kingdom of the dead ruled by *Hades and Persephone. It had four entrances and several rivers, across which the ferryman *Charon transported the deceased. *Cerberus admitted them to the area likewise called Hades, from which he permitted no one to return. Minos, Aeacus, and Rhadamanthys officiated as judges of the dead, letting the pious enter *Elysium but driving sinners to eternal penance in *Tartarus. Greek conceptions of the underworld had certain variations.—In Roman religion, the realm of the dead was called Orcus.

Upis *Opis.

Urania 1. One of the *Muses, and daughter of Zeus and Mnemosyne. Assigned to astronomy, she was usually portrayed with a celestial globe and a pointer. 2. Epithet of *Aphrodite. 3. Daughter of Oceanus and Tethys.

Urania One of the Muses

Uranus The oldest of the gods in Greek mythology, he personified the heavens. He was generally referred to as a son of *Gaia (Earth) and later also as her husband, to whom she bore the Titans, Cyclopes, Hecatoncheires, and Giants, among others. Since Uranus was jealous of his children and hid many of them in the womb of the earth (i.e., Tartarus), Gaia incited her son *Kronos to topple his father from the

303

throne. Kronos castrated Uranus with a sickle, threw his genitals into the sea, and seized world dominion for himself. Later, he in turn was dethroned by his son Zeus.

Ursa Major The constellation of the *Great Bear.

Ursa Minor The constellation of the Lesser Bear.—*Great Bear.

Vacuna An ancient Sabine divinity; the etymology of her name and her significance were already obscure in antiquity. She was often identified with Bellona, Venus, Minerva, Victoria, and other deities.

Vaticanus In Roman religion, the spirit who opened the mouths of newborn infants so that they could let out their first cry.

Venus An old Italian goddess of spring and gardens, closely connected with the notions of grace and charm. She was later equated with the Greek goddess of love, *Aphrodite, whose qualities she assumed for the most part. This identification may have originated in Eryx on Sicily. Several sanctuaries were built for the goddess in Rome, including the temple on the Circus Maximus dedicated in 295 B.C. and the temple on the Capitol pledged in 215 B.C. Ultimately Venus's importance as the national and tutelary goddess of Rome did not rest on the tradition that Aphrodite was the mother of Aeneas and that Venus therefore (being equated with her) figured as the ancestress of the Roman people, who were descended from Aeneas. Her veneration was given special impetus in the 1st century B.C. by prominent contemporary politicians such as Sulla, Pompey, Caesar, and Augustus, each of whom saw the goddess in a different light. For Sulla, she was Venus Felix; for Pompey, Venus Victrix (a victorious goddess); for Caesar, founder of the Julian dy-

Venus Birth of Venus from a shell; after Botticelli

Venus of Melos; famous late Hellenistic marble statue (late 2nd century B.C.) from Melos

Venus Medicean Venus; ancient marble statue once in the possession of the Medici; Roman modification of the Aphrodite of Cnidos by Praxiteles

Venus with Cupid (ivory), by Georg Petel (1601–1634)

nasty. Her chief festivals were celebrated on April 1 and August 19.—In antiquity and afterward, Venus was a favorite subject for artistic representation.

Verplaca Roman goddess of family harmony.

Vertumnus A Roman vegetation god, probably of Etruscan provenance. *Pomona is often named as his wife. His cult, initially evident in Volsinii, traveled from there to Rome in the 3rd century B.C. The god's main festival, the Vertumnalia, was celebrated on August 13. Vertumnus had a temple on the Aventine in Rome. Known as a god of business and trade, he was endowed with a boundless capacity for transformation, which he put to use during his courtship of Pomona.

Vertumnus Roman vegetation god

Vesper Venus as the evening star.

Vesta In Roman mythology, goddess of the hearth, first and foremost of the state hearth, which symbolized the stability of the state. She was probably associated with the Greek *Hestia, whose authority certainly extended to the

Vesta

Vestal Virgins Probably
a Vestalis Maxima

Vestal Virgin

private hearth. Vesta was originally worshiped in the cities of Latium, but her cult arrived in Rome at an early date. In the round temple erected to her there, the *vestal virgins were charged with ensuring that the sacred fire never went out. At her main festival, the *Vestalia, the matrons of the city walked barefoot to the sanctuary of the goddess, and the animal consecrated to Vesta, the donkey, was crowned with garlands of flowers and bits of bread. The storeroom of the temple of Vesta remained open in June for a few days to give the women of Rome an opportunity to restock their provisions.

Vestalia The chief festival of the Roman goddess *Vesta, celebrated in Rome on June 9.

Vestal Virgins Priestesses of the goddess *Vesta, who tended the sacred fire of the state. Maidens from noble families, they numbered four at first and then six. Living communally in the vicinity of the temple of Vesta, they were subject to a "mother superior," the Vestalis Maxima, but also maintained close ties with the Pontifex Maximus. The vestal virgins pledged themselves to absolute chastity; transgression of this vow brought with it the severest punishment, including death under certain circumstances. As a rule, the vestal virgins were still children when they entered the novitiate, in which they served for ten years. For the following ten years, they practiced the cult and instructed the novices who succeeded them. Then they were permitted, if they wished, to return to civil life and to marry.—The vestal virgins enjoyed high esteem. Traditionally their office could be traced back to the beginnings of Rome, for it was already said of *Romulus and Remus, the founders of the city, that their mother was a vestal virgin.

Victor Epithet for various Roman gods, including Jupiter and Mars.

Victoria Roman goddess of victory, she was the Roman equivalent of the Greek *Nike.

Viminal (*mons Viminal*) One of the seven hills of Rome.

Virbius Companion of Diana in the sacred grove of Nemi. His genealogy is obscure. In antiquity he was often identified with the Greek Hippolytus, son of Theseus, who was said to have been dragged to death by horses, recalled to life by Aesculapius, and brought to Italy by Diana. In Naples, Virbius seems to have had his own official cult.

Virgil (*Publius Vergilius Maro*) A Roman poet born in 70 B.C. near Mantua, who died in 19 B.C. at Brundisium (on the way home from Greece). Virgil was probably a farmer's son whose family was dispossessed in connection with the program of public assistance to veterans. Virgil may have been compensated through the intervention of Maecenas with a villa near Naples, where he lived in retirement. He was considered the most important poet among classical Latin authors, and his art achieved canonical status in antiquity, the Middle Ages, and the Renaissance. His fourteen early poems, handed down in the *Catalepton*, show him under the spell of the Neoterics. The ten eclogues in his *Bucolics* refer back to the pastoral poetry of Theocritus; the fourth eclogue was frequently interpreted as a prophetic allusion to the birth of Christ. The four books of the *Georgics* comprise a didactic poem about farm management, the cultivation of vines and fruit, cattle breeding, and beekeeping. The twelve books of the *Aeneid*, revolving around the figure of Aeneas, present a justification of the Augustan empire: divine wisdom has called the Romans to world dominion so that they may usher in a reign of peace.

Virgo A constellation and the sixth zodiacal sign: that of *Astraea or *Erigone.

Virtus ("virtue") The Roman conception and personification of "manliness," understood in the sense of warlike excellence but also in an essentially ethical sense.

Volcanalia The festival celebrated on August 23 in honor of the god *Volcanus. It was solemnized in Rome in a temple dedicated to Vulcan on the Field of Mars.

Volcanus *Vulcan.

Volscians (*Volsci*) In antiquity an Italian people who spoke an Umbro-Sabellian language and inhabited the region of the Volscian mountains (named after them). In 338 B.C., they became subject to Rome.—In legend, the Volscians were allies of *Turnus in his struggle against Aeneas and were governed by their queen, Camilla.

Volturnalia The chief festival of *Volturnus.

Volturnus An ancient Roman river god, usually identified with the Tiber. Whether his provenance was Etruscan remains disputed. His chief festival, the Volturnalia, was celebrated on August 27.

Vulcan (*Volcanus*) The Roman god of fire, taken over from the Etruscans, he was later equated with the Greek *Hephaestus because of the close connection between smithing and fire. His most important festival was the *Volcanalia, during which living fish from the Tiber were thrown into the fire.

Vulture The bird sacred to Mars (Ares), which also played an independent role in ancient mythology.

Walnut tree *Caryae.

Winds In the ancient imagination, divine beings of a lower order who were usually considered to be sons of the Titan Astraeus and *Eos. In the *Odyssey*, *Aeolus, among others, was mentioned as their supreme lord. He lived with them on the legendary island of Aeolus and gave Odysseus a leather bag filled with winds to ease his homeward journey. The winds were also personified as winged figures like the *Harpies or as windswift, winged horses like *Xanthus and *Balios. The individual winds had different names depending on their direction. Insofar as they were objects of cult veneration, the aim was generally to ward off their harmful influence. Control over the weather was not the province of the winds but rather of Olympian gods such as Zeus and Poseidon.

Wolf *Lycaon. *Romulus and Remus.

Wooden horse The device used by the Greeks to gain entry into Troy. Counseled by Odysseus, *Epeios constructed it, and a number of important Greek warriors hid inside it. The Trojans were then persuaded by *Sinon, disguised as a deserter, to drag the horse into their city, despite the contrary advice of the priest *Laokoon. Once inside the walls, the heroes who had hidden in the belly of the horse opened the gates of Troy and let their compatriots in. After bloody battles, the fate of Troy was sealed.

Woodpecker The bird sacred to Mars.— *Picus.

Xanthus 1. With his brother *Balios, one of the immortal, windswift horses of Achilles. From Hera he received the gift of speech, and he warned Achilles of the latter's imminent death. Xanthus wept over the death of Patroclus at the hands of Hector in the Trojan War. 2. In the language of the gods, the name of the river god *Scamander.

Xenios An epithet of *Zeus.

Xenodamos Son of the nymph *Knossia.

Xenodike 1. Daughter of *Minos and *Pasiphae. Among her siblings were *Ariadne and *Phaedra. 2. Daughter of *Syleus.

Xuthus Son of *Hellen and *Orseis, brother of Aeolus and Dorus. He married *Creusa (2), a daughter of Erechtheus of Athens. His wife bore him Achaeus and *Diomede; but Apollo fathered her son *Ion. Xuthus was banished by his wife's brothers and emigrated to Aigialos. According to another version, Xuthus was a son of Aeolus and Creusa (2) and the father of Achaeus and Dorus. In this tradition, too, Ion was a son of Apollo.

Zagreus Originally probably a hunting, vegetation, and underworld god who played a role in the Orphic myths. He was a son of Zeus and Persephone. When the Titans dismembered him, Zeus (in another version, Semele) swallowed his still-warm heart. Zagreus was identified with Dionysus.—The myth has a series of variants.

Zelos Son of Styx and her husband Pallas, and brother of *Bia, *Kratos (2), and *Nike, he was an ally of Zeus in that god's combat with the Titans.

Zemelo Thracian and Phrygian name of *Semele, mother of Dionysus.

Zephyrus Son of Astraeus and Eos, the west wind. By Podarge he became the father of Xanthus and Balios. One strand of the tradition relates that he lived in Thrace.

Zephyrus

Zetes The winged son of Boreas, twin brother of *Calais. He was an Argonaut, and on the island of Chios, where Heracles was searching for his beloved Hylas, who had been captured by water nymphs, he sided with those who advocated continuing the voyage without Heracles. Later Heracles encountered both sons of Boreas on Tenos and killed them.

Zethus The twin brother of Amphion. *Amphion and Zethus.

Zeus The highest god of the Greeks, and the only one whose Indo-European origin can be conclusively demonstrated. His name, derived from the Indo-European root for "shining," probably coincided with the name given to their highest god by other Indo-European peoples. Ac-

Zeus The highest heavenly god of the Greeks

Zeus The god driving his chariot

cording to the myth, Zeus was a son of *Kronos and Rhea; he had numerous siblings, among them *Poseidon, *Hades, *Hera, and *Demeter. Kronos, who had once dethroned his father, *Uranus, with a view to seizing power for himself, was anxious lest the same fate befall him. For this reason, he swallowed all of his children except Zeus, whom Rhea hid in a cave. Instead of Zeus, she handed Kronos a stone wrapped in swaddling clothes, which he took to be his son. Later Zeus forced his father to spit out his siblings. After he had defeated the Titans with his brothers' help, he divided the government of the world with Poseidon and Hades: Poseidon was allotted the sea and Hades the underworld, while Zeus reserved the heavens and the earth for himself. Once the *Giants and *Typhon had been eliminated, Zeus's ascendancy was uncontested. From that point on, he acted as *Nikephoros*, or bringer of victory, and his only possible rivals were the *Moirai.—At first the Greeks saw Zeus as a weather god, whom they imagined on a mountain (Olympus especially), or enthroned in the sky, hurling lightning and thunderbolts down onto the earth. Yet his functions gradually extended far beyond weather. He was the father of the family of gods but seen by humans as the pater familias protecting their

Zeus
His wives and the children they bore him:
  Metis (Athena)
  Themis (the Moirai, the nymphs, the Horae)
  Dione (Aphrodite)
  Mnemosyne (the Muses)
  Eurynome (the Charites)
  Demeter (Persephone)
  Leto (Apollo, Artemis)
  Hera (Ares, Hephaestus, Hebe, Eileithyia)
The tradition regarding the children is not fixed, and at a later stage Hera was considered to be the only legitimate wife of Zeus. Apart from his wives, the god indulged in a great many liaisons, which gave rise to numerous progeny.

Zeus hurling a thunderbolt; Greek bronze statuette, first quarter of the 5th century

possessions. He was concerned about custom and the political order, he guarded freedom and justice, as *Zeus Xenios* he patronized strangers and hospitality, as *Zeus Meilichius* he granted petitionary prayers, he received propitiatory sacrifices, and he figured as the great *Soter. There was hardly any area of life in which he played no role. He was often called "Father Zeus," but in the framework of a kind of Zeus monotheism, his name was sometimes used simply to mean "God."—Although he was recognized on all sides as the supreme deity, in the historical period his cult had a relatively modest appearance. His most important cult places were *Dodona, the oracular seat with the famous oak tree of Zeus, and Olympia, where originally an oracle of Zeus had likewise operated and where the Olympian games honored him. There, too, the most splendid temple of Zeus in all Greece stood, housing the cult statue of gold and ivory created by *Pheidias, which was counted among the *Seven Wonders of the World. At Athens the festival of the *Diasia was celebrated in honor of the god.—On the one hand a god of the highest dignity who guaranteed the world order, on the other hand Zeus exhibited qualities verging on the burlesque in his relationships with women. He had several goddesses in succession as wives, although part of the tradition mentions the ever-jealous Hera as his only wife. In addition, he engaged in liaisons with mortal women that produced a proportionally vast progeny. Almost every aristocratic family in Greece could trace itself back to a descendant of Zeus and thereby enhance its reputation.

Zeuxippe In the tradition she was often referred to as the wife of King Pandion of Athens and as the mother of Butes, Procne, and Philomela. Since Butes was a son of Poseidon or of *Teleon, it is possible that two persons named Zeuxippe were meant.